Voices of Women Writers

Voices of Women Writers

Using Language to Negotiate Identity in Transmigratory Contexts

Elena Anna Spagnuolo

ANTHEM PRESS

Anthem Press
An imprint of Wimbledon Publishing Company
www.anthempress.com

This edition first published in UK and USA 2024
by ANTHEM PRESS
75–76 Blackfriars Road, London SE1 8HA, UK
or PO Box 9779, London SW19 7ZG, UK
and
244 Madison Ave #116, New York, NY 10016, USA

Copyright © Elena Anna Spagnuolo 2024

The author asserts the moral right to be identified as the author of this work.

All rights reserved. Without limiting the rights under copyright reserved above,
no part of this publication may be reproduced, stored or introduced into
a retrieval system, or transmitted, in any form or by any means
(electronic, mechanical, photocopying, recording or otherwise),
without the prior written permission of both the copyright owner
and the above publisher of this book.

British Library Cataloguing-in-Publication Data
A catalogue record for this book is available from the British Library.

Library of Congress Cataloging-in-Publication Data
A catalog record for this book has been requested.
2023939174

ISBN-13: 978-1-83998-798-4 (Hbk)
ISBN-10: 1-83998-798-7 (Hbk)

This title is also available as an e-book.

CONTENTS

Introduction	1

1. Revoicing Female Migrant Identities through Creative
   Multilingualism | 9 |
   1.1 Identity and Migration | 9 |
   1.2 Self-translation: 'A Territory without History?' | 11 |
   1.3 Code-switching | 14 |
   1.4 The Existential Connotation of Writing and Self-translating | 17 |
   1.5 Adding a Linguistic Perspective | 18 |
   1.6 Transnational Italy | 21 |
       1.6.1 What's an Italian's Mother Tongue? | 21 |
       1.6.2 Migration Literature in Italy | 23 |

2. Gianna Patriarca: Self-Translating as a Strategy of Re-grounding | 27 |
   2.1 Finding a 'Voice' as an Italian-Canadian Woman | 27 |
   2.2 Rethinking Home and Belonging through Poetry | 33 |
       2.2.1 Rethinking Politics of 'Home' for Italian-Canadian
   Women | 39 |
   2.3 Code-switching, or the Language of Memory | 42 |
   2.4 Self-translating Strategies in *Italian Women and Other
   Tragedies/Daughters for Sale/Ciao, Baby/What My Arms Can
   Carry/My Etruscan Face* | 48 |

3. Dôre Michelut: Coming to Terms with the Mother Tongue | 57 |
   3.1 The Emergence of a Multilingual Paradigm | 57 |
   3.2 The Overarching Mother Tongue | 61 |
   3.3 Writing One's Cultural and Linguistic Otherness | 68 |
   3.4 The Importance of Self-translating in *Loyalty to the Hunt* | 75 |

4. Licia Canton: Rewriting the Italian Mother (Tongue, Land)'s
   Legacy in Self-Translation | 85 |
   4.1 Growing Up in a Cavarzeran Community in Montréal | 85 |
   4.2 Italian-Canadian Spaces and Narratives of (Up)rooting | 91 |

	4.3	Juggling Two Cultural Heritages through Code-switching	99
	4.4	A Model of Collaborative Self-translation in *Almond Wine and Fertility/Vino alla mandorla e fertilità*	104
5.		Francesca Duranti: 'Trans-Writing' the Self through Acts of Narration and Acts of Living	111
	5.1	The Link between Author, Character and Narrator in the Autofictional Novel	111
	5.2	Remembering or not Remembering, That is the Question	116
		5.2.1 Rebuilding Memories of Home and Belonging	121
	5.3	Multilingualism as an Authorial and Existential Imperative	125
	5.4	*Sogni mancini* and *Left-Handed Dreams*: Why and How to Self-translate	130
Conclusion			143
References			147

INTRODUCTION

In 2022, the Haslemere Educational Museum hosted an exhibition about bird migration, aiming to expand people's knowledge of this phenomenon, and to inform and arouse concern about the decline of many summer migrants, a problem that is being increasingly reported worldwide. For instance, in January 2023, an article in the Guardian signalled that, due to the climate crisis, the number of UK's winter birds is in sharp decline.[1]

In the meantime, European newspapers and TV news talk about the migrant crisis in Europe, highlighting its effects and consequences for society. As an Italian, I am very familiar with these discourses; our press coverage continuously reports about a supposed migrant invasion, portraying the country as invaded by refugees and asylum seekers.[2]

Taking these two facts into account, two considerations emerge. The first one concerns the different attitudes towards birds and people's migration. Bird migration is considered natural, necessary and unavoidable; like Dingle and Drake state, we tend to see animal migration as an 'essential component of the life history and ecological niche of the organism' (2007, 113). On the other hand, we are reluctant to accept human migration. In order to stop and delimit it, we build walls and make citizenship laws stricter and stricter. Nonetheless, the movement of people is not an unprecedented phenomenon. The general assumption is that 'because a phenomenon is highly visible, contested and difficult to administratively manage, nothing like this has happened before' (Mayblin and Turner 2021, 10). This is not true. People have always moved, and their movements have shaped the world as we know it.

The second consideration is that, far from being in decline, human migration is increasing more and more. According to Global Trends (2022), over the last decade, the number of refugees has doubled.[3] On the one hand, this increased mobility is the result of people's innate curiosity and restlessness, of free borders and movement, which leads them to leave their comfort zone and explore new shores; on the other hand, it is the consequence of war, persecution, poverty and global warming.

As a natural outcome of this surge, migration has gained the full attention of the media and political debates. The dominant narrative is based on a dichotomy: the rhetoric of *us* versus *them*, which sees migrants in contraposition to local people, exacerbating the linguistic and socio-cultural divide.[4] Concepts such as nationhood and ethnicity are constantly used to discriminate against migrants and mark them as outsiders, in a process that leads to their dehumanisation and invisibility (Mazzara 2015).

Migration has also gained the attention of academic research. Migration scholarship has flourished over the last decade, and new theoretical developments and approaches have emerged in response to the need 'to develop modified concepts suitable to and adequate for these changing situations of migration/immigration in contemporary societies' (Bachmann-Medick and Kugele 2018, 1). Within the field of humanities, the new studies specifically attempt to shift the attention to individuals, thus moving beyond statistics and 'disrupting and challenging any representational system that aims at reducing migrant subjectivities to mere bodies without words and yet threatening in their presence as a mass, a multitude, a haemorrhagic stream of anonymous and unfamiliar others' (Mazzara 2015, 460).

This approach has naturally spawned interest in the connection between migration and identity. This is not surprising as, like Humpál and Březinová claim, 'migration almost always leads to a disturbance of identity' (2022, 7), specifically challenging conventional views that are shaped by what Yasemin Yildiz calls the monolingual paradigm (2012). The latter constitutes a socio-political construct that emerged in the eighteenth century, displacing 'previously unquestioned practices of living and writing in multiple languages' (2012, 6). Such 'reforms' established the idea that having one language is the norm. People are believed to possess one mother tongue and, through this linguistic connection, to be intimately and exclusively tied to a specific nation, community and culture. According to this paradigm, the mother tongue defines people's identities both as individuals and as members of a society. Nevertheless, migration breaks this pattern of continuity, forcing migrants to rethink the terms that define their identity and to redefine their connection with places, languages and cultures. Migrant stories show that people can inhabit multiple linguistic and cultural spaces, opening up routes to several languages and establishing connections with many sites.

Against this backdrop, a multilingual paradigm is now affirming itself. While multilingual practices have always existed, the increasing visibility of migration today gives multilingualism an increased visibility as well. Multilingual practices have affirmed themselves as instruments through which migrants can claim their voice and retrieve their agency, counteracting

INTRODUCTION

dominant narratives and defeating prejudices. This is the reason why focusing on these practices, and on the people involved in them, is essential to change the current discourse about migration.

The connection between language and identity makes multilingual practices a privileged *locus* for investigating how displacement affects subjectivity and belonging and how this connection shapes human mobility. This is the focus of the present volume, which examines how migrant authors use language to negotiate identity within the context of transmigration. In order to illustrate this point, I analyse a corpus of migrant narratives, written by four authors who were born in Italy and then moved to English-speaking countries: Gianna Patriarca, Dôre Michelut, Licia Canton and Francesca Duranti. Gianna Patriarca, Dôre Michelut and Licia Canton are representatives of the literary movement known as Italian-Canadian writing. They all moved to Canada as children and use English as their main writing language. Francesca Duranti instead is an Italian author who lives six months of the year in Tuscany and six months in New York. She moved abroad as an adult and uses Italian as her main writing language, occasionally (self)translating between Italian and English.

Two things can be noticed with respect to this corpus. Firstly, all the authors can be considered transmigrants. Transmigration constitutes the process through which migrants 'forge and sustain simultaneous multi-stranded social relations that link together their societies of origin and settlement' (Schiller, Basch, and Szanton Blanc 1995, 48). Transmigrants are 'simultaneously embedded' (Schiller, Basch, and Szanton Blanc 1995, 48) here and there, now and then. Their lives happen across multiple linguistic, cultural, social and physical places, as they live and operate in the interspace between their origin and host country.

According to Bachmann-Medick and Kugele, the concepts of transmigration and transnationalism are more suitable to describe current patterns of migration, as 'it is no longer sufficient to work with framings and concepts based on naturalizing and essentializing assumptions [...] or the presumption of a linear migration process' (2018, 1). In this volume, the concept of transmigration has two dimensions. On the one hand, it refers to the actual physical dislocation of the writers, and their constant movements between Italy and English-speaking countries. On the other hand, it acquires a metaphorical connotation. The authors are considered transmigrants because they find new meanings and forms in the space between more languages and cultures. In this stance, their transmigration represents a form of mental mobility. It defines a specific way of conceptualising reality, which is characterised by the attempt to create spaces of interaction and connection. To this end, transmigration will be figuratively described as a journey articulated around multiple movements both backwards (to the country of origin) and forwards (to the host country). These directionalities refer to migrants' positions with respect to both countries. Moving backward leads them closer to the country of origin, while moving forwards increases their proximity to the host society. Transmigration instead originates from their continuous movements both backward and forward, which help them establish several links with both countries.

Secondly, all the authors in the corpus are women, which allows adopting a gendered perspective. Through a parallelism between the mother and the mother (tongue, land), it will be illustrated how the authors' writing and translating are also connected to their desire to express their voice as women. The movement away from the mother (tongue, land) coincides with a movement away from the legacy of womanhood. Like stated by de Rogatis, these authors 'mettono in campo non solo i modi specifici con cui una figlia destabilizza il legame materno con la lingua primaria e/o viene destabilizzata dalla sua perdita, ma anche le strategie di rinascita, traduzione o compresenza spettrale della voce materna perduta nella nuova lingua' (2023, 8). Envisaging multiple linguistic and cultural affiliations, they can also envisage and express alternative forms of femininity, away from concepts of womanhood and motherhood, that are inscribed in the mother (tongue, land).

The transmigrant experience of the writers is at the core of both their writing and translating activities. Transmigration is recreated in the text through writing and translating strategies that help the authors put forward a specific migrant and 'identitarian' discourse, which expresses and exploits the creative and existential possibilities of a transmigrant existence. To illustrate this point, the analysis of the texts will follow a three-fold approach. Firstly, I conduct a thematic investigation into how the authors rewrite traditional migrant tropes from their transmigrant perspective. For example, concepts of home and belonging are reconceptualised beyond the dialectical and oppositional dimensions that conventionally characterise them. Examining these tropes is essential, because 'it is also through the selection of specific themes, characters, voices, language(s), settings and/or narrative devices that authors express and perform their subjectivity' (Dagnino 2019, 382). This means that the authors' identity emerges both in *what* they choose to narrate, and *how* they choose to narrate it. The thematic analysis will allow to focus on *what* they narrate, while the linguistic analysis will highlight *how* they do it. The latter will first address the use of code-switching. Looking at specific semantic domains, such as food and cultural references, it will be demonstrated how the shift from one language to another mirrors the authors' physical transmigration from one place to another, also suggesting how to read their relationship with, and conceptualisation of, each mother tongue. Finally, a specific form of self-translation will be examined.

INTRODUCTION

This typology of self-translation establishes a *continuum* between writing and translating, and it is characterised by revisional changes.

All the texts in the corpus fall into the category of literary texts. Contrary to Hokenson and Munson, who understand literary 'as a broad umbrella term encompassing at various times philosophical, political, and theological treatises, commentaries, letters' (2007, 14), in this volume the term 'literary' refers exclusively to texts that fall into the fiction genre. In analysing how language is used in these narratives, the insights of linguistic research are applied to the field of literature, thus supporting and demonstrating the conceptual and methodological strength of an approach that relies on the collaboration between both fields of study. In the book *Literature as translation/translation as literature*, Conti and Gourley stress 'the "play"' that occurs 'at the border of literature and translation', that enables 'the one to be bought in terms of the other' (2014, viii) and suggest examining 'literature through translational practices of reading and writing' (2014, ix). Likewise, in 'Reading Literature through Translation: The Case of Antonio D'Alfonso in Italian', Maria Cristina Seccia examines 'how translation as a practice can be a form of literary criticism' (2018, 153) because it can be 'an expansion of a literary work and can enhance its understanding' (2018, 154). In her work, she illustrates how misunderstanding the literary world of an author can lead to incorrect translation strategies, which fail to convey the author's view and message.

Taking her study as a starting point, the present volume combines literary criticism and linguistic analysis, aiming to improve the understanding of the texts, of the role played by language in them, and of the subjectivity involved in the process. Literary criticism supports the first part of the analysis, which in turn informs the second part, displaying a sharper focus on language. This combination will allow to understand *why* the authors chose to narrate specific topics and *why* they decided to do it in a specific way. This approach is even more useful in the case of migrant literature, where the connection between literature and language becomes particularly evident. Language is shown to hold great importance, both as object of metalinguistic reflections and as the channel through which multilingual writers reflect on, and recreate, their multilingual experience. Moreover, given that the authors' motivations for self-translating cohere with those for writing (Anselmi 2012, 41), both practices should be analysed together, as different but connected expressions of the subjectivity involved in the creative process.

This book is composed of five chapters. Chapter 1 defines the theoretical and methodological framework, introducing main concepts and notions, such as code-switching and self-translation.

Chapter 2 is dedicated to Gianna Patriarca, one of the representatives of Italian-Canadian literature. Migrating from Italy to Canada was not easy for

Patriarca, who had to deal with stereotypes and prejudices within Canadian society, and with the patriarchal and conservative attitude of the Italian migrant community. Her life was characterised by the struggle to find a space and a voice of her own, and it is therefore not surprising that she uses literature as an instrument of expression and recognition. Patriarca finds in the written page the space where she can finally express 'her self'. The search for recognition is essential to her poems, whose thematic and linguistic features testify to her attempt to reposition herself between Italian and Canadian worlds. For instance, from a thematic perspective, she offers a new reading of the traditional concept of home, no more conceived of as a physical place but as a mental attitude. Her rewriting asserts the possibility of inhabiting multiple homes. The same purpose is achieved with code-switching, through which her mother tongues are allowed to coexist on the page, eventually finding space for a mutual dialogue.

In Chapter 3, the focus is on the life experience and career of Dôre Michelut. The reconstruction of her linguistic biography begins with the movement from Italy to Canada. The analysis specifically investigates what this physical movement entails from a linguistic perspective, leading Michelut to redefine the relationship with her three linguistic systems: Friulian, Italian and English. She experiences the 'impossibility of the monolingual paradigm' (Yildiz 2012), as she finds herself in the condition of having to live with several languages. 'Deprived' of Friulian, 'forced' to communicate in Italian by her parents, exposed to English in the wider community: these are the stages of Michelut's linguistic journey, which reaches an end only when she manages to redefine the relationship with the mother tongue(s) on her own terms. This redefinition is possible only through multingualism, which allows her both simultaneity of existence and expression. The movement towards a multilingual paradigm emerges in her poems, where she extensively conceptualises and narrates the experience of being displaced.

Chapter 4 focuses on Licia Canton, examining what the movement beyond a monolingual paradigm entails in both her professional and personal life. She moved to Montréal, a bilingual city in Canada. There, her family settled down in an area where there was a strong community from Cavarzeran, Canton's hometown. All these factors shape her migrant experience, as inherently defined by multilingualism and multiculturalism. Within this scenario, it does not surprise that, throughout her life, her life and career choices have been driven by the need to bridge and combine multiple worlds. Her multilingualism and multiculturalism are reflected in her writing and translating as well. For instance, in Canton's narratives, the thematic rethinking of home is intertwined with a specific use of code-switching, where lexical choices serve the function of expressing her relationship with

INTRODUCTION

her Italian and Canadian cultural heritages. Her use of Italian words is part of a wider discourse put forward by the author, whose mixed feelings towards her Italian home are voiced through both criticism and sentimentalism. *Almond Wine and Fertility/Vino alla mandorla e fertilità* are striking examples of this aspect. Moreover, they offer interesting insights from a purely translational point of view. They represent a specific form of self-translation, known as collaborative. Through the analysis of the short stories in these collections, I illustrate how the author's voice connects with the translators' voice, and what this entails in the transfer from one linguistic and cultural system to another.

Chapter 5 is dedicated to Francesca Duranti. Both her life and literary career constitute a perfect example of what it means to live and write across multiple linguistic and physical spaces. To begin with, Duranti spends six months in New York and six months in Italy every year, thus engaging herself in a constant process of transmigration. Her transmigration is also a linguistic one, as she writes and (self)translates in both Italian and English. The attempt to move beyond borders and boundaries is therefore at the core of her personal and professional lives. This aspect is further reinforced in her autobiographical novels, where she manages to bridge the gap between author, character and translator. *Sogni mancini/Left-Handed Dreams* is a perfect example of this. The main character is Martina, whose Italian-American life seems to reflect Duranti's experience. The stratagem of the *alter ego* thus generates an overlap between the two figures, and it prompts a wider discourse about identity. Duranti also writes this novel in both Italian and English, thus finding in self-translation the instrument, which allows her to relocate in a hybrid literary and existential space.

In each chapter, the thematic and linguistic analyses are preceded by the reconstruction of the authors' 'linguistic biographies'. The translation scholar Paschalis Nikolau claims that a combined study of translation and autobiography 'strengthens understanding of shared ground between translating, "original" writing and self-expression' (2006, 31). This means that the biographical component has an impact on an author's literary production, and it can therefore illuminate the latter. In the present book, I take his statement as a starting point, but reformulate and narrow the biographical component, as I exclusively focus on reconstructing the authors' 'linguistic biographies'. Following Yildiz's notion of monolingual paradigm (2012, 2), I investigate the authors' relation to language(s), their rethinking of the concept of a mother tongue, and how this rethinking is intertwined with their experience of mobility. To this end, I use a varied range of resources, including biographical information and metalinguistic reflections in their texts, interviews, essays and papers.[5] These sources are examined as language memoirs, intended as narratives of 'what happen[s] to [one's] identity when [one's] language changes' (Kaplan 1994, 59).

The reconstruction of these linguistic trajectories maps the terrain for a reading and understanding of the writing and self-translating performances of the authors. Within the context of mobility, literary practices acquire specific meanings and values and fulfil a specific function, as mobility makes migrant authors individuals with a story to reclaim and tell. In the case studies under examination here, the writers aim to narrate the story of their transmigrant experience. The narratability of their story is the key to their agency, as by telling their story, they can express and reclaim both an authorial and an existential voice. The possibility of being heard/read validates and reinforces their voice.

The connection between writing and living is well expressed by the philosopher Adriana Cavarero, in her *Relating Narratives: Storytelling and Selfhood* (2000). She focuses on the relation between the self and the act of narration and looks at individuals as 'unique existents', who long to narrate and reveal the uniqueness of their identity. The awareness of its uniqueness 'announces and promises to identity a *unity* that the self is not likely to renounce' (2000, 37). For this reason, the self desires its tale 'but, above all, the unity, in the form of a story, which the tale confers to identity' (2000, 37).[6] If the mother tongue constitutes 'a condensed *narrative* about origin and identity' (Yildiz 2012, 12), for migrants, stepping out of the mother tongue (Yildiz 2012, 120) must undermine the grounds on which this narrative is based, replacing their condensed narrative with a fragmented one. Within this scenario, the transmigrant authors in this volume must long to reconstruct a sense of personal unity, which is achieved through writing and self-translating, which help them to make sense of their linguistic, physical and cultural in-betweenness.

Notes

1 https://www.theguardian.com/environment/2023/jan/08/uk-wintering-birds-sharp-decline.
2 In 'Nostalgia and Hybrid Identity in Italian Migrant Literature: The Case of Igiaba Scego', also Erichsen Skalle talks about how the mass media often use labels such as 'a *wave, masses,* or an *invasion*' (2017, 73).
3 https://www.unhcr.org/globaltrends.html.
4 For a detailed account of the history of migration scholarship, see *Migration Studies and Colonialism* (Lucy Mayblin and Joe Turner, 2021).
5 I focus exclusively on written forms of representation. Other forms, such as oral or visual products, are excluded from my investigation.
6 Concerning this point, I disagree with Cavarero. For her, the narration of one's self can only be done by 'an other'. On the contrary, I identify self-narration as essential to migrant's self-validation and self-empowerment.

Chapter 1

REVOICING FEMALE MIGRANT IDENTITIES THROUGH CREATIVE MULTILINGUALISM

1.1 Identity and Migration

In her book *Beyond the Mother Tongue: The Postmonolingual Condition*, Yasemin Yildiz introduces the notion of the monolingual paradigm (2012, 2).[1] This paradigm establishes that people possess one language only: their mother tongue. The relationship with the mother tongue is believed to set the boundaries defining who we are. It links us to a well-defined and exclusive ethnicity and culture, affecting the way we operate and function within a specific community (2012, 2). This paradigm does not exist in nature; rather, it is a sociopolitical construct that emerged in the eighteenth century, and which reminds us that this world 'is not one but is ruled as one' (Ponzanesi and Merolla 2005, 6). As a matter of fact, the monolingual paradigm serves the purpose of organising our world, defining individuals and communities on both a personal and a collective level (Yildiz 2012, 2). Despite the attempts at imposing this paradigm on individuals and society, Yildiz claims that multilingual practices nonetheless continued to exist and survive. She defines them as postmonolingual, a term which describes their 'struggle *against* the monolingual paradigm' (Yildiz 2012, 4).

As mentioned in the Introduction, this struggle has become particularly evident in contemporary societies, where people are constantly on the move, crossing and inhabiting multiple linguistic, physical and cultural spaces. Their movements trigger a rethinking of the relation between individuals, place and language. Indeed, 'traditional representations based on the supposed unity of people, culture and territory do not hold' (Wilson 2020, 214). The alleged unity of people and language is also challenged. Constituting a movement to a different linguistic environment, migration breaks the constitutive relation between language and identity. It disrupts the grounding of the self in the mother tongue, forcing migrants to renegotiate and redefine their selfhood and rethink taken-for-granted concepts, such as home and belonging. For this reason, migrants have often been defined as 'translated beings' (Cronin 2006, Polezzi 2012). In order to function within the new community, the way they perceive and relate to reality has to be redefined and transferred from one linguistic and cultural dimension to another:

> translation takes place both in the physical sense of movement or displacement and in the symbolic sense of the shift from one way of speaking, writing about and interpreting the world to another. (Cronin 2006, 45)

Against this backdrop, several studies are now paying attention to the connection between language and identity, specifically analysing what kind of identity emerges in migratory contexts, and how language is involved in this process. One way to do this is through the analysis of multilingual practices. They are examined as self-reflexive practices, through which an author 'translates' him/herself across different linguistic and cultural spaces.

The present title follows this ontological point of view, as it investigates language as a site of identity reconstruction during migration processes; as the instrument that migrant authors use to negotiate and frame an identity, which is at the crossroads between multiple linguistic, cultural and physical spaces. More specifically, this book explores the connection between writing, self-translating and the transmigrant experience of the authors in the corpus. The argument is that both writing and self-translating are rooted in their transmigrant experience. On the one hand, the latter represents the reason behind their literary activity, as they use both writing and self-translating to achieve a simultaneous existential embeddedness, by means of a simultaneous linguistic embeddedness. On the other hand, the transmigrant experience constitutes the object of their activity. It is reproduced in the text, on both the level of content and language. To illustrate this point, the analysis will be conducted on three different levels. First, the linguistic biographies of the authors will be reconstructed, specifically looking at how the transmigrant experience redefines the relationship with the mother tongue(s) against the monolingual paradigm. Second, a thematic analysis will be conducted; by examining how the authors rewrite traditional migrant tropes, the thematic analysis will highlight how they create what Tiziana de Rogatis calls 'un immaginario traslingue' (2023, 44). The thematic analysis will then inform a linguistic analysis, which will take into account self-translation and code-switching (CS).

1.2 Self-translation: 'A Territory without History?'

Self-translation can be defined as a practice involving those authors who write a text in one language, and then translate it into another language. In doing so, they engage in a process that is at once linguistic, cultural and self-reflexive. This definition suggests a 'metaphorical' interpretation of the translatorial act, to be understood as a process, through which authors 'translate' themselves across different linguistic and cultural spaces.

Self-translation was recognised as an official branch of translation studies in the 1998 edition of the *Routledge Encyclopaedia of Translation Studies*. Since then, a huge wave of interest in the practice has emerged, as demonstrated by the increasing number of conferences, events and publications dedicated to this phenomenon. Before that, self-translation was overlooked and ignored in the field of translation studies for quite a long time.[2] In *The Bilingual Text: History and Theory of Literary Self-translation* (2007), Hokenson and Munson list a number of reasons that might explain this neglect. First, they refer to the fact that self-translation was seen as a rare phenomenon. As such, it was considered as quantitatively unimportant and therefore unworthy of critical attention. For instance, in his book *The Experience of the Foreign*, Antoine Berman stated that 'self-translations are exceptions, as are the cases where a writer chooses a language other than his own' (1992, 3). Over the years, some scholars have approached the practice from a historical and diachronic perspective, in an attempt to debunk such a wrong assumption. They have demonstrated that self-translation does not constitute an exclusively modern phenomenon but has a much longer history. Indeed, bilingual authors translating their own works is not as uncommon as it has been assumed (Santoyo 2005, Hokenson and Munson 2007, Peñalver 2011, Kippur 2015). In *Autotraducciones: Una perspectiva histórica* (2005), the philologist Julio César Santoyo states that self-translation emerged in Greco-Roman antiquity and identifies the Hebrew historian Flavius Josephus as the first self-translator. He wrote his book *The Jewish War* in his native Aramaic language, self-translating it into Greek years later (2005, 859). Self-translation was extensively practised during the Middle Ages when diglossia was common. Many authors wrote their texts in Latin, in order to reach a wider audience and achieve greater prestige. During the Romantic age, however, this practice became despised and marginalised, as writing in another language was seen as a betrayal of the Romantic concept of the mother tongue, upon which the consolidation of nation states, national languages and literature was based (Hokenson and Munson 2007, 1). Nevertheless, the number of self-translators continued to be high in the eighteenth and nineteenth centuries. The Italian playwright Carlo Goldoni used to write his plays in both French and Italian. Other such examples are John Donne, Étienne Dolet and Frédéric Mistral. Self-translators flourished in the twentieth century, including important names such as Samuel Beckett, Rabindranath Tagore, Vladimir Nabokov, Rosario Ferré and Nancy Huston. Nowadays, self-translation is a widespread and popular practice, especially in multilingual countries such as Spain, India, South Africa and Ireland. Living in translation seems to be an essential feature of contemporary societies, where people are constantly on the move, global encounters are frequent and borders are constantly reshaped. Different cultures and languages meet and overlap, generating a dynamic process of connection, interaction and transformation.

The second motivation lies in the 'ambiguous' nature of self-translation. Whether it should be considered straightforwardly as translation, or as a practice of rewriting was – and to some extent still is – hotly debated. As Grutman pointed out, for a long time 'translation scholars themselves have paid little attention to the phenomenon, perhaps because they thought it to be more akin to bilingualism than to translation proper' (1998, 17).[3] Hokenson and Munson identify also a third reason for the relative neglect of self-translation, closely connected to this notion of its ambiguous nature and the perception that it sits between translation and bilingualism. The special status of self-translation seems to question and complicate the foundations of translation theory. While the latter is based on a series of dichotomies (author/translator, original/translation), self-translation moves away from these 'polar extremes and oppositions' (Hokenson and Munson 2007, 165) and focuses on everything that exists in between. For instance, it blows away the classical idea that the translator is a second person, other than the writer of the source text (ST), and it creates a third figure, where the author and translator coexist. It also challenges the concept of an original text, forcing scholars to wonder which version should be given textual priority, or whether both versions should be given the same consideration and attention.

The current position of self-translation as a burgeoning source of interest to scholars is the result of conceptual and methodological development over the past years. Initial investigations into self-translation were mainly monographic and investigated the practice from a literary perspective. Concentrating on a single author, they followed a descriptive approach and, through a side-by-side reading of an original text and its self-translated counterpart, they analysed the linguistic and stylistic transformations experienced by the latter.[4] The aim was to identify similarities and differences between the two versions, in order to detect whether self-translation could be properly considered as translation. This research question rested on the assumption that translation is mainly a normative activity, aiming at producing a faithful and equivalent transfer of material from the ST to the target text (TT). That which did not fit within this structure could not be understood as translation. As such, self-translations were traditionally discounted as unrepresentative of common translating practices, because they generally show a higher degree of creativity. Being both the authors and the translators of the text, self-translators are at greater liberty and have a larger scope to intervene creatively on the TT. They can choose to re-enact their authorial voice and make substantial changes to the ST, freely following the need of their creative genius, again at work in what has been understood as a 'repetition of a process rather than the reproduction of a product' (Wilson 2009, 187). Thus, they can produce a TT that has nothing or little in common with the ST, so much so that the former could be seen as a new original.

This distinction, though, seemed to draw on an understanding of translation as a process that produces an equivalent copy of the ST. This idea has now been extensively challenged and questioned by translation studies. Against the backdrop of the 'creative turn', translation has been 'rethought and redefined in the light of "creativity"' (Perteghella and Loffredo 2006, 1–2). Since translations are performed by individuals, they undergo a process of interpretation and mediation. In this process, the form of the ST can be (and normally is) altered and modified. Moreover, as translation scholars Manuela Perteghella and Eugenia Loffredo claim, 'the variance in translation practices and subsequent strategies is also generated by the fact that translators inhabit different cultural, temporal, and spatial spaces' (2006, 7). This means that translation is an activity that takes place within a social context, which accounts for some of the transformations the ST undergoes.

If a certain degree of creativity is accepted and required when translating, however, we must not forget that the degree of intervention of translators is constrained and delimited by the existence of the ST. Such an assumption holds true for self-translators as well; their activity must be sketched according to the referential frame provided by the ST. As Helena Tanqueiro states, 'the author, when deciding to self-translate, plays more the role of translator and rather less that of author, mainly because he is constrained, like any translator, by the existence of a preestablished fictional universe in the literary work' (2000, 62–63). Ignoring the presence of a previously existent text would break that dimension of continuity, which is essential to build the relation between ST and TT.

These assumptions are now fully recognised in the field of translation studies. The fact that research about self-translation would still refer to so old and outdated notions shows that they were not only chronologically but also conceptually hindered. The newest studies have originated exactly against this backdrop; rethinking translation as an act of writing, they have moved beyond the clear-cut distinction between translation and self-translation. This new approach does not implicitly stress a distance between

14 VOICES OF WOMEN WRITERS

both practices. It rather acknowledges that the bond between them is so deep that there is no need for a comparative and contrastive approach. These new studies have also questioned the 'myth' of the freedom of the self-translator, acknowledging that self-translators are subjected to the same constraints faced by translators. Translator and self-translator, therefore, meet in a 'border zone', both roles being anchored to specific norms and rules, which make their activity not too limited in the first case, and not too free in the second one. Reformulating Venuti's words, the translator is not completely invisible, and the self-translator is not completely visible (1995).

Rethinking translation as a creative practice has entailed a shift towards a translator-oriented approach. This takes into account the relation between the translator and the text, examining how the translator's subjectivity is inscribed in the final product. This approach has been adopted by several studies of self-translation (Jung 2002, Anselmi 2012, Hokenson 2013, Grutman 2013b). They have shifted their focus from the relation between source and TT to the relation between the text and the self-translator. They investigate the different approaches taken by self-translators, as well as the purposes and motivations behind their self-translations, analysing whether and how these impetuses are enacted in linguistic performance. The aim is to detect the reasons that lead self-translators to translate in a specific way, instead of analysing whether their performances match ideal and abstract models of translation and self-translation. A parallelism can be drawn between the cultural turn and this branch of studies that focus on translators, the so-called sociology of translators (Chesterman 2009, 16). While the cultural turn stressed the necessity to place the translated text in its environment, the sociology of translators aims to place translators in the specific social, political and cultural contexts where they operate. As Hokenson (2013, 44) states, it is now time 'to situate the self-translator as a singular figure in the historical interchanges between languages and between social milieus, in part by looking not only at the *what* and *how* of their work but also at *why* the translating practice was undertaken in the first place'. In examining the self-translating experiences of the authors in this corpus, the analysis will consider rightly the reasons that lead them to self-translate their works, and how their motivations define their self-translating performance, leading them to engage with a specific form of self-translation.

1.3 Code-switching

In looking at how the authors use language to recreate their transmigration, the role played by CS in their texts will be also considered. The argument is that, through CS, they establish a linguistic and cultural continuity between the multiple linguistic spaces they inhabit. Exactly like they dismantle the boundary between writing and translating through self-translation, they abolish the borders between the languages they speak, as CS allows each language to move into the territory of the other.

CS can be defined as the mixing of two or more languages and codes, as 'the alternative use by bilinguals of two or more languages in the same conversation' (Milroy and Muysken 1995, 7–8). The phenomenon is frequent in bilingual communities, as it necessarily implies a certain degree of competence in all the languages involved. Indeed, Hoffman describes CS as 'the most creative aspect of bilingual speech' (1991, 109). In defining the authors in this book as bilinguals, the terminological and conceptual complexity of such a term is acknowledged. The reference will be to a broad definition of bilingualism, one which includes 'not only the "perfect" bilingual [...] or the "balanced" bilingual [...] but also various "imperfect" and "unstable" forms of bilingualism, in which one language takes over from the other(s) on at least some occasions and for some instances of language use' (Dewaele et al. 2003, 1). This definition applies to the writers in this volume, who show diverse degrees of proficiency with respect to each language and different skills (speaking, writing, reading, listening). Furthermore, they learned each language at a different age, and in diverse contexts. Despite these differences, all of them can be considered as bilinguals inasmuch as they use at least two languages in their works, regardless of their quantitative or qualitative importance.

There is a lot of disagreement with respect to the terminology to use when talking about mixed language use, and a lot of confusion and overlaps emerge with terms such as code-mixing, CS, and borrowing; as Milroy and Muysken claim, the field 'is replete with a confusing range of terms descriptive of various aspects of the phenomenon' and any attempt to standardise the terminology constitutes 'an impossible task' (1995, 12). In fact, defining CS has proven quite complicated and scholars' views still differ greatly. In order to overcome this terminological issue, this study refers to Anna De Fina, who uses the term CS as 'an umbrella expression for different phenomena including word insertion and intrasentential and intersentential switching' (2007, 380); that is, to describe all kinds of language contact, both within and beyond the sentence boundary. While such a definition might seem too inclusive, it is exactly its wide applicability that makes it useful to the present analysis, as it allows to investigate various cases of language interaction. This approach is also supported by Daniel Weston and Penelope Gardner-Chloros, who extensively investigated CS in literature (2015). In trying to build a terminological and conceptual framework of CS, they pointed out that, in distinguishing between bilingual phenomena, scholarly research normally adopts the parameter of the spontaneity of production.

Nevertheless, Weston and Gardner-Chloros contend that spontaneity cannot be a parameter to consider in written CS, because the latter involves a process of reflection. In the case of written CS, language mixing should be considered as the result of the writer's intentional and conscious choice. Given that all phenomena of language mixing in texts are conscious and purposeful, there is no reason for distinguishing between different phenomena of bilingual mixing in written texts (2015, 196).

In analysing CS, this study will mainly draw on a sociolinguistic approach. Scholars such as Blom and Gumperz (1972) and Myers-Scotton (1993) claim that CS is socially motivated. Even Stroud (1998, 322) states that it should be looked at from a social perspective and that it 'cannot really be understood apart from an understanding of social phenomena'. Some studies also foreground the extra-linguistic nature of CS. For instance, Vogt (1954, 368) claims that 'code-switching in itself is perhaps not a linguistic phenomenon, but rather a psychological one, and its causes are obviously extralinguistic'. Bandia (2008, 148–149) also claims that CS 'is distinct from other multilingual phenomena such as interference, transfer, borrowing and shifts in that the latter can occur in the speech of monolingual speakers while codeswitching is rooted in a multilingual existence'. On these grounds, the use of CS will be investigated rightly in relation to the authors' transmigrant experience, exploring what personal significance it acquires, and what specific message it conveys. Given that the linguistic process exists in conjunction with an existential one, through CS the authors attempt to express a simultaneous linguistic embeddedness, which offers them the possibility to enact a simultaneous existential embeddedness. The switches in the text allow them to articulate multiple backward and forward movements. For instance, the choice of English as the main writing language, on the one hand, establishes a point of connection and communication with the new society. On the other hand, the presence of Italian and dialectal words can be read as a sort of return to the Italian motherland. In analysing examples of CS in these texts, both quantitative and qualitative analyses were conducted. However, the focus is on the latter, providing examples that better illustrate the migrant and 'identitarian' discourse put forward by the writers. As Delabastita and Grutman point out, 'the actual quantity of foreignisms in a text is rather less important than the qualitative role they play within its overall structure' (2005, 17). In some of the works that will be considered, English is the matrix language (Myers-Scotton 1993, 67), in which lexical items from the Italian language are introduced. This is mainly the case for the Italian–Canadian writings. Duranti, instead, offers an example of a text predominantly written in Italian, with the insertion of English terms. In all of the texts, code-switched terms are generally italicised, as conventionally accepted.

1.4 The Existential Connotation of Writing and Self-translating

Michael Cronin (2006) and Loredana Polezzi (2012) have widely investigated the role played by translation in the era of globalisation. They have highlighted that translation and self-translation impact differently on the construction of migrant identity. Heteronomous translation constitutes a mediated communication, which shapes migrants as passive objects of an external act of interpretation and representation, thus limiting their subjectivity and agency. By contrast, self-translation is seen as an autonomous practice that restores migrants' voices and reduces their diversity and distance from the new society. Voice in this instance refers to the ability to actively communicate and operate within a given community. This term has linguistic, cultural and social connotations, as it regulates and determines the mechanisms that renegotiate and redefine migrants' spaces of action and interaction within the new society. Through self-translation, migrants move from being passive objects to active subjects, from being 'translated beings' to 'translating ones'. As translating beings, they are able to express their voice and set the boundaries that define their level of integration, exclusion, participation and adaptation to the new community. They can redefine the personal and collective identity they choose to adopt, as well as the role they choose to play, and what position they aim to occupy within the new society. Therefore, for migrants, 'the right to exercise autonomous forms of translation', rather than receiving them, 'is seen as a crucial element in [their] emancipation [...] and an important factor in their social and psychological well-being' (Cronin 2006, 53–54).

Cronin and Polezzi's analysis will be taken as a starting point, but it will be expanded to include multilingual practices in general, and it will be put in connection with Federica Mazzarra's analysis of arts in migratory contexts. In her essay 'Spaces of Visibility for the Migrants of Lampedusa: The Counter Narrative of the Aesthetic Discourse' (2015), Mazzara examines arts as a practice, which creates spaces of visibility for migrants, thus counteracting processes of dehumanisation and invisibility. Like Cronin and Polezzi, she also claims a voice for migrants and advocates for the need to change 'the position and the roles of observers and observees, in order to gain different perspectives' (2015, 460). This aspect is essential for the transmigrant authors in this volume. Their writing and self-translating are instruments through which they claim their voice, intended as the possibility to tell their own story with their own words, and on their own terms. This possibility has two meanings. On the one hand, they reclaim a voice as women, managing to speak up in a patriarchal and sexist society. They write against gendered norms and societal expectations, rewriting and translating notions of womanhood and motherhood across multiple linguistic, cultural and physical spaces. On the other hand, these authors write against the monolingual paradigm and the notion of a single and fixed allegiance to one country, one language and one culture. Through translingual practices, they textually reproduce the heterogeneous nature of their self, which is made up of several linguistic and cultural identities. The fact that these linguistic and cultural identities are allowed to coexist on the page reflects their coexistence within the individual as well. For instance, this aspect is represented in their choice to self-translate, rather than producing different texts in different languages. In the latter case, bilingual writers keep their languages in a binary relationship, stressing the distance between their linguistic and cultural worlds and producing separate products, which do not overlap or communicate. In self-translation, instead, they create two (or more) versions of a single complex product, textually reproducing and voicing the hybridity of their self:

> self-translators seem instead to juggle or equilibrate both the old and new literary languages and legacies at once, and usually together in frequent interliterary reference, in texts in either language. The sheer act of self-translating is an opening out onto both languages, rather than a binary tension or foreclosure. (Hokenson 2013, 52)

These authors are aware that they belong to more cultures, languages and worlds at the same time. Multilingualism is precisely the instrument they use to take advantage of this position. It constitutes the linguistic transposition of their transmigrant experience. On the page, the word moves across diverse linguistic systems, exactly like these mobile subjects move between different physical spaces. Multilingualism, therefore, helps them to overcome 'the problematic of *inclusion* into the monolingual paradigm' (Yildiz 2012, 121), to escape from the mother (tongue, land)'s claims to exclusivity and to establish affective and creative connections and identifications with dialectal, Italian and English spaces. Belonging to both contexts means to accommodate, that is, to detach the self from exclusive and absolute identifications with specific linguistic, cultural or geographical spaces. Source and target languages, in merging with one another, contribute together not only to the creation of the text but also to the redefinition of their subjectivity, which is inscribed in multiple linguistic and cultural contexts.

1.5 Adding a Linguistic Perspective

Taking this assumption as a starting point, it will be investigated what the bond between language and identity exactly entails on a linguistic and literary level. A study of the connection between language and identity cannot disregard the linguistic dimension because writing and translating are activities where language takes centre stage. By incorporating linguistic elements into the theoretical framework, it will be possible to substantiate theories and provide them with a concrete example of what the practices of writing and self-translating really imply, especially with respect to the use of language. Such an approach is even more useful with respect to the case studies in this volume. Given that they use linguistic means to negotiate identity in transmigrant contexts, it is necessary to analyse how they do this from a linguistic perspective, that is, to move beyond simple metalinguistic reflections on the interconnection between identity and language in migrant narratives. Instead, attention must be paid to language, illustrating what this interconnection entails on a linguistic level.

To this end, the texts will be examined from both a thematic and a linguistic perspective. The aim is to highlight how the transmigrant experience is voiced and inscribed in the text, through storytelling and the translational act. In the first case, it emerges through the rethinking of a series of traditional migrant tropes, which are rewritten from the authors' liminal position. In the second case, it is articulated through CS and a specific form of self-translation, which I define as a *continuum*, intended as a performance in-between writing and translating. In moving from the source to the TT, self-translators do not simply perform translating tasks, but re-enact their authorial voice. In *The Writer's Double: Translation, Writing, and Autobiography*, Rita Wilson paraphrases Ancet and defines translation as 'the conscious side of an activity (writing) that is never totally conscious' (2009, 193). Since translation and writing, in self-translation, are performed by the same individual, self-translation can be considered as the conscious moment of the creative process, which allows writers to rethink and rewrite their work.

Looking at self-translation as a *continuum* requires the relation between original and translation to be reconsidered. If the creation of the ST continues during the translating phase, then the boundary between the source and TT does not exist anymore. The two are in a meta-textual relation, as each version simultaneously determines and is determined by the other one, through a linguistic and cultural exchange demonstrating that the ST has several potential meanings, which still need to be explored. The difference between both versions is simply chronological, and it has nothing to do with matters of status, or authority. As Fitch claims, the 'original' and the self-translated text are in a meta-textual relation (1988, 155). They constitute 'variants of something that enjoys no tangible textual existence but whose existence is none the less implicit in their very co-existence' (1988, 135). The complex literary work that is eventually created arises from the combination and interaction of the authors' voices in the multiple linguistic spaces they belong to.

20 VOICES OF WOMEN WRITERS

For this reason, the definition of self-translation as a *continuum* is deeply interrelated with the self-reflexive dimension of the practice. Writing and translating constitute transitory spaces of continuous rethinking and rewriting, not only of the text but also of the writer's selfhood.

This specific performance of self-translation can be seen in those changes and modifications to the ST that are not required by its re-contextualisation, or by any grammatical or syntactical problems. With respect to this point, I draw on the study offered by Verena Jung *in English-German Self-Translation of Academic Texts and Its Relevance for Translation Theory and Practice* (2002). Even if Jung exclusively analyses academic texts, her study offers useful insights into the analysis of literary self-translation as well. She identifies four types of changes in translated texts:

– Systemic: changes due to the lack of a grammatical or syntactical category in a language.
– Cultural: changes requested to pander to the cultural world of the target audience.
– Skopic: changes made to adjust the text to the expectancy frame of a new readership.
– Optimisational: changes 'in the structure or the information level of the text', that improve its quality (2002, 47–49).

In self-translation, another category of changes can be added. Jung calls them 'revisional' and states that they do not fall within any of the previous categories. She defines them as 'the actual decision of the author at any specific point to rewrite his text, rather than translate the original' (2002, 49). An example of this extreme degree of intervention is represented by changes to the plot; for instance, the Spanish author Suso de Toro, in one of his self-translations, decided to bring back to life one of the characters in the novel.[5] As revisional changes 'defeat any effort to explain them linguistically' (Hokenson and Munson 2007, 198), they are usually seen as the proof that self-translators, having greater freedom of intervention than normal translators, perceive self-translation more as the chance to perform creative tasks rather than translating ones. On the whole, I agree with Jung's classification. Nonetheless, an overlap between 'optimisational' and 'revisional' changes can be identified, because self-translators can decide to rewrite the ST in order to improve it. In light of this, the use of 'revisional' in this volume encompasses 'optimisational' approaches as a single category. The focus on 'revisional changes' constitutes the point of departure for this study of self-translation as a *continuum*. The revisional changes in the narratives are substantial. For instance, Duranti adds or removes several parts in the passage from Italian into English; the Italian text, with its 230 pages, is longer than the English version, which counts up to 118 pages. Moreover, the writers use pronouns and articles dissimilarly to convey diverse meanings in each language. For example, Patriarca's distinct use of definite and indefinite articles sometimes serves the purpose of expressing her diverse relationship with Italy and Canada.

If re-contextualisation is unable to account for revisional changes, then we need to tackle the issue from another perspective and take into consideration other explanations and factors. Within this scenario, the concept of motivation becomes extremely useful, especially in a study of self-translation as a complex human activity. As previously mentioned, recent investigations have shifted the focus of attention to the persona of the self-translator, mainly looking at the drives behind the decision to self-translate, and whether and how these drives affect the writing and translating performance. These studies place emphasis on the why of the self-translation because it is believed to determine the how.[6] The present volume follows exactly this path and examines revisional changes as an overt manifestation of the self-translating subjectivity. Their presence in the TT entails the authorial presence of self-translators and undermines the idea of their invisibility.

1.6 Transnational Italy

1.6.1 What's an Italian's Mother Tongue?

In drawing on the concept of monolingual paradigm, it is necessary to rethink what it means with respect to the Italian context. In his book *Mother Tongues and Other Reflections on the Italian Language*, the linguist Giulio Lepschy states that 'there are some questions concerning the mother tongue that seem to be even more disturbing for Italian than for other languages' (2002, 17). He refers to the complex linguistic situation in the peninsula, which is characterised by the coexistence of dialect alongside standard and regional Italian. This already complex linguistic situation is further complicated because dialects, as well as regional Italian, undergo further inner distinctions. For instance, similarities can be identified between varieties spoken in different regions, while differences can be noticed within the same region, from one city to another, from one town to another. Anna Laura and Giulio Lepschy stress this point also in *The Italian Language Today* (1988). Here, they try to make sense of this linguistic panorama, identifying four linguistic strata: national and regional Italian, and regional and local dialect (1988, 13). They claim that 'there is no polar opposition' between these strata and that 'one can move between the two varieties of the standard and the two varieties of the dialect with an indefinite number of intermediate stages' (1988, 14). They suggest leaving open 'whether these varieties are more appropriately considered to be distinct entities between which one has to switch, or rather dimensions which allow movements along continuous gradients' (1988, 14). This point has to be constantly kept in mind in reading terms such as Italian and dialect in this book. These terms define linguistic entities, which constantly interact and intertwine with each other, because they are characterised by fluid borders.

Given the complex linguistic situation in Italy, concepts such as mother tongue and monolingualism are challenged, acquiring new significance and connotations. One might question which language should be considered an Italian's mother tongue, and whether it would not be more correct to talk about mother tongues. Against this backdrop, the concept of a monolingual paradigm acquires a specific significance for the authors in this corpus. To begin with, none of them truly experiences a 'monolingual condition' before migrating. This is because, as Italians, they grow up speaking regional dialects, alongside the official national language. Despite this multilingual makeup, they initially operate through a monolingual framework, which leads them to identify and forge connections with one language only. However, migration breaks this pattern of continuity and familiarity with an exclusive language, as it relocates these 'monolingual subjects' to a new environment, where new languages are spoken.

In talking about the Italian language, it is necessary to define its relation to English. This is even more important with multilingual practices, where 'le relazioni tra le lingue non sono mai paritarie' (de Rogatis 2023, 46). For instance, the language pair the authors work with is particularly important in self-translation, as the relation between the languages involved plays an essential role in affecting the self-translating performance. To date, a number of studies have mainly focused on 'vertical translation' (Grutman 2013a, 54), which occurs in contexts characterised by languages in an unequal power relation, such as the Iberian Peninsula. Self-translators operating in these contexts mainly self-translate for 'utilitarian' reasons, to reach a wider audience and gain more literary prestige. Hence, they tend to domesticate the ST, in order to bring it closer to the target reader. For instance, translation scholar Xosé Manuel Dasilva (2013) investigated this point in the context of the Iberian Peninsula, addressing the self-translations undertaken from Catalan and Galician into Castilian. He identified the tendency to domesticate the ST, in order to conform to the canon of the dominant language. The same domesticating tendency was identified by Hokenson and Munson in Tagore, who self-translated his works from Bengali into English. His self-translations are so domesticated ('he changed the diction, tone, register, imagery, and form, to resemble stylistic models in contemporary English') that 'today the poems read like plodding love lyrics, more awash in Victorian rose-water than in visionary seas' (2007, 169).

This aspect is particularly important for Italian and English, two languages that cannot be considered as structurally similar. Italian's global position and role also seem to be less predominant than other languages, such as French and Spanish. This aspect is highlighted by Grutman who, in *Beckett e oltre: autotraduzioni orizzontali e verticali*, refers to Marco Micone's self-translation between Italian and French as an example of vertical self-translation (2013a, 45–58). I nonetheless challenge this assumption. Italian cannot be considered a minor language in the same way that Catalan and Gaelic are, for example. Kippur characterises French and Spanish as major world languages (2015, 18). As Italian has a political and literary history which does not greatly differ from them, it is possible to consider it as a major language as well. To further support this, in the aforementioned paper, Grutman himself admits that 'i rapporti tra il francese e l'italiano non sono sempre né dappertutto asimmetrici' (2013a, 55). In her paper 'Breaking the Linguistic Minority Complex through Creative Writing and Self-translation' (2019), Arianna Dagnino argues for a more contextualised definition of a minority language, in relation to literary writing and translation. To do so, she refers to Deleuze and Guattari's investigation into the potential of minor literature to destabilise dominant ones (1975). Taking this point as a starting point, Dagnino contends that 'minor languages in self-translation may act as tools to subvert, escape from and, possibly, decentralize the dominant role of any language perceived as "major" in a particular cultural context' (2019, 114). In looking at the relation between Italian, dialect and English in this book, the same approach will be followed. Italian and dialect will be therefore analysed through their subversive potential. Indeed, the authors in this book use them also to disrupt 'the binary ideological framework of what is minor and what is major, what is dominant and what is subaltern, what is relevant and what is irrelevant' (2019, 115). Through multilingual writing and self-translating, they also fight against the dominant position of a language over another, attempting to decentralise a major language – English – and redefining the power dynamics between dominant and dominated languages.

1.6.2 Migration literature in Italy

In their book *Transcultural Italies: Mobility, Memory and Translation* (2020), Charles Burdett, Loredana Polezzi and Barbara Spadaro claim that 'the history of Italians and of Italian culture stems from multiple experiences of mobility and migration' (2020, 1). Historically, Italy has been a country of emigration since the unification of the peninsula in the 1870s. Italian communities are scattered all over the world, with more than '60 million people around the world currently identifying as having Italian origins' (Burdett et al. 2020, 2). From the 1990s, instead, Italy became a country of immigration, as it was the main destination of several Albanians, following the political and economic instability in their country (Skalle 2017, 76). Contemporary Italy offers a quite unique case, as it is simultaneously a country of emigration and immigration. On the one hand, the country's unstable economic situation pushes many young people to move abroad, either to study or to find a job. On the other hand, Italy is the first stop for migrants coming from African countries (Bonifazi, 2009). From this perspective, the Italian context offers interesting and unique insights into the phenomenon of migration.

Despite Italy's long history of migration, the dominant narrative imposes and sustains homogeneous and fixed notions of citizenship and belonging: 'even though Italian society has become fully multicultural in recent decades, it is still considered quite homogenous, which consequently accentuates the difference between the Italian us and the migrant them' (Skalle 2017, 76). Italian migrant literature, that is, the literature produced by migrant authors in Italy, attempts to counteract this dominant narrative, challenging discourses of nation and belonging, and constantly redefining the notion of Italianness. For this reason, this literature has become an interesting and fruitful area of investigation among scholars and researchers. The first scholar to acknowledge the existence of such literature was Armando Gnisci. In his works *La letteratura italiana della migrazione* (1998) and *Creolizzare l'Europa. Letteratura e migrazione* (2003), Gnisci analysed the role and impact of the literature produced by migrant authors in Italy. In the introduction of *Creolizzare l'Europa*, perhaps too optimistically, he celebrated the extraordinarily lucky case of Italy, in comparison to other nations such as France and Germany. Unlike those countries that had had a longer and more controversial history of immigration, Italy could identify and enjoy *'fin dal primo momento'* (2003, 7) what he thought would be the birth of a creole literature, emerging from the encounter and connection between national and migrant literature. Sadly, Gnisci had probably underestimated the rigid rules of the publishing industry that, to date, is still reluctant to include migrant authors within the Italian literary canon. As claimed by Wilson a few years later, 'the individual and different histories of literature and migration in various national contexts show that the national frame is still a powerful and influential aspect. The Italian literary canon [...] has traditionally excluded authors who did not conform to the ideal of Italian national identity' (2020, 215). Despite the closure and resistance of the publishing field, current research is taking into account the importance of migration in Italy and is paying more and more attention to the literary production of incoming migrants. For instance, in her *Migration Italy: The Art of Talking Back in a Destination Culture*, Parati talks about what she calls 'Italophone literature', intended as the set of 'texts written by migrant authors in Italy and in Italian' (2005: 54). In this book, she analyses texts such as *Volevo diventare bianca* (1993), by Nassera Chohra, and *Lontano da Mogadiscio* (1994), written by Shirin Ramzanali Fazel. Rita Wilson, in *Parallel Creations* (2012), examines several texts, such as *Traiettorie di sguardi. E se gli altri foste voi?* (2001), by Geneviève Makaping, and *Madre piccola* (2007), by Ubax Cristina Ali Farah. Comberiati Daniele focuses on incoming migration in his book *Scrivere nella lingua dell'altro. La letteratura degli immigrati in Italia* (2010). Current research aims to trigger a rethinking of the concept of national and linguistic belonging, to challenge conventional interpretations and beliefs, and to show the benefits deriving from intercultural and interlingual encounters, in opposition to current discourses, which denounce what is seen as 'an infiltration into a monolithic Italian identity under siege' (Parati 2011, 7).

Less attention has been paid to Italian authors abroad. Outward migration has been mostly neglected, possibly in an attempt to ignore the range of social, economic and political causes behind it. Nevertheless, the experiences of Italian authors abroad are interesting because they dismantle the notion of Italianness from within, equally contributing to the construction of a new Italianness, one that transcends physical, cultural and linguistic borders. Essentially, they also take part in what Emma Bond calls the 'transnational turn' in Italian studies (2014, 21). Writing in Italian (and other languages) from abroad, these authors push the boundaries of Italian literature, rewriting national imaginaries and engaging with what I call 'literature in motion', that is, the literature emerging from, and reflecting, their experience of mobility and dislocation. The literature of Italian immigration and emigration shows that there is not a single and invariable way of being Italian and that it is necessary to acknowledge and accept its multiple facets and trajectories. In this book, the focus is exactly on Italian authors abroad, thus aiming to fill in a gap in current research and to demonstrate and validate the importance of their experiences as well. Their personal and literary worlds also call into question traditional discourses and homogeneous representations of Italian identity. They demonstrate that, in our globalised and mobile society, fixed and stable identities cannot be long sustained, and highlight processes of translation at work in contemporary Italian society.

Notes

1 Her investigation deals with the German geopolitical context, where the monolingual paradigm has played a fundamental role. The focus on this context allows her to illustrate in depth the effects of this paradigm, and the changes and transformations brought by new forms of multilingualism. For instance, she illustrates the work of Kafka, highlighting the role played by the Jewish language in his literary and intellectual activity.

2 The title of this section refers to Santoyo's definition of self-translation as 'another vast territory without history' (2006, 22).

3 This emphasis on bilingualism is demonstrated by the fact that the term bilingualism features in the title of many texts dedicated to self-translation. See, for instance, Fitch's (1988), Beaujours' (1989), Oustinoff's (2001) or Hokenson and Munson's (2007) texts.

4 To date, Beckett and Nabokov are the most studied authors. For instance, consider Fitch's analysis of Beckett's self-translation practices, in his *Beckett and Babel: An Investigation into the Status of the Bilingual Work* (1988) and *Self-translation in Vladimir Nabokov's Pnin* (Besemeres, 2000).

5 This happens in *Sete Palabras* (2009), which he self-translated into Spanish as *Siete Palabras* (2010).

6 As Hokenson notices, 'motive is not a common rubric in Translation Studies [...] Yet it is a loss, eliding an important constituent of translation history' (2013, 44).

Chapter 2

GIANNA PATRIARCA: SELF-TRANSLATING AS A STRATEGY OF RE-GROUNDING

2.1 Finding a 'Voice' as an Italian-Canadian Woman

Gianna Patriarca is one of the major voices in Italian-Canadian literature.[1] The term refers to a body of literature produced by over one hundred authors of Italian background living in Canada; some of them were born in Italy and moved to Canada afterwards, while others were born in Canada to Italian parents. Their literary products show two main features. Firstly, they principally deal with the phenomenon of migration and its related issues; secondly, their works are characterised by an extensive multilingualism, which constitutes 'one of the distinctive features of the literatures of the Italian emigration' (Loriggio 2021, 805). Their texts are written in Italian, French, English and regional dialects. Alongside the extensive use of CS, several Italian-Canadian writers also practise self-translation; for instance, Mario Duliani translated his French novel *La ville sans femmes* (1945) into the Italian *La città senza donne* (1946). Likewise, the Quebec author Marco Micone self-translated *Gens du silence* (1996) into the Italian *Non era per noi* (2004).[2]

The beginning of Italian-Canadian writing dates to 1978, thanks to the writer Pier Giorgio Di Cicco, who was also editor of the literary magazine *Books in Canada*. He was the first to realise the existence of an impressive literary production that attempted to express itself and be recognised alongside the official Canadian literature in English and French.[3] To this end, in 1978, he published *Roman Candles*, an anthology of literary works produced by seventeen Italian-Canadian writers. Moreover, in 1978, D'Alfonso, one of the most influential figures in the group, founded Guernica Editions, the publishing house that played a key role in promoting Italian-Canadian writers.[4] The date therefore marks the birth of Italian-Canadian writing as an officially recognised body of literature. It also marks the emergence of an increasing self-awareness and self-consciousness about the relevance and importance of these works; as the writer and academic Joseph Pivato claimed, '[...] we had

28 VOICES OF WOMEN WRITERS

discovered a literature about ourselves, and the great responsibility which this entailed' (1998, 13). These writers became aware that they had created a set of writings that required and deserved the same space of expression and accreditation as mainstream literary productions written in English and French.[5] They also acknowledged the political and ideological importance of their literary productions, through which the story of Italian migration to Canada could finally find a space to be heard.

The specific use of literature as an instrument of expression and recognition emerges both in Patriarca's writing and self-translating activity. The urge to transmit a message shapes her literary career and is deeply interrelated with her life experience. Through her writing and self-translating, she affirms her voice as an Italian-Canadian woman, fighting off a sense of non-existence and non-agency:

> I write because I can, I write because I choose to do so, because it is an action that I control and it will not abandon me unless I want it to abandon me. Writing allows me the choice I was not granted as a child and it is proof that I exist and that I am here (*Exploring Voice: Italian Canadian Female Writers* 2016, 243).

Her poetry has appeared in several anthologies, journals and magazines, as well as being heard on radio and television in Canada. Her books appear on the course lists of many Canadian and American universities, and she has held several lectures at universities such as Yale and Calumet in the U.S., and Udine, Milan and Naples in Italy. Her poetry has been adapted for the stage in a production called *Ciao, Baby* (2001), like the eponymous collection (1999). This production had a very successful three–week run at the Canada Stage Berkeley Street Theatre in Toronto in 2001 and received many great critical reviews.[6] Her work has received several recognitions and awards. For instance, in 2010, her book *My Etruscan Face* was shortlisted for the Bressani Literary Prize. In the same year, Patriarca also became the first recipient of the Science and Culture Award from the Italian Chamber of Commerce of Ontario. In 2012, she received the Jackie Rosati Award for Literature and for promoting women's issues. Her road to success and self-realisation, though, has not been easy and steady. Her poems testify to this long and possibly unfinished struggle to find a space and a voice of her own.

Gianna Patriarca was born in Ceprano, a small town in the province of Frosinone, in Lazio. In 1960, when she was nine years old, she moved to Canada with her sister and her mother in order to reunite with her father, who had migrated five years earlier. At that time, migration from Italy to Canada was common, and it mainly involved peasants from rural areas in

Southern Italy or the North-East. Canada became one of the main destinations for Italians from the late 1940s to the 1970s, during what the sociologist Clifford J. Jansen has defined as the 'postwar boom' (1988, 15). Thousands of Italians arrived in Canada as a consequence of the tragic political and economic situation in Italy. Moreover, thanks to the new sponsorship system, they were allowed to enter the country if they had relatives residing in Canada who could sponsor and support them financially during the settlement phase. The cities that saw the greatest Italian settlement were Toronto and Montréal, where Italian communities constituted up to 2% of the population (Ramirez 1989; Perin and Sturino 1989; Iacovetta 1992). Italy became 'second only to Great Britain as the source of Canadian immigration' (Ramirez 1989, 7), with Pier 21 in Halifax constituting the main port of Italian immigration after World War II. The influence of Italian migration in Canada was officially recognised in 2017, when June was declared Italian Heritage Month in the whole country.

Italians migrated in pursuit of a dream, hoping to improve the conditions of their lives. Most of the time, though, their dreams were unrealised, and their conditions worsened. They had to face economic difficulties, language barriers and alienation, which made settlement in the host country extremely complicated.[7] Patriarca's family encountered the same destiny. In the following passage, the comparison of their Canadian life to living in a dungeon, as well as the use of words such as 'hidden' and 'buried alive', powerfully express and recreate feelings of entrapment and confinement:

> We learned too quickly that dreams often become nightmares. [...] It was as if we had walked from light into the darkness of a dungeon. This dungeon represented our new life: we were hidden, tucked away, buried alive ('Espresso, Camaros and Gianni Morandi', *Daughters for Sale*; 1997, 10).[8]

Once in Canada, Patriarca's parents started working in factories all day, leaving her and her sister alone. In such conditions, her childhood 'became a fading photograph', as she had to become 'the surrogate mother' to her younger sister and 'an adequate homemaker' ('Espresso, Camaros and Gianni Morandi', *Daughters for Sale*; 1997, 10). The movement from Italy to Canada therefore marks her passage into adult life. The refashioning of her role within a familiar and personal space, from daughter and sister to surrogate mother, anticipates and symbolises the redefinition of her role within a public and collective space, too. With the move to a new community, the structural relationship between her identity and specific linguistic, physical and cultural factors is broken. Patriarca must engage with a process of identity reformation, learning to negotiate her condition in between two different spaces: old and new contexts, childhood and adulthood. Her writing and self-translating offer her a way to make sense of, and come to terms with, this in-between condition. The act of self-translating becomes the act of translating 'her self'. It does not surprise, then, that the identity issue recurs often in her poems, which narrate the long journey that has led her to accept her Italian-Canadian identity. Her literary activity can be seen as a novel of re-formation, intended as the narration of individuals' unceasing process of rethinking and re-adapting their selfhood.[9] Her multilingual poems and her self-translations testify to the challenges entailed in this process of personal reconfiguration, while she attempts to cope with her sense of un-belonging and peripheral existence. Patriarca's loss of identity is deeply interrelated with her loss of agency, which is represented by the lower-case 'i' that recurs throughout her poems. By dismissing the uppercase 'I', which seems to impose itself on the page and upon the other words, she metaphorically reduces the self to the same level as the other terms, thus breaking and decreasing its legitimacy and hegemony, as well as questioning the precarious grounds our conventional sense of the self is built on. A coherent and independent self is therefore replaced by a fragmented and dialogic one that lacks an overarching nature.

A parallel can be drawn between the notions of agency and voice, as both refer to individuals' ability to actively communicate and operate within a given community. Both terms have linguistic, cultural and social connotations, as they regulate and determine the mechanisms that negotiate and define individuals' spaces of action and interaction within society. Nonetheless, given the focus on writing and self-translating, preference is given to the term 'voice', as it carries a more overtly linguistic connotation. Three factors determine Patriarca's loss of voice. To begin with, the movement to a country where another language is spoken makes her lose the ability to speak. If agency is mostly 'constructed through linguistic means' (Pavlenko and Lantolf 2000, 164), movement to a different linguistic community limits the ways in which she can exert her agency. It therefore makes her realise the empowering dimension of language, which can impact participation in the host society. Her need to master the host language is linked, rightly, to its conceptualisation as a factor in integration and emancipation. As expressed in the following passage, Patriarca must master English to overcome the connotations of inferiority her linguistic ignorance carries:

> They put us back a year thinking that, because we could not speak the language, we must also be slow-learners. We fooled them. We learned the language quickly and this helped us survive ('Espresso, Camaros and Gianni Morandi', *Daughters for Sale*; 1997, 10–11).

Speaking English becomes a strategy of survival, thus anticipating one of the most recurring tropes in her literary production: the possibility to speak and write is deeply interwoven with the possibility to exist. Pavlenko and Lantolf (2000, 167) identify the migrant's appropriation of other voices as one of the first stages in the process of recovery from the loss of the mother tongue. For Patriarca, the internalisation of 'the voice of the other' – that is, the English language – operates precisely as a rooting factor. It grants her recognition and participation, as it allows her to renegotiate her position within the new community.

Her loss of agency is also linked to her gender. More specifically, it is related to her being a girl in a patriarchal society. The Italian community she grew up in was strongly male-dominated. Women were subjected to conscious and unconscious mechanisms of control and were trapped in submissive and traditional roles. This aspect is encapsulated in Patriarca's struggle to affirm and pursue her literary ambitions. At first, she decides to comply with what her family expected her to become – a primary teacher. Like she narrates in 'Espresso, Camaros and Gianni Morandi' (*Daughters for Sale*; 1997, 10), she knew she had 'no choice', 'the decision had already been made' for her, and she simply accepted a fate that seemed too difficult to escape. Nevertheless, as a result of migrating to Canada, a more liberal and tolerant society than Italy in the 1960s, she realises that alternative forms of femininity exist. She understands that the reconstruction of her selfhood can happen only in relation to a process of deconstruction of a gendered identity and of disidentification with the traditional roles expected of Italian women. Within this scenario, for Patriarca and other Italian-Canadian female authors, writing becomes an instrument of emancipation and liberation: 'many Canadian women writers raised in an Italian immigrant environment were not encouraged to "speak," and therefore many of them used their writing "to speak up" or "to speak out"' (Canton 2018, 89).[10] In reshaping their own subjectivity through the act of writing and self-translating, they also write against patriarchal authority. Their agency in redefining their identity, therefore, is also played out in terms of gender. If traditionally 'women's experiences have been interpreted for them by men and according to male norms' (Pavlenko 2001, 226), for Italian-Canadian women writers, the possibility to interpret and tell their stories according to female rules constitutes a further way to regain and express agency. This is the reason why they often talk about migration from a female perspective. Most of their writings deal with women's struggles to find a voice of their own in such a controlled context. Their stories illustrate the contrast between Italian and Canadian values, highlighting how the movement to a new country eventually led Italian women to rethink conventional ideas of femininity. Their writings

32   VOICES OF WOMEN WRITERS

therefore possess a revolutionary connotation; they introduce change and empower Italian women (De Luca 2007, Canton 2018, Saidero 2018).

Lastly, Patriarca loses her voice when she ceases to be identified as an individual and starts to be seen as a category, that is, as an Italian migrant. Seeing human beings as a category means focusing exclusively on their shared attributes, neglecting the personal and unique traits that make everyone inherently different from one another. This aspect is evident in the poem 'My Etruscan Face' (*My Etruscan Face*; 2007, 28), where the author presents her outer appearance through the eyes of the local community:

> my Etruscan face betrays me/faded with time/my profile etched on stone/disintegrates/i am a museum piece/a fresco stumbled upon/ by the curious art student/who observes history/in the lines/the grandmother/of another century/everything about me sings the past/ my skin/my eyes/the fullness of my belly/the art student takes me home/ a souvenir.

The representation of her body as a souvenir inserts Patriarca into a narrative of tradition and history. Souvenirs are 'material objects which serve as reminders of people, places, events or experiences of significance in a person's biography' (Cohen 2000, 548), because people attach functional and symbolic meanings to them. In looking at her Italian body, Canadians construct Patriarca's identitarian narrative by means of a series of socio-cultural and historical associations. The image of the souvenir therefore has a negative reading. Souvenirs are mass-produced; they adjust to a specific model, which is usually reiterated with slight variations. By perceiving her as a 'souvenir', the Canadian gaze undermines Patriarca's sense of self. As such, her Italian body operates like a mask: it conforms to 'what' the others perceive and hides 'who' she really is because it is emblematic and representative of a specific idea of Italianness.

In this context, Patriarca's struggle to find her voice represents her struggle to express 'who' she is rather than complying with 'what' she seems to represent. Her writing and self-translating express this need and desire to redefine herself on her own terms, both as a woman and as a hyphenated individual. They constitute attempts to break the silence, moving beyond any form of constraints, manipulations and external representation and letting the truth behind her personal story emerge. The urge to write coincides with the urge to exist, and it derives from the experience of being voiceless, both on a linguistic and existential level. In giving herself a narrative voice, Patriarca manages to give herself an existential voice, too. This is exhibited in 'Woman in Narrative', one of the poems in the collection *My Etruscan Face*, where the overlap between being and writing reaches its zenith: 'i speak/i am the words/the words are me/there is nothing deeper/hidden' (2007, 13). To be is to write, and vice versa.

Patriarca's migration can therefore be seen as both a physical and a psychological journey. It is not only a journey outside – from one country to another – but also inside, as she must engage with a process of personal reformation in the attempt to heal the dualistic sense of self she has long been haunted by. Exposed to alternative forms and possibilities, she must translate 'her self'; in order to re-ground, she has to negotiate and locate her identity at the crossroads of Italian and Canadian spaces. Her split identity results precisely from her perpetual movement of inclusion and exclusion from both Italian and Canadian communities and from being trapped between contrasting ideas of Italianness and Canadianness. This feeling of eternal displacement, which is generated by the impossibility of finding a place where she fully belongs, can be overcome only by learning to live in between push and pull factors, creating a space where these opposite poles can interact dialogically. This space is a linguistic one: if identity is dependent on language, then its redefinition cannot disregard the linguistic means. The distance between Italy and Canada can be annihilated through her literary activity. Through this, she can invent and tell her personal story ('i am ciociara', *My Etruscan Face*; 2007, 26). For her, the need to write and self-translate therefore has ontological roots; the tale eventually coincides with existence (Cavarero 2000, 56). The practice of writing and self-translating her story is not separated from the experience of living it. On the contrary, writing, self-translating and living are combined and connected in what constitutes a process of self-recognition and self-affirmation. Her literary activity reflects her condition as an individual situated between different spaces, one who manages to defeat her sense of 'being out of place, uprooted', with a sense of 'being in a hybrid place, hybrid-rooted'.

2.2 Rethinking Home and Belonging through Poetry

Gianna Patriarca has written seven collections of poems:

- *Italian Women and Other Tragedies (1994);*
- *Daughters for Sale (1997);*
- *Ciao, Baby (1999);*
- *Invisible Woman (2003);*
- *What My Arms Can Carry (2005);*
- *My Etruscan Face (2007);*
- *Too Much Love (2012).*

Moreover, she has written a children's book, *Nonna and the Girls Next Door* (2004) and a collection of short stories, *All my Fallen Angelas* (2016). The autobiographical component in her books is strong. For example, several poems are dedicated to the relations between her and her family members, such as those where she explores the relationship with her daughter; adopting the perspective of a mother, Patriarca rethinks the relation to her own mother. Despite her attempts to not retrace her mother's steps, she ends up experiencing the same dynamics with her own daughter. Eventually, she realises that every mother-daughter relationship is characterised by phases of continuity and discontinuity, identification and disidentification. This relation is destined to be constantly reproduced in a cycle where each part is continuously reminded of what 'being mother' and 'being daughter' entail, in what Anna Pia De Luca calls 'passaggio di consegne generazionale' (2007, 34). Many of her poems are dedicated to her experience as a primary teacher in a poor and migrant area of Toronto. Her stories abound with abused or neglected children, illustrating the intergenerational conflict within the context of mobility and examining how migration redefined the relationship between Italian parents and their 'figli canadesi' (Ciao, Baby 1999, 84).

The reconstruction of Patriarca's linguistic biography is a prerequisite for an understanding of her literary activity. If her subjectivity is expressed through writing and self-translating, then the topics she writes about, the choice to self-translate and how she does it can be understood only in relation to her linguistic trajectory and her life experience. This connection can emerge only by combining literary criticism and linguistic analysis, an approach that will be adopted in each chapter. This paragraph specifically adopts the perspective of literary criticism, to conduct a thematic investigation of Patriarca's poems. The aim is to illustrate how she refers to conventional themes of migrant literature but rethinks and rewrites them from her transmigrant perspective. To this end, the focus is on the concepts of 'home' and 'belonging'. While in migrant narratives these imaginaries usually follow a dialectical framework, in Patriarca's poems the transmigrant experience emerges from her continuous back-and-forth movement between these opposite poles. The author depicts them as transitory spaces whose features and attributes are constantly demolished and re-built through her perceptions, memories and feelings. In this hybrid space, borders and oppositions do not exist, but everything is connected and interwoven; nothing is fixed and immutable, but everything is changeable and shifting.

'Home' constitutes one of the most recurrent tropes in migrant and diasporic literature. It is a prototypical image that, rich in symbolism, allows migrants to address issues such as 'nostalgia, and roots, and the conflicts between the values of the old and new worlds' (Nyman 2009, 37). This traditional view of home is dependent upon a native/foreign place dialectic. Home represents the physical space where one was born and is made of familiar images, people, tastes and sounds. It exists in contraposition to the foreign place, which represents a site of alienation and estrangement.

However, the transnational dimension of contemporary migration has led to a rethinking of these conventional dualities. This aspect emerges in the narratives of contemporary migrant authors, where 'home' and 'away' are not constructed as opposites set against one another but are used to question dualities and binaries and to articulate new meanings and significances. This tendency is evident in the Canadian literary scene; contemporary writers rewrite the literary tropes of the first wave in transnational terms (Caporale-Bizzini 2018, Hutcheon 2019), as they overcome the trauma of displacement and successfully reposition themselves between Italy and Canada. For instance, in Patriarca's poems, home is reconfigured as a space that is no longer geographically or linguistically bound. It is rather a mental attitude, a way to perceive and conceive of the relationship with her origin and host lands. The author experiences what Nannavecchia calls 'the permeability of borders' (2014, 14), as her 'home' resurfaces at different points in time and space through a complex and variable layering of associations, perceptions and positions. Her relationship with Italy and Canada is the result of continuous mental and emotional uprootings and re-groundings, which move her between numerous and transitory feelings of homeliness and un-homeliness. This attitude emerges through her entire literary output, which covers different periods of her life and her writing career. Such an extended chronological dimension defines her transmigration not only as a movement over space but also over time. To illustrate this point, I examine the collection of poems entitled *What My Arms Can Carry* (2005), which is representative of the discourse I have put forward. In representing her relationship with her native country, Patriarca continuously switches between an idyllic recall and a recognition of home as a place that displays some level of strangeness and unfamiliarity. The first attitude emerges in the following poem:

> it is the landscape i miss/it is the unbelievable beauty/of a mimosa in bloom/of a fig tree with its ripe/sensuous fruit/it is the market on Saturday/the red tomatoes/the goat cheese salty and sharp/the birds on the windowsill/it is the smell of extinguished/wax candles at evening mass ('What I Miss'; 2005, 104).

She is articulating a backwards movement, reclaiming a sense of rootedness in, and belonging to her native country. The phrase 'I miss' expresses her need to establish a form of continuity and connection with her native land.

36 VOICES OF WOMEN WRITERS

The objects and practices she lists metaphorically function as points of reference along the path that leads her back home. The poem is articulated around two blocks. In the first part, Patriarca alludes to Ceprano: her hometown is recreated through a series of items (a fig tree, the birds on the windowsill, wax candles) and ritual practices (the evening mass, the market on Saturday). They help her to recreate a sense of home (Jones 2011; Drozdzewski, De Nardi, & Waterton 2016), as they trigger a series of associations with specific people, scenes and moments of her life in Italy. Indeed, habitual routines and practices contribute to constructing 'a liveable structure of security, familiarity, community, and comfort' (Ratnam 2018, 4). Objects also constitute effective reminders of home by virtue of two specific features. Firstly, they give Patriarca's memories a tangible and concrete dimension, thus reducing the elusiveness of all distant things and increasing her feeling of closeness to home. Secondly, their sentimental value helps her connect to the emotional dimension of home despite being in diverse and unfamiliar territory. Objects thus offer her a way to preserve and access past emotions, to evoke and recall events and feelings belonging to another time and space, and to restore lost linkages and relations.[11] In the second part of the poem, the author refers to Rome. The eternal city is evoked through the reference to Bernini's 'magnificent statues'. This reference to Rome, the capital of Italy, functions as a point of departure for a broader appreciation of Italy and its beauties, occupying the concluding lines of the poem.

However, alongside this sentimental and nostalgic description of the native land, in the same collection, Patriarca inserts poems that deliberately foreground the foreignness of Ceprano, expressing it through the traditional image of the 'return home':

> i am a tourist now/in this town i once called home/this place i keep coming back to/looking for whatever it is/i might have left behind/ [...] but it is not home/that i come back to/i am simply a stray cat/bewitched by/curiosity ('Ceprano/Carnevale'; 2005, 110–111).

The idea of home as spatially and temporally fixed reveals itself to be necessarily misleading because it ignores the mutable essence of reality. This idealised image is destined to fall when migrants make the 'return home', which 'reveals the inability of memory [...] to produce a determinate image of the native "home"', and forces migrants 'to rework the terms which identify the native "home" as such' (Facchinello 2005, 116–117). This aspect is expressed in the passage above, where Patriarca defines Ceprano as the place that she 'once called home' but which 'is not home' anymore. Her estrangement from the 'once familiar place' is expressed also through terms such as 'tourist' and 'stray cat'. Defining herself as a tourist in Ceprano means denying any intimate bond with the place; comparing herself to a stray cat further disrupts this connection, as stray literally means to be homeless. In 'Ritorno' (*What My Arms Can Carry*; 2005, 115), this feeling of unfamiliarity becomes even stronger, expanding from places to people. In visiting her relatives still living there, Patriarca realises the formality and shallowness of their relationship: 'my cousin's wife is polite/she offers me coffee/ [...] there is insignificant/ chatter between us/we are strangers'.[12] By destabilising the traditional view of the family as a site of intimacy and closeness, she unveils the unfamiliar potential of the familiar space. Migrants' sense of home is recreated through their relationships with relatives and friends, which guarantee them a form of rooting in the country of origin (Romoli, Cardinali, Ferrari, and Migliorini 2022). For Patriarca, the sentimental connection to her cousin is fundamental to generating her emotional attachment to Italy. However, the failure to establish this connection destabilises her relationship with Italy and further unveils the illusory and misleading connotation of 'returning home'.

Return journeys occupy an important space in Italian-Canadian writing. In the narratives of the first and second generations, the return home often represents a starting point to rethink and redefine their positioning in both Italian and Canadian spaces (De Luca 2013; Saidero 2021). This is evident in Patriarca's poems, where the original opposition between 'here' and 'there' is undermined and further complicated. 'Home' now emerges through multiple backward and forward movements, where no place can be identified as origin or host. Devoid of any physical, temporal, or linguistic connotation, 'home' can be constantly destabilised and recreated. Indeed, 'home' is not only where your roots are but also where your routes lead you.

Her reconceptualisation of the concept of 'belonging' must be understood against the same backdrop. Belonging and un-belonging refer to the perspective that migrants use in looking at and judging the habits and behaviours of the host society. Nira Yuval-Davis differentiates between 'belonging' and the 'politics of belonging'. 'Belonging' is about emotional attachment, feeling at home and feeling safe. The 'politics of belonging' concerns 'specific political projects aimed at constructing belonging in particular ways to particular collectives that are, at the same time, themselves being constructed by these projects in very particular ways' (2006, 197). In this analysis, the term 'belonging' is used to refer to Yuval-Davis' concept of the 'politics of belonging'. The latter is more relevant and useful to the present analysis, as it identifies belonging as a process rather than a state. Talking about the 'politics of belonging' refers to the idea that belonging is not something that individuals naturally possess but something that they can intentionally and consciously perform.

38 VOICES OF WOMEN WRITERS

Migration affects individuals' sense of community belonging as they find themselves operating in a new context where old norms do not function anymore. The most common activities cannot be done naturally but need to be understood and learned. This aspect is often highlighted in migrant narratives, where migrants narrate the complex process of assimilation into the host country and the struggle to internalise local customs and habits. From a transmigrant perspective, the concept of belonging is nonetheless further complicated because even the native land can reveal itself as a site of un-belonging. The country of origin becomes a place that does not naturally grant inclusion and affiliation as migrants struggle to fully identify themselves with the origin society. At the same time, the latter does not recognise them as members anymore. The belief in individuals' natural belonging to the place where they were born is therefore dismantled.

This aspect recurs quite often in Patriarca's poems, where it is again explored through the 'return home'. For instance, this point is evident in her description of her return to Ceprano and of her relation to the local community, which perceives her as an outsider and labels her as an 'American tourist': '*you come from America*/they ask/i answer/no/i come from here/America is where i live' ('Marzo 21, 2003', *What My Arms Can Carry*; 2005, 71). On the one hand, these words emphasise her feeling of exclusion, as she is recognised as an outsider in both Italy and Canada. On the other hand, they reinforce her attachment to Italy. As she identifies Ceprano as the place 'where she comes from', and America as the place 'where she simply lives', she makes a backwards movement. Her statement is an assertion of rootedness in a specific and unique place. Nevertheless, being labelled as an American tourist makes her realise her fictitious and incomplete affiliation with Italy. It breaks her illusory view of home as a place where she naturally belongs. This failed return to a community she feels part of, yet which perceives her as a stranger, makes her realise that she is trying to rearticulate a narrative of belonging that instead excludes her. She experiences the country of origin as 'an uncomfortable location of belonging' (Parati 2005, 7); as one that problematises and questions her belonging there as a natural gift of birth. In the end, she realises that she does not belong in Ceprano any more than she does in Toronto. Unable to claim a place where she totally belongs, she tries to forge a sense of hybrid belonging that could suit both her Italian and Canadian cultures. By consequence, there are no spaces that can be identified as origin and host but only intermediate spaces, emerging from her continuous movement backwards and forwards. In the same poem, in fact, she admits being 'another immigrant/another torn and broken soul/forever in a storm/two moons/two hearts/two deaths' (2005, 70). Eventually, she recognises that she belongs to a hybrid space,

GIANNA PATRIARCA

which is created by the continuous contact between her two linguistic, cultural and physical systems. In this space, she is constantly engaged with processes of translation, negotiation and mediation.

2.2.1 *Rethinking Politics of 'Home' for Italian-Canadian Women*

In migrant narratives, the movement to another country is often explored as a metaphor of 'liberation and transgression' (Burns 2013, 103). The physical distance from the mother (land) can enact migrants' process of detachment from its psychological and emotional legacy, freeing them from social, familiar and cultural constrictions. The concept of 'home', in this context, takes on a metaphorical status. It refers not only to the physical place where one was born but also to a set of elements and features that define the individual's personal and social identity. Against this backdrop, reassessing the meaning of 'being home' coincides with developing a form of criticism towards the culture of the country of origin. Martin and Mohanty call this process 'not being home', intended as the recognition of the illusory construction of home: 'Not being home is a matter of realising that home was an illusion of coherence and safety based on the exclusion of specific histories of oppression and resistance' (1988, 196). Migrants start feeling an emotional and psychological distance between themselves and the native land: 'the relationship of continuity [...] is substituted by a relationship of detachment' (Burns 2013, 102), which gives them a 'strange lucidity' (de Certeau 1997, 71). They are now able to look at the origin land from the position of an external observer, as the physical distance allows them to develop some critical potential.

This aspect is particularly strong for Patriarca, who articulates her criticism of Italian values and traditions through stories of domestic violence and oppression. The notion of home as a site of harmony and safety is problematised and re-conceptualised as a space of power relations and misogynist attitudes. Home becomes a limiting and suffocating place, sometimes even violent and dangerous, as depicted in the poems, where she tells the stories of many children who are neglected or ill-treated by their parents. This is the case of Marilisa, a young girl who is abused by her father:

> when Marilisa told me/*Jesus keeps telling me to do things*/i knew it wasn't Jesus talking/i brought it/to my superior/ [...] Marilisa's father was eventually/charged/her tiny abused body/taken away/i never saw her again/the social worker's report quoted/the mother's testimony at the inquiry/better at home than outside the home/she had said ('Better at Home', *My Etruscan Face*; 2007, 61).

40 VOICES OF WOMEN WRITERS

This poem contests the idea of home as a site providing a sense of security. Home demonstrates its potential as a space that can also be dangerous and unsafe. For Marilisa, danger is inside the domestic space. The traditional relation between external place/unsafe place and internal place/safe place is overturned. The internal place, which is represented by home, proves to be more dangerous than the external one, which is represented by school. Within this scenario, the sentence 'better at home' appears ironic.

Patriarca's rethinking of 'home' is intrinsically linked with rethinking women's conditions.[13] She describes how Italian women's existence was constrained by gendered discourses, dynamics of power and oppression. In the poem 'Marisa' (*Italian Women and Other Tragedies*; 1994, 65), the woman's subjugation finds a brilliant figurative representation in the image of her bending over: 'Marisa/si piega/verso i figli/si piega/verso il marito/ si piega/verso tutto'. The act of bending over represents her tendency to surrender to the needs of her family members. In 'Taking (a) Place: Female Embodiment and the Re-grounding of Community' (2003, 91–112), Gedalof claims that women serve the symbolic function of representing 'home', intended as the place where traditions and values are preserved and where continuity and stability are reproduced.[14] This function becomes particularly relevant within migratory contexts, where the connection with the origin home is broken. The movement abroad breaks the sense of community belonging and of collective identity because migrants find themselves operating in a different context with new rules and practices. In order to provide 'the appearance of sameness and stability in ever-changing contexts' (Gedalof 2003, 101), women are 'called upon to *be* place' (Gedalof 2003, 94); more specifically, to be home in those contexts where home has been torn away. This aspect is evident in the following passage, where Patriarca illustrates how the personal and social positioning of women within the Italian migrant community was tied to fixed identities and roles:

> Growing into young women we were made to believe we had roughly three choices for our future. The first choice was going to a commercial high school and learning the skills to become a good secretary. The second choice (if we were pretty enough) was to get married before or after graduation, and become good wives and mothers. The third choice (if we were slightly more ambitious) was to become school teachers or bank tellers. We bought into these role models without question. And although there was nothing wrong with these choices we were convinced there were no other options ('Espresso, Camaros and Gianni Morandi', *Daughters for Sale*; 1997, 11–12).

This description is in line with the portrait of Italian women that can be found in most works written by female Italian-Canadian authors. In these narratives, women are often described 'as the "homey-churchy" type: a submissive, chaste, plump creature closely guarded by protective fathers, husbands and brothers who was not allowed to socialize outside the family circle and the parish neighbourhood' (Saidero 2018, 110). The same approach prevails in the paragraph above; as Patriarca narrates, Italian girls believed they had only 'three choices' for their future, were convinced that 'there were no other options' and 'bought into these role models without question'. By accepting and reiterating these models of femininity, they preserved beliefs and practices that forged a sense of belonging within the Italian migrant community, thus contributing to guaranteeing a form of 'rooted belonging' in a context of 'rootless mobility' (Ahmed, Castañeda, Fortier and Sheller 2003, 3).[15] The necessity of confirming a specific private and public idea of femininity was a way to counteract the revolutionary model incarnated by Canadian women.

However, in her paper 'Women and Religion in Italian-Canadian Narratives', Saidero explores the empowering dimension of several narratives written by female Italian-Canadian writers. She highlights how they attempt to debunk 'conventional patriarchal inscriptions of womanhood' (2018, 107), instead 'creating an interstitial space in which a new, empowered image of the Italian-Canadian woman can emerge' (2018, 107). Patriarca's poems must be read against this backdrop. If 'to challenge the association of women with "place"', it is necessary 'to argue for women's "right to travel"' (Gedalof 2003, 106), then the author shows how the movement to the more tolerant and open Canadian society led Italian women to develop and explore new forms of femininity, thus counteracting the patriarchal oppression they were exposed to:[16]

> As girlfriends we spent much of our spare time in each other's homes, usually in the basements drinking espresso, sneaking cigarettes, exploring new feelings and talking about boys and marriage ('Espresso, Camaros and Gianni Morandi', *Daughters for Sale*; 1997,13).

Patriarca takes as a starting point the image of home as a concrete physical space and uses it to symbolically refer to home as a set of community values and beliefs. The Italian girls she talks about operate within the domestic space, as they meet in each other's houses, specifically in the basement. The reference to the basement, which constitutes the lowest part of the house, further reinforces their physical and existential confinement. As we keep reading, however, we realise that Patriarca rethinks this 'physical enclosure', reimagining home as a place of tension between tradition and transformation, between fixity and change. Inside the domestic space, Italian girls perform an alternative femininity, by 'drinking espresso, sneaking cigarettes, exploring new feelings'; that is, by performing behaviours that, within the Italian community, were not considered acceptable for girls. In doing so, they find a balance between 'traditionalism and progressivism' (Saidero 2018, 107), as demonstrated by their chats about 'boys and marriage', which show their attempt to explore their sexuality, at the same time showing allegiance to tradition. Thus, they resist dominant discourses and renegotiate their female identity, experiencing the transformative power of movement even in a traditionally enclosed and confining site. As they oppose the pulling forces of the Italian migrant community, which wants to tie them down to their Italian legacy, they shift from a position of being to one of becoming.[17]

For Italian women, 'being home' is neither safe nor fulfilling; on the contrary, 'being away' is stimulating and reassuring. The affirmation of their selfhood is therefore deeply interrelated with breaking the attachment to 'home' and creating a bond with the host country. They feel the tension between being constantly pushed back to their distant homelands and being pulled towards the new community, between their cultural and social Italian heritage and the Canadian context. The only way to overcome this tension is to position themselves between these opposite poles and mediate between these conflicting drives. For Patriarca, rethinking 'home' means precisely moving beyond the conventional opposition between roots and routes (Clifford 1997), origin and host country, departure and arrival. She does not ascribe a path that simply goes backwards or forwards. Her path is characterised by multiple comings and goings that can lead her closer to the host or to the country of origin. Both uprooting and re-grounding thus cease to be dichotomous processes and are redefined as constant practices of 'crossing borders', spanning several phases, levels and locations.

2.3 Code-switching, or the Language of Memory

Patriarca's rethinking of home will now be further informed by the linguistic analysis of her poems. The latter will illustrate how she uses language to locate herself at the crossroads between Italian and Canadian spaces. CS becomes an instrument to negotiate her belonging to both sites, alternatively expressing her insider or outsider's gaze. She writes and translates her poems in English, Italian and the dialect of Ciociaria, an area in the region of Lazio. Through the extensive use of CS, she creates a mainly monolingual text presenting traces of her other languages, thus establishing a constant dialogue between her multiple mother (tongues and lands) and translating her existential

GIANNA PATRIARCA 43

transmigration into a linguistic one. In this paragraph, this function will be illustrated through three semantic domains: food, nouns referring to family members and comfort nouns (*piazza* and *paesani*). The latter refers to things and people that have become 'signifiers of Italianness' (Tamburri 2003, 149).[18]

In migrant narratives, food constitutes one of the domains where CS occurs most frequently. This type of CS constitutes a form of lexical need because the field of food is invested with a high degree of specificity, which 'enhances a word's chances of being used as a codeswitch' (Backus 2001, 127). When addressing a culinary item, it is often necessary to use the original term because a correct equivalent in the other language does not exist. However, in migrant narratives, CS in the domain of food also fulfils an 'identitarian' function. As several studies (Giachetti 1992, Caplan 1997, Lentz 1999) have pointed out, in the context of mobility, retaining some food habits can enact processes of personal and collective identification. As they trigger specific cultural, social, religious and geographical associations, cooking practices guarantee migrants a form of placement in the context of displacement, and of affiliation within the context of alienation. This point has been specifically stressed by Comellini within the context of Italian-Canadian literature: 'gli autori canadesi contemporanei si avvalgono del vino e del cibo come metafora della ricerca tanto dell'identità individuale quanto di quella collettiva' (2004, 105). In Patriarca's poems, references to traditional dishes are invested with both emotional and social meanings, as they become instruments with which she forges memory and affiliation. They allow her to make a journey backwards, re-inscribing herself within an Italian territory and voicing her Italian identity. Essentially, she uses food references not only to define *who* she is but also *where* she is (Padolsky 2005, 19); that is, to negotiate and reconcile her position in both Italian and Canadian spaces. The poem 'Two Fat Girls' (*Ciao, Baby*; 1999, 52), demonstrates this function well:

> grocery stores crammed with all/the delicacies from Sicily and Calabria/ from Molise to Lazio/artichokes and eggplants like shiny trophies/ on the sunny open market/Tre Mari[19] Bakery where we stopped for *zeppole*/on the feast of St. Joseph/and that one treasured café/where we spent our street life/sipping cappuccino before they were cool.

Here, she adopts her childhood perspective, as she remembers the days spent with a friend, walking along St. Claire Avenue, dreaming about their future, and interacting with other Italian migrants. In her childhood memories, this circumscribed space -'the St. Claire Avenue from Dufferin to Lansdowne'- is described as a piece of Italian land within Canadian territory. As she says, her *paesani* had claimed this space to be theirs and had created an

44 VOICES OF WOMEN WRITERS

Italian *locus* where their religious, culinary and social traditions and norms could be preserved and reproduced. The delicacies she mentions function as signposts and lead the reader on a journey through the different Italian regions, from south to north. For instance, eggplants are popular in Sicilian gastronomy, while artichokes are used in several recipes in Lazio. The same effect is achieved through the reference to the 'Tre Mari Bakery'. This 'Italian-Canadian' café is named after a famous Italian bakery brand, Tre Marie, which started in the Milanese area. Referring to food in this passage serves the function of recreating a familiar space, which is opposed to the unfamiliar Canadian one. This goal is achieved through the reference to 'zeppole' and the festivity of Saint Joseph. In Italy, the festivity of Saint Joseph coincides with Father's Day. In Christian tradition, Saint Joseph represents the loving and caring father, chosen by God to be the Virgin Mary's husband and Jesus' father.[20] His figure, therefore, hints at the sense of protection and love that individuals normally experience within the family unit. In referring exactly to this festivity when talking about her life within the Italian community, Patriarca expands this sense of protection and love to the entire community. As already mentioned, this aspect is further reinforced by the reference to 'zeppole'. In the South of Italy, on Saint Joseph's Day, tradition requires that 'zeppole' be made. They are Italian pastries consisting of fried dough, which is usually topped with sugar and filled with cream, custard or jelly. Within the Italian migrant community in Toronto, the 'Tre Mari Bakery' preserves this tradition. In baking them for the entire Italian community on Saint Joseph's Day, the Tre Mari bakery looks after this community exactly like a father normally takes care of his children. If the act of making and sharing food is itself perceived as a way to express love and affection, Patriarca's words portray the bakery as a familiar space where Italian migrants would find their traditional food but also enjoy a form of sociality that is perceived as typically Italian. The café also contributes to forging and reinforcing a sense of collectivity as it preserves the culinary traditions of a specific group. The reference to the café therefore 'takes us from the domain of individuals and families to that of groups' (Padolsky 2005, 24), as Patriarca constructs the identity of Italian society in sharp contrast with the individualist nature of the Canadian one. It is for this reason that she resorts to code alteration. Switching to Italian allows her to voice her Italian half, describing the Italian circle from an internal perspective. Codeswitching helps her to articulate a backward movement; by linguistically re-grounding herself in the Italian community, she claims her belonging there.

In the following passage, however, CS is used to achieve the opposite effect, that is, to question her relationship with the native land and to undermine the significance of the 'return home'. While she longs to go back and claims

GIANNA PATRIARCA

her belonging to the Italian community, her specific use of the word 'piazza' highlights her impossibility to do so;

> i stand back and watch/the *piazza* ignite/costumes, music, laughter/ children's limitless cries [...] it is not *my* town anymore/home is not about material/it is not the cobblestones/or the *piazza*/it is not the church or the/bells/although the umbrella pines and/the cypress trees by the cemetery/always felt like home ('Ceprano/Carnevale', *What My Arms Can Carry*; 2005, 110).

Patriarca is visiting her hometown on Carnival Day. Going back home, though, she realises that she does not feel part of that place anymore. The image of her 'standing back and watching' depicts her as an outsider, whose physical confinement symbolises her feelings of estrangement and exclusion. These feelings become even stronger in contrast to the image of the square. In Italian cities and towns, the square plays an important social role of aggregation, as the life of the community is articulated around this public space.[21] This is evident in the passage above, where Patriarca describes the piazza as the centre where the community has gathered to celebrate Carnival. The reference to the 'piazza', therefore, hints at its social function and at a lifestyle that can be seen as typically Italian and that is missing in the Anglophone world. If 'landscapes in poems are often interior landscapes [and] are maps of a state of mind' (Atwood 1996, 49), the constant reference to the 'piazza' might symbolise Patriarca's nostalgia for a different form of sociality. It is, however, also one for which she is no longer entitled to be part and can, therefore, only 'stand back and watch'.[22] This meaning is further highlighted by the italicisation of the possessive adjective 'my'. This stylistic stratagem signals that 'my' is the focus of attention and that it must be read in combination with piazza, the other term that appears italicised in the poem. The possessive in the broader context of the poem makes it clear that italicisation has an ironic and contrastive function, as it reinforces the awareness that her connection with Ceprano is now broken. The town that she defines as 'mine' is not hers anymore. CS, then, acquires social and emotional value as it conveys her feeling of alienation. In standing alone and observing 'the others' having fun and celebrating, Patriarca reinforces her outsider position and rethinks the relationship with her past. In her paper 'Landscapes of return: Italian-Canadian writing published in Italian by Cosmo Iannone Editore', Baldo analyses the 'landscape of return' (2013, 200) in Italian-Canadian writing. She claims that, in these works, scattering Italian or dialectal words in an English text, or translating into Italian is a way to rethink and rewrite the return to the homeland.

46 VOICES OF WOMEN WRITERS

This aspect emerges in the example above, where CS does not equal return (2013, 200); it rather signifies its impossibility.

The use of language as an instrument to create and claim affiliation and allegiance to the origin country becomes evident in Patriarca's use of the term 'paesani'. This colloquial word was used by Italian migrants in Canada to refer to their fellow countrymen. By adopting it, Patriarca foregrounds her belonging to the Italian community, expressing her emotional and social closeness to the people she is talking about. As such, CS in the following examples is 'indicative of group identification' (Alvarez- Cáccamo 1998, 36):

> he worked with great/slabs of stone/marble, granite/carved the names of/dead relatives and *paesani* ('A Man Named Pete', *What My Arms Can Carry*; 2005, 83).

The sense of closeness and intimacy is intensified by the juxtaposition of 'paesani' and family members, whose ties are equally strong. The author appeals to a communal sense of estrangement felt by displaced people and their subsequent attempt to recreate a sense of placement. They bond together to overcome the sense of estrangement and loss caused by migration, establishing a sense of community and belonging within the new territory. This idea also appears in the poem 'Piazza Navona' (*What My Arms Can Carry*; 2005, 54). Patriarca is visiting Rome by herself and stops to eat dinner in a local restaurant. Here, her Italianness allows her to find an immediate connection with the Italian waiter who is serving her. Despite being strangers, their intimacy and solidarity ground in the terrain created by their common geographical, linguistic and cultural origins. Indeed, Patriarca claims that 'by the end of the meal we are/as close as *due paesani*'. In this case, CS is used to enhance affinity and closeness. In stressing her identification with the Italian waiter, she reclaims her Italian origins. CS, then, becomes a statement of personal and social identity.

Her use of CS as an instrument of re-grounding and affiliation also emerges in the use of the word 'mamma', which has the highest degree of occurrence in her poems: up to 61 times. It is sometimes used when she is talking about her mother (I want mamma) (*Daughters for Sale*; 1997, 22). At other times it appears in the vocative form, like in dialogues, when she addresses her mother directly (it's only land, mamma, only land) (*Ciao, Baby*; 1999, 64). It is often in a focalised position, or it is repeated several times throughout a single poem, thus further stressing the importance of the mother in her real and fictional world (mamma is the baby/mamma insists I accompany her) (*Ciao, Baby*; 1999, 37). Patriarca's understanding and use of the term 'mamma' can be fully understood only if we examine it in relation to her biography, especially considering the impact that migration had on the dynamics of her family. This aspect is evident in 'Painted Windows' (*Daughters for Sale*; 1997, 20–25), where she narrates the first months after her arrival in Canada, mainly describing how the relations between the family members changed:

> Mamma is crying in her room downstairs. I hear mamma crying every night since we got here in this dark, tall house with all these stairs. [...] I'm not sure why mamma cries. I think she misses nonno and nonna, like I do. Maybe she cries for them. My father is never home. Maybe she cries for him. [...] Mamma left for work at six. Papa didn't come home at all. Got to get Nina ready. Get myself ready and go to school. I'm cold. I want mamma, I want nonna. I want somebody.

Alfonzetti (1998, 193–194) suggests the existence of a link between the plot and CS. The latter helps to create the narrative, as it foregrounds all those elements essential for the reader to understand the plot. CS can provide 'information beyond referential content' (Nilep 2006, 9) and force readers 'to look beyond the referential meaning for the inferential meaning' (Callahan 2005, 17). Patriarca's constant use of the word 'mamma' in the example above helps her contextualise the scene around the topic of family relations. It orients the reader towards a specific interpretation of the dynamics within her family after their migration to Canada. Given this, the word 'mamma' acquires a specific value and can be understood as an example of CS. Rorato claims that 'migration [...] functions as a litmus test in revealing how women, and particularly mothers, often find themselves in a vulnerable position' (2018, 75). This situation is exemplified by Patriarca's mother. Once in Toronto, she started working all day in a factory. Patriarca and her sister had to learn to look after each other, as they could no longer rely on their mother all day. The author's perception of her life in Italy and Canada, then, can be articulated around the binary presence/absence of the mother. Against this backdrop, her switch to Italian acquires a specific function: she uses the actual mother's tongue to call her mother. Her written voice, which keeps pronouncing the word 'mamma', sounds like an invocation; she attempts to concretise and materialise a presence, which is inevitably turning into an absence. In being unable to call her 'mamma' in English, she expresses her incapacity to match her current perception of her mother with the incarnation of the maternal role she has in her mind, which is sketched against her memories of her family life in Italy. She cannot reconcile these contrasting views, and this impossibility is expressed linguistically through CS. She cannot pronounce the word 'mother' because her mother's role and presence have blurred in Canada. Switching to Italian, then, represents an attempt to grab at a childhood world that she seems to be

48 VOICES OF WOMEN WRITERS

losing. Through this form of resistance to translating, she is trying to resist the reality around her. By grounding herself in the language of her mother, she attempts to re-establish a connection with her mother. This aspect becomes more evident if we consider that, in the poem above, 'father' is the only familial term appearing in English. Again, some background information can help us understand this point better. In the poem above, as well as in her entire literary production, Patriarca often talks about the difficult relation with her father: 'i have written about you/enough/the conflicts/ the reconciliation/enough/ confessions' ('Another November Visiting You', *My Etruscan Face*; 2007, 39). In the first example provided, she uses the 'unfamiliar' English language to refer to her father. In this context, unfamiliar must be understood as 'not the usual language of the interaction within the family'. By refusing to use Italian (her family language) when referring to her father, she wants to express his estrangement from the family.

The use of CS to restore familiar dynamics recurs in the poem 'Mother Tells Me Stories' (*Italian Women and Other Tragedies*; 1994, 42). The author recounts how her mother would often tell her stories about Italy and their lives over there in an attempt to interrupt her memory erasure and thus prevent the deterioration of what Giorgio calls 'the mother-daughter dyad' (2002, 124). Nonetheless, Patriarca does not manage to completely engage with this process of remembering, as the distance in time and space has broken the relation with the mother (tongue, land), as expressed in this line: 'do you remember?' she asks/her fingers making ringlets in my hair/I want to scream 'I don't!'. By code-switching, her mother is trying to restore the connection with her half-Canadian daughter. The Italian term conveys a shift in focalisation, as it arouses their Italian memories. In doing so, it also articulates a backwards movement, reminding Patriarca and her mother of their communal past and legacy. The attempt to restore the dynamics of their mother/daughter relation is further demonstrated by the fact that Patriarca is addressed as 'bimba', thus revealing her mother's desire to put her daughter in a more vulnerable position of dependence: 'her eyes/are always wet/as she calls me/*bimba*'. Through the word 'bimba', her mother attempts to exploit the emotional and formative legacy of the mother-tongue, in order to exercise her authority over her daughter.[23]

2.4 Self-translating Strategies in *Italian Women and Other Tragedies/Daughters for Sale/Ciao, Baby/What My Arms Can Carry/My Etruscan Face*

The same attempt to recreate the transmigrant experience on the page is at the core of Patriarca's self-translating performance. She intentionally performs a specific form of self-translation, which I have defined as a *continuum*, because it breaks the conventionally understood binary between writing and translating. This form of self-translation satisfies her desire to bridge and connect because it establishes a form of continuity between her multiple spaces of existence and expression, dismantling borders and boundaries in living as well as in writing. By self-translating her Italian voice into English and vice versa, Patriarca overlaps her Italian and Canadian lives, demonstrating that one cannot exist without the other. Narrating her story in both languages allows her to look at her Italian life through her Canadian gaze and vice versa, thus mirroring and doubling each experience. To this end, let us consider the following example, which appears in the poem 'The Old Man', in the collection *Italian Women and Other Tragedies* (1994, 45). Its Italian counterpart is entitled 'Il Vecchio' (1994, 46). This poem is about an old man, possibly a migrant, as the reference to his 'old stories of a distant land' seems to suggest:[24]

The Old Man	Il Vecchio
a fireplace	un focolare
an old wooden bench	**un vecchio banco**
potatoes buried	**di legno**
under hot ashes	patate coperte
an old man	da ceneri calde
chews tobacco	**un vecchio mastica tabacco**
and tells stories	a racconta storie
of a distant land	di un paese lontano
he discovered in letters	scoperto in lettere
outside the trees	fuori gli alberi
are furious with the wind	sono furiosi col vento
his **hands** tremble	le **dita** tremano
too many years loving	troppi anni amando il grano
the wheat in borrowed **fields**	di una **terra** prestata
his eyes are wet moons	i suoi occhi sono lune bagnate
too many tall sons	**troppi figli**
and slenders daughters	**sono ombre lasciate**
have left shadows behind	nella notte
somewhere in the night	grilli scherzano
crickets are clowning	a calde ceneri rinfrescano
and hot ashes are cooling	

Although the main structure of the 'original' poem is retained, it is still possible to identify a few differences between both texts. Firstly, the English version is slightly longer than the Italian one: the former has 21 lines, while the latter has 20. In fact, the Italian poem counts a number of omissions, such as the words 'tall' (line 16) and 'somewhere' (line 19). The lines 'too many tall sons and slenders daughters' in Italian are translated into the more generic 'troppi figli'. In Italian, Patriarca uses these omissions to continue her exploration of the relationship between Italian migrants and their Italian-Canadian sons. Throughout this chapter, it has been highlighted that her poems often tell the stories of parents who are unable to communicate with their children. The cultural distance caused by migration exacerbates the intergenerational conflict. In the poem under examination here, the omissions in the Italian text express, rightly, the weakening of the family unit. Metaphorically speaking, Patriarca is telling us that the old man is so distant from his children that he does not distinguish between sons and daughters anymore. The more generic word 'figli' in the Italian version conveys the shallowness and superficiality of their relationship.

This poem also presents some cases of stanza restructuring, which alter the metrics and the rhythm. They give the impression that words are floating in the text, moving from one space to the next, without being anchored to a specific space on the page. The word's experience of the space of the white page echoes Patriarca's movement between physical and linguistic sites. Words undergo a process of uprooting and re-grounding, which mirrors the same process experienced in her constant transmigration. Thus, the page is rearticulated as a site of transgression and reinvention, and words are not demarcated, neither spatially nor linguistically:

an old wooden bench	un vecchio banco di legno
an old man chews tobacco	un vecchio mastica tabacco

A side-by-side reading of the Italian and English versions of her works shows that she intentionally uses articles and pronouns in different ways, to express the relationship with both host and origin country. This is illustrated in line 14, where the plural 'fields' is replaced by the singular 'terra':

too many years loving the wheat in borrowed **fields**	troppi anni amando il grano di una **terra** prestata

In the Italian version, this shift seems to reinforce the idea of the intimate relationship individuals possess with one unique land, that is, their mother land. The singular 'terra' resounds as an open and direct reference to Italy. This aspect is also confirmed by the semantic value of the Italian term 'land' with respect to the English term 'fields'. The latter lacks the specific connotation that 'terra' has, which can also be understood as 'country'.

This point validates the idea that Patriarca decides to use 'terra' instead of a more generic 'campo' in order to refer to her native Italy. This lexical switch places a stronger emotional emphasis on the Italian term and indicates that she is using the Italian mother tongue to reinforce the connection to the Italian mother land. This reading is further confirmed by her use of the term 'borrowed' to refer to Canada. Such a term entails a fictitious relationship between the man and the land, which is depicted as not inherently his.

This use of the Italian language to reinforce the connection to the Italian land also appears in the following poem, 'Paesaggi'. The English version is in the collection *Italian Women and Other Tragedies* (1994, 12), while the Italian version appears in *Donne Italiane ed Altre Tragedie* (2009, 15). I do not reproduce the whole poem, but only the part that is relevant to the analysis:

she waved her dark hand	salutò con la mano scura
by the open gate	vicino al cancello aperto
in a town that grew	**in quel paese** che cresceva
like a mole from the	come una talpa
side of a hill	sul fianco di una collina

This poem about migration features a man and a woman. The author does not specify it, but they are possibly in a relationship. The man is leaving for an unspecified country, which can be associated with Canada, as Patriarca writes that he spent 'thirteen days' sailing an 'endless ocean'. Against this backdrop, her use of the demonstrative adjective in the Italian text serves the purpose of strengthening the tie between the migrant and the place he is leaving. In English, the indefinite article weakens this bond, as the reference is to a generic town. In Italian, the demonstrative adjective 'quel' instead reinforces the reference to a specific and well-identifiable town. Patriarca therefore uses the Italian language as an instrument of re-grounding within the context of uprooting. As it was pointed out with respect to the previous poem, her use of the term 'paese' has to be analysed against this backdrop. In Italian, 'paese' has a double meaning, as it refers both to village and country. Thanks to this double meaning, Patriarca can use the word 'paese' to refer to the small town the migrant is leaving as well as to Italy.

The following poem 'May' appears in the collection *Italian Women and Other Tragedies* (1994, 15) together with its Italian version (1994, 14). The use of singular and plural here offers some interesting reflections. It further shows how the author intentionally plays with language, using it as an instrument to reflect upon her migrant experience. Writing and self-translating are not merely linguistic exercises; they represent existential necessities that allow

52 VOICES OF WOMEN WRITERS

her to reassess her liminal and dualistic positioning. Bearing this in mind, let us consider the following example:

Maggio	May
gli alberi	the trees
hanno finalmente	**have finally decided**
deciso	to laugh
di ridere	the way my mother laughed
come mia mamma rideva	before the **changes**
prima del **cambio**	the new country
della nuova terra	before she woke up to
prima di svegliarsi	the dark stranger
accanto	**in her bed**
allo scuro estraneo	before she recognized
prima di riconoscere	my sister didn't care
che mia sorella	for ribbons
non voleva più	this month the
fiocchi	flowers appear **most**
questo mese	beautiful
i fiori apparono	this month **i can put**
belli	**aside** anything
questo mese	i am drunk with trees
scanzerò tutto	
sono ubriaca	
di alberi	

Another version of the poem appears in the Italian version of the collection, *Donne Italiane ed Altre Tragedie* (2009, 73), that Patriarca translated into Italian with the help of her cousin Maria Grazia Nalli. The Italian version was published by a Canadian publishing house. Despite the high number of Italian migrants in Canada, it would be difficult to conclude that she was motivated to publish the book in Italian merely to communicate with Italian readers. As such, the publication of her Italian book in Canada can be understood as responding to two principal needs. Firstly, it can be seen as representing her need to bridge Italian and Canadian spaces by bringing one into the territory of the other. Secondly, it satisfies her personal necessity to retrieve and express her Italian voice:

1994	2009
gli alberi	gli alberi
hanno finalmente	hanno finalmente
deciso	deciso
di ridere	di ridere
come mia mamma rideva	come rideva mia mamma

1994	2009
prima del **cambio**	prima dei **cambiamenti**
della nuova terra	**prima** della nuova terra
prima di svegliarsi	prima di svegliarsi
accanto	accanto
allo **scuro estraneo**	all'**oscuro estraneo**
prima di **riconoscere**	prima di **rendersi conto**
che mia sorella	che mia sorella
non voleva piú	non voleva piú
fiocchi	fiocchi **nei capelli**
questo mese	questo mese
i fiori apparono	**i fiori sembrano ancora più**
belli	**belli**
questo mese	questo mese
scanzerò tutto	scanzerò tutto
sono ubriaca	sono ubriaca
di alberi	di alberi

There are just a few changes of note between the Italian and the English versions in *Italian Women and Other Tragedies*. However, they are enough to change the overall effect of the poem as well as its length and rhythm. Patriarca cannot be defined as perfectly bilingual, but her spelling and grammar 'inaccuracies' give an additional value to her literary productions. Her authorial and existential voice exists in and through these inaccuracies that emerge from the interaction between her linguistic and cultural worlds. Indeed, in our private interview, she confessed that, even if her self-translated poems are not always written in a very accurate Italian, she prefers them this way because her 'mistakes' are more effective in expressing her voice than other, more polished versions.[25] This point is evident in the poem above; the translation with her cousin shows a tendency to clarify. For instance, 'apparono' is replaced by 'sembrano', or it is specified that her sister did not want ribbon in her hair. Particularly interesting is the rendering of 'lo scuro estraneo' as 'l'oscuro estraneo'.[26] In this case, it is made clear that the author is not referring to her father's physical features; rather, she is using the term dark to represent his ambiguous and complex presence in the family. These modifications have a positive effect on the one hand, because they make the meaning of the poem more accessible. Nevertheless, polishing Patriarca's voice obscures the fact that language, in her literary activity, is the channel through which broader and deeper meanings are expressed. As she stated, this polished Italian is less effective in communicating her voice. It is mediated and tamed and ends up losing its essential traits.

This analysis has demonstrated that Patriarca's self-translations are the result of a dynamic and dialogic interaction between the act of writing

54 VOICES OF WOMEN WRITERS

and the act of translating, as well as between her multiple mother tongues. As Fitch points out, 'the bilingual writer is not merely *aware* of the existence of a multiplicity of tongues but lives in the continual presence of this awareness during the very act of writing' (1988, 158). In this process of contact and exchange, new forms and meanings emerge, as both languages are activated and affect the creative process. Through multilingual writing and self-translating, Patriarca can articulate a dialogue between Italian, English and her dialect from Crociaria, thus bridging her linguistic divide. The notion of linguistic purity becomes a fictitious territory as one language makes an incursion into the territory of the other, ending up 'physically' embedded in the other. Simultaneously, she manages to solve the 'dilemma of belonging to two cultures but existing in neither one comfortably' (Zucchero in Canton and Di Giovanni 2013, 44). Her physical and linguistic journey is inevitably and intimately an existential one, too. 'Being at home', for her, means moving across languages, cultures and places: 'Ces trois langues, comme toutes les autres choses ordinaires du quotidien, font pleinement partie de ma vie. Dans ma routine quotidienne j'utilise les trois langues sans difficulté, plutôt aisément, comme si elles étaient, et selon moi elles le sont, les différentes parties d'un tout, la trilogie d'une langue' (Patriarca 2015, 94).[27] Her languages coexist, meet and cooperate, thus shaping her identity and reality.

Notes

1 To expand upon this literary movement, please refer to the following works by Pivato: *Contrasts: Comparative Essays on Italian-Canadian Writing* (1985) and *The Anthology of Italian-Canadian writing* (1998).

2 Multilingualism in Italian-Canadian writing has been investigated by several scholars, such as Saidero (2011, 2018, 2020), Baldo (2019), Camarca (2005), Casagranda (2008) and many others.

3 Pivato defines Italian-Canadian writing as an 'ethnic literature', that is, a literature that 'has traditionally been defined as writing in the unofficial languages of Canada' (1985, 27).

4 Most of the texts written by Italian-Canadian authors have been published by this editor.

5 Italian-Canadian literature has started to attract more attention in Italy since Gabriella Iacobucci's Italian translation of Frank Colantonio's book *From the Ground Up: An Italian Immigrant's Story*, which was published by Cosmo Iannone Editore in 2000.

6 http://canadian-writers.athabascau.ca/english/writers/gpatriarca/gpatriarca.php.

7 For a detailed account of the approaches and directions in old and new studies of Italian migrants to the US, Canada and Australia, please see the article 'Deprovincialising Italian Migration Studies: An overview of Australian and Canadian research' (Susanna Iuliano and Loretta Baldassar, 2008).

8 To expand upon this point, see also *Canadese: A Portrait of the Italian Canadians* (Bagnell 1989), and *Such Hardworking People: Italian Immigrants in Postwar Toronto* (Iacovetta 1992).

9 In the article 'The Quest motif in the Travelogues and Memoirs of Migrant Writers' (2021), Saidero also stresses the link between travelling and the formation of selfhood in the migrant narratives of female authors.

10 Particularly interesting is the paper 'Literary Women: Exploring the Voices of Delia De Santis and Venera Fazio' (2018), in which Canton illustrates the role played by Italian women as cultural agents in the context of Italian-Canadian writing.

11 Objects have been widely investigated in the context of Italian diaspora, mainly in works exploring their transcultural and transnational dimension (Burdett, Polezzi and Spadaro 2020), with respect to women's domestic work (Sciorra and Giunta 2014), and in connection to identity and translation (Bartoloni 2016, Wilson 2020, Chianese 2022).

12 I do not know whether these poems were written during the same period, or if they were written at different times and they only happen to be in the same collection. The fact that Patriarca decides to insert them in the same book is nonetheless indicative of her attempt to dismantle a traditional view of home.

13 Feminist writers have widely investigated the roles of women at home, representing home primarily as a site of oppression: 'Rather than see home as a solely gendered space, usually embodied by women, such writings also reveal domestic inclusions, exclusions and inequalities in terms of class, age, sexuality and 'race'' (Blunt 2005, 7).

14 This function granted to women connects to the romantic view that women, as mothers, reinforce the link among the members of a family.

15 From this perspective, it does not surprise that being mothers and teachers were seen as traditional female roles; both play a fundamental part in the education and formation of individuals.

16 This topic is one of the most popular among female Italian-Canadian writers.

17 A detailed analysis of the female world in Patriarca's poems has also been conducted by Anna Pia De Luca, in her paper 'Mondi Femminili ed Altre Tragedie Canadesi: le Poesie di Gianna Patriarca' (2007).

18 Among these words, for example he mentions *piazza* and *nonna*.

19 The name is mispelled, as the correct version is 'Tre Marie'. I have no information to detect whether this is a typo or a 'mistake' made by Patriarca, and I simply report it like it is written in the book.

20 The reference to 'zeppole', through its connection with this religious festivity, also hints at the important presence of religion. It stresses how religion permeated and affected the practices of everyday life for Italian migrants.

21 For an in-depth analysis of the role of the *piazza* in Italian cities, please see *The Politics of the Piazza: The History and Meaning of the Italian Square* (Canniffe 2012).

22 In Patriarca's poems, together with mamma, piazza is the term with the highest degree of occurrence. It appears 8 times, excluding appearances in names such as Piazza Navona.

23 The relation between Patriarca and her parents is also analysed by Anna Pia De Luca in her paper 'Mondi Femminili e Altre Tragedie Canadesi: Le Poesie di Gianna Patriarca' (2007).

24 Please note that there are a number of typos in the poem.

25 In general, in the collection translated with her cousin interventions mainly concern the correction of typos. For instance, this occurs in the poem 'Tu' (2009, 49). Patriarca also adds a new poem, written in her dialect from Ceprano: 'sta vita' (2009, 76). Here, she engages with a dialogue with her daughter, reflecting upon her life and her literary career.

26 Patriarca and I met in Toronto, in May 2017. I was a PhD student back then and was planning to travel to Toronto to attend a conference on self-translation. At the beginning of my PhD, I had contacted Patriarca to introduce myself, tell her about my research and ask her to fill in a questionnaire. On that occasion, she had been extremely kind; she had answered my questions in a very detailed way and had also sent me some unpublished self-translations. Remembering her kindness, before my trip to Toronto I contacted her again and asked for a meeting, to which she agreed. We met at 'Il gatto nero', a famous Italian restaurant that she often mentions in her poems. We had lunch together and talked about her migrant experience, her writing and self-translating, her relationship with her Italian origins and so on.

27 The image of a triangle is also used by the author Jhumpa Lahiri, to describe her relationship with her three languages: Bengali, English and Italian (2016, 152).

CHAPTER 3

DÔRE MICHELUT: COMING TO TERMS WITH THE MOTHER TONGUE*

3.1 The Emergence of a Multilingual Paradigm

Dorina Michelutti, better known as Dôre Michelut (the Friulian version of her name), is also an Italian-Canadian author. She was born in 1952 in Sella di Rivignano, a town near Udine, in the region of Friuli. Her family migrated to Canada in 1958 and settled in Toronto. After graduating from high school in 1972, she spent five years in Florence, studying Italian at the University of Florence. She returned to Canada in 1981, where she continued to study at the University of Toronto. Meanwhile, she began to write and publish in literary magazines. Her first book of poems, *Loyalty to the Hunt*, was published in 1986 by Guernica Editions. In 1994, this book also appeared in the French version, entitled *Loyale à la chasse*. In 1989, she published *Coming to Terms with the Mother Tongue*. In 1990, in cooperation with five writers, she published *Linked Alive* and the simultaneous French edition, *Liens*. In 1990, she also published *Ouroborous: The Book That Ate Me*, containing poems in English, Italian and Friulian.[1] In 1993, she published *A Furlan Harvest*, a collection of poems written in Italian, English and Friulian, by women of Friulian descent living in Canada. After 1996, Michelut started travelling and working around the world. In 2005, she received a Master of Arts in Applied Communication from Royal Roads University in Victoria, BC. She died of cancer in Oman in March 2009. She was teaching advanced speech, multimedia and technical communication at Al Akhawayn University in Ifrane.[2]

Michelut's works have appeared in many literary publications and have been anthologized both in Canada and Italy. Her literary production constitutes a form of experimental fiction, that is, a form of writing defined by its innovative nature. She continually breaks linguistic, narrative and stylistic norms and conventions, combining different styles and discourses. On the level of content, her poems are thematically obscure, difficult to analyse, and engage the reader with different levels of interpretation. Through this innovative approach to writing, 'discursive borders are constantly

58   VOICES OF WOMEN WRITERS

relativized and transgressed, thereby intensifying the work's migratory character' (Frank 2008, 20). This inventive approach is also evident in her experiments with different poetic forms, such as a series of *renga*, an Asian form of social poetry. It constitutes a form of collaborative poetry, as it is written by different authors working together. Her self-translating experience, as well as the essays where she explores her multilingualism and narrates what it means to live in between multiple linguistic and cultural heritages, can also be understood as examples of her original and experimental writing. *Coming to Terms with the Mother Tongue* (1989) and *Il Lei: Third Person Polite* (1990) are prominent examples of metalinguistic essays. Michelut describes her relationship with the three linguistic systems constituting her multicultural background: Italian, English and Friulian. The result is a linguistic polyphony, which characterises her writing and self-translating as instruments to articulate the relations between these languages, redefining their spaces of existence and expression, and breaking linguistic, cultural and identitarian borders. To her, bridging Italian, English and Friulian represents a way to reach personal unity and to regain possession of her pluricultural and plurilingual identity. As Romaine claims in *Bilingualism*, multilingualism enhances metalinguistic skills, that is, the use of language 'to talk about or reflect on language' (1995, 114). Michelut displays a strong metalinguistic awareness; she uses her writing and self-translating to reflect on language. She perceives literature as a linguistic experiment, which allows her to explore what can be said through languages, and how. Indeed, the relationship between languages is the focus of her literary production. She investigated the bond between language and identity throughout her life, analysing 'her self' as indissolubly tied to her mother tongues. The reconstruction of her linguistic biography will demonstrate rightly that her transmigrant experience undermines notions and beliefs that are affected by the monolingual paradigm, pushing her to move towards a multilingual paradigm, and rethink linguistic narratives and dynamics.

Michelut offers an interesting case study in this respect. This is because, being immersed in multilingual contexts, she was 'never firmly *included* in the monolingual paradigm' (Yildiz 2012, 121). Nevertheless, her initial approach to language shows that she initially conceives of herself as monolingual and, despite her multilingual makeup, attempts to build links with one exclusive linguistic system; essentially, she refers to a monolingual 'conception of subjects, communities, and modes of belonging' (Yildiz 2012, 31). Her rethinking of the concept of a mother tongue, in both her personal and literary experiences, comes at a later stage, as the result of a process of negotiation between a multilingual and a monolingual frame of reference. As her life events make her realise and experience the impossibility of the monolingual paradigm, she eventually challenges her claims to an exclusive mother tongue and opens up channels of connection and identification with multiple mother tongues.

Like anticipated, Michelut was never immersed in a monolingual environment. Her first years in Italy exposed her to both Italian and Friulian, which is the linguistic variety spoken in the area where she grew up. While Italian was the official and standardised language, Friulian belonged to daily communication and family interactions. This distinction initially marks Michelut's perception of both languages; Italian is acquired in school through a conscious and mediated process. Friulian, instead, is naturally and spontaneously possessed. For her, it represents the pure mother tongue, transmitted and received within the family unit. This perception will eventually change through a process responding to both external and internal forces and motivations. Migration is at the outset of this process. In 1958, when Michelut is six years old, her family migrate to Canada. Her physical movement from Italy to Canada coincides with a linguistic movement from Friulian to both Italian and English. The transition to Italian occurs because, in most cases, migration acted as an instrument of linguistic unification beyond Italy's linguistic fragmentation. Mobility increased the importance of standard Italian for migrants because they had to resort to Italian to overcome the communication barrier posed by their dialects. Italian thus became an instrument to achieve understanding and communication on a national level.[3] Within this scenario, Michelut had to silence Friulian and speak Italian in order to interact with the other Italian migrants in Canada.

However, it is necessary to specify that, in this context, the reference is not to standard Italian. First generation Italian migrants were normally poorly educated and expressed themselves mainly or exclusively in dialect, or in their regional Italian: 'Popular Italian, a fossilized interlanguage between dialect and Standard, served frequently as H variety for first generation immigrants' (Haller 2011, 59).[4] Once living together abroad, migrants affected each other's speech, thus creating and speaking a highly heterogeneous variety of Italian.[5] One more level of complexity was added by the merging of Italian and English, which marked the birth of a specific linguistic variety known as Italiese.[6] Therefore, the concept of Italian language, with its inherent complexity, acquired even more specific features within migrant communities.

Michelut's encounter with English also follows her migration to Canada. The new language suddenly invades her personal and collective territory, imposing itself on the way she experiences and expresses the reality around her. An ontological imperative spurs her novel linguistic ability: the 'I that speaks' must necessarily coincide with the 'I that lives'. Life must correspond to its narration. Immersed in an English-speaking environment,

60 VOICES OF WOMEN WRITERS

Michelut must master English to be able to communicate with and function within the community around her. Like for Gianna Patriarca, speaking English becomes a strategy of survival and expression. Remapping her linguistic territory also means remapping the terrains of her identity and agency. Within this scenario, at first Friulian is forced to take a step back. Regionally circumscribed and expelled from the migrant community, it seems unable to coexist with the other languages: English and Italian. Michelut's return to this mother tongue will happen only later in her life, as the ultimate step to take in her journey towards the multilingual paradigm. Returning to the Friulian mother tongue will represent a way to move towards all her mother tongues since her hybrid language can only exist in the interspace where Italian, English and Friulian meet and dialogue. This coexistence will be possible only when she realises that her languages can – and possibly must – occupy different yet related spaces in her life. This acknowledgement is thoroughly analysed and described in the following passage, in *Coming to Terms with the Mother Tongue*. Here, she describes how her Friulian, Italian and English express different 'concepts and sensibilities' because they voice inter-related yet diverse aspects of her identity. She specifically explains how Friulian and English affect her persona in diverse ways, to the point that she becomes a different person in each language:

> It might be fruitful to explain the person I become in these languages in terms of what I can imagine within them. For example, in Furlan, the thought that beyond highway 11 in Ontario there are no other roads going north, only a vast expanse of forest wilderness, makes me panic. I cannot enter into relation with this threatening emptiness unless I think of hewing out a plot of land, building solid shelter and planting a garden for food. I would worry about how to get seeds and nails. Perhaps when things become stable I would tame a wild creature, a bear comes to mind. If I approach the same territory in English, I do not worry about food and shelter, somehow they are granted to me and do not cause anxiety. I would perhaps learn to fly so I could enter into some kind of relation with the immensity before me. It would not occur to me to tame animals, I would rather observe them in their natural state and learn small things about myself through watching them (*Coming to Terms with the Mother Tongue* 1989, 70).

As she states, in Friulian, she is completely overwhelmed by emotions such as panic, concern and feelings of emptiness. In English, instead, she recovers control over life. While in Friulian she is overcome by the 'vast expanse of forest wilderness' around her, in English she manages to 'enter into some kind of relation with the immensity' before her. Coming to terms with the mother tongue, for Michelut, means rightly acknowledging and accepting how her multiple languages shape and convey different approaches to life, diverse values and ideas. This awareness grants her a new sense of self; piecing together the linguistic and cultural fragments of her identity, she can finally discover and appreciate the empowering value of multilingualism and multiculturalism.

In Chapter 1, I referred to Yildiz's definition of multilingual practices as postmonolingual, as they 'persist or reemerge' (2012, 5) against the monolingual paradigm. This aspect is particularly important for Dôre Michelut. Her literary activity can be considered postmonolingual because it emerges from, and against, the monolingual paradigm. Against her parents and her communities' attempts at imposing a monolingual approach to life and reality, she cultivates and embraces her multiple languages, both in living and in writing. Therefore, it is only by considering the tension between this persistent paradigm and her multilingual necessities that it is possible to understand why and how she uses her writing and self-translating to overcome the monolingual paradigm. Her poems 'intentionally produce hybrid discourses that radically destabilise meaning and identity' (Moslund 2010, 6), which are shaped by this frame of reference. Michelut uses her literature to demonstrate the potential of multilingualism in the making of her identity across languages, cultures and countries.

3.2 The Overarching Mother Tongue

The essays *The Third Person Polite* and *Coming to Terms with the Mother Tongue* are perfect examples of language memoirs. In these works, she reflects upon what it means to live in-between multiple languages and cultures, describing the different steps of her linguistic trajectory, and her journey towards a multilingual paradigm. To do so, she recurs to a common trope in migrant narratives: the identification of the mother tongue with the figure of the mother (de Rogatis 2023, 56). Through this overlap, she attempts to redefine her new linguistic identity against the backdrop of her relationship with her mother, thus inscribing the former within specific family dynamics and accounts. The maternal genealogy is intertwined with the linguistic one, as the author analyses the impact of both figures on her persona. Stepping away from the mother tongue, in this context, also means to escape from the mother's tongue, that is, from the sociocultural and gendered legacy of motherhood and daughterhood.

The parallelism between the mother tongue and the mother derives from the maternal connotation of the former, which is traditionally considered the language that emanates from the mother. This relationship is biological and organic, as the mother is the one who gives birth, simultaneously passing the mother tongue on to the daughter. On these grounds, the mother-daughter relationship can also be defined as a 'family romance' (Yildiz 2012, 12), as it signifies a specific mode of belonging and natural kinship (2012, 11), which shapes the individual's subjectivity. Given the gendered connotation of this relation, the mother plays an important role in the development of the daughter's identity; she offers a specific model of femininity, to which the daughter will refer in becoming a woman. However, this model is the product of the sociocultural system the mother belongs to. It is therefore bound to a precise linguistic, cultural and physical space. With the movement to a new context, where different sociocultural rules apply, the model which is proposed by the mother does not work anymore. Migration disrupts the grounding of the daughter in the mother, forcing the former to move away from the latter in order to fully realise and express her potential. Exactly like stepping out of the mother tongue, even moving away from the mother determines a process of redefinition of identity and translation of the self.

In the essays mentioned above, Michelut takes the relationship with her mother as a starting point, to explore the new forms and meanings that this relation assumes in migratory contexts, and what these new forms entail for the reframing of her female subjecthood. Marianne Hirsch claims that 'the bond between mother and daughter, daughter and mother, must be broken so that the daughter can become woman' (1989, 43). At first, Michelut's new female identity is reconfigured through a process of detachment from the mother (tongue). She must break this biological, linguistic and familial attachment to become 'who' she really is and develop an identity that is truly hers; that is, to escape from the restrictions of the patriarchal culture her mother represents. As a matter of fact, the model of femininity offered and transmitted by her Italian mother does not function in the Canadian context, where women are allowed to envisage and embrace alternative identitarian possibilities. Migration therefore prompts the separation from the mother, whose model ends up being challenged and questioned. The movement to another country sustains and supports new models of womanhood.

Michelut's detachment from the mother must necessarily involve a rupture with the mother tongue as well, as the latter is passed on to the daughter rightly by the mother. On these grounds, the switch from one linguistic system to the other represents the ideological and cultural route she undertakes in the process of redefinition of her female identity. Speaking English against this backdrop is essential. English is a language that exists outside the family unit, and is therefore free from biological and organic connotations. English allows Michelut to exist and express herself beyond the borders and boundaries established within the family. Moreover, English is not the product of the patriarchal culture that she is trying to escape. English is, therefore, a promise of freedom and liberation. Michelut embarks on a new linguistic journey, seeking the identitarian promise that the new language conveys.

The movement away from the Friulian mother tongue is enacted rightly within the family unit. After migrating to Canada, Michelut's parents stop speaking Friulian at home and start communicating exclusively in Italian. This is because they think that Friulian will not be useful to their daughter in the new context, where new linguistic necessities emerge. The choice of Italian, the official national language, also seems to be linked to the idea of the nation. The Italian language must remind Michelut of her national identity, in opposition to the Canadian one. The national structure prevails over the familial one (represented by Friulian) because the mother tongue ceases to be a means of private belonging and becomes an instrument of national affiliation. Affected by the monolingual paradigm, Michelut's parents believe that Friulian and Italian cannot coexist; the former must be silenced for the latter to speak. Michelut must adopt Italian as the dominant language, while Friulian is 'relegated to a circumscribed private territory' where she can still sense its 'feeling and presence' but where it has become 'speechless' (*Coming to Terms with the Mother Tongue* 1989, 63–64):

> When my family emigrated to Canada, my parents decided that Furlan was such a minority language that it would not be of use to their children in the future. Therefore, in our house, our parents spoke Furlan amongst themselves and they spoke what Italian they knew with the children (*Coming to Terms with the Mother Tongue* 1989, 65).

In nullifying the bond with Friulian, her parents attempt to forge, for their daughter, a specific identification with one language only: Italian. They are purposefully acting according to the monolingual paradigm, enacting linguistic dynamics that show a homogenising tendency. They operate according to a dialectical pattern, where the two languages are seen as opposites, excluding each other.

However, by imposing Italian over Friulian, they contribute to destabilising Michelut's monolingual beliefs, offering her a way to break with monolingualism. What she perceives as her real mother tongue, Friulian, is replaced by what she identifies as an artificial mother tongue, Italian. Her parents' attempt at imposing the latter as the native language undermines her perception of the mother tongue as given. The L1 (i.e., the native language) is not necessarily the language that individuals naturally possess, but it can be acquired through a mediated process. As her parents refuse to talk to

64 VOICES OF WOMEN WRITERS

her in Friulian, Michelut is symbolically denied any access to what to her represents the actual maternal language. Friulian ceases to function as a site of familiar belonging, as the family becomes the site where it is contested and rejected. As the intimate and almost sacred bond between individuals and their mother tongue is denied, Michelut begins to foresee the illusory connotation of the myth of the mother tongue.

This process takes a step further when English begins to conquer spaces of existence and expression in her life. Over time, even if she can still understand both Friulian and Italian, she starts to reply in English only, because she cannot express herself well in neither Italian nor Friulian: 'It took only a few years for me to reply to both languages exclusively in English. In my teens, I could understand both Italian and Furlan, but I spoke them badly' (*Coming to Terms with the Mother Tongue* 1989, 65). The 'speechlessness' of these languages – that is, the impossibility and inability to speak them – is also existential, as they are unable to voice events that are now lived in a different language. At this stage, she experiences a role reversal between her three linguistic systems. English replaces both Friulian and Italian, and what used to be background noise eventually becomes foregrounded (*Coming to Terms with the Mother Tongue* 1989, 65). She is still operating in accordance with the monolingual paradigm, as she cannot foresee the coexistence and co-expression of her multiple linguistic systems. For her, moving towards English means moving away from Friulian and Italian. The movement towards English is both a natural consequence of the new linguistic environment, and an active and intentional decision. On the one hand, she must master English to navigate within Canadian society. On the other hand, the choice of English grounds itself in her search for a space for freedom and autonomy, a point that has been outlined at the beginning of this paragraph. Migration to Canada leads Michelut to reconsider the relationship with the mother (tongue) as limiting and suffocating. In the new context, the legacy of the mother (tongue) becomes a burden. This aspect is thoroughly described in her essay *Il Lei: Third Person Polite*, where the identitarian and social legacy of the L1 is explored through the metaphor of the mother-daughter relationship:[7]

> Furlan is my mother tongue. [...] In Furlan, I can still focus on anything and say "no" with utter certainty. Perhaps that's the reason I lose the capacity to speak Furlan when we emigrate. When my mother speaks, I reply in English [...] Mother's iron grip is loosened; she can't reach me in English, I can stop the nos she insists on passing on (1990, 113).

Moving beyond Friulian and towards English means 'to abandon the legacy of the mother (tongue) and to re-ground in a free space, where she can express her voice; to interrupt the emotional involvement that the use of the L1 entails and to overcome its formative influence. Her linguistic freedom also determines her existential freedom' (Spagnuolo 2019, 15). For Michelut, the restrictions of the monolingual paradigm cohere with the strictures of the Italian misogynist culture. Speaking English, therefore, signifies her search for a different existence as a woman. English embodies the possibility of a diverse female existence and constitutes a way to resist the gendered expectations of her mother's Italian culture:

> Such complete re-immersion into an unknown body of sound [...] reminds me of my birthright, that I have a choice, that I can be anything, that I am free to feel life surging. [...] In English, I feel the surge again, and I let myself be carried out, over and above the dams, released from all those excavated places (1990, 113).

Rethinking language, then, also means to rethink gender. The return to the mother tongue can be articulated only by rethinking its identitarian and social legacy, thus ceasing to perceive its rooting and defining power. From this perspective, speaking another language helps Michelut rearticulate the relationship with her mother as well. Reconsidering conventional concepts of mother language, she can also rewrite traditional models of motherhood and daughterhood:

> A turning point comes when mother finally learns to say the word *love* in English. In Furlan there is no equivalent, tender words happen in an intimate space that acknowledges a difference conquered from familiarity. The English word for love is an awareness that the other is another, and responds independently. The moment mother utters the words *I love you*, the countess within her starts to decay (1990, 115).

At this stage, we glimpse the emergence of a multilingual paradigm. The latter coincides with her rejection of the notion of the mother tongue as unique, primary and overarching. Indeed, 'through the metaphor of the mother being able to utter the words "I love you", Michelut is weakening the identitarian charge of the mother (tongue), which gives up on a dominant role and eventually acknowledges the presence and the autonomy of "the other"' (Spagnuolo 2019, 16). Questioning the centrality of the mother tongue leads her to experience the emergence of new linguistic family romances, offering her the possibility to live across languages, not beyond them. The mother's 'I love you' therefore has a performative force; it enacts a process of transformation, as the mother (tongue) ceases to possess a dominant nature and the daughter loses its

66 VOICES OF WOMEN WRITERS

position of subjugation. The mother's words break the core structures and features of the mother tongue, thus enacting the daughter's autonomous and independent becoming. This process ultimately debunks the intimate and essential connection between mother, language, culture and identity. Michelut's existential and linguistic transmigration consists exactly of this: rethinking languages as hybrid spaces where the individual is free to operate and express itself. She can transmigrate between her languages because they are not separate and independent but constitute connected entities.

In *Nonostante Platone: Figure femminili nella filosofia antica* (2009), Cavarero proposes a new reading of the myth of Demeter and Persephone, which she believes to celebrate the eternal bond between mothers and daughters. According to Greek mythology, Hades kidnaps Persephone, the daughter of Zeus and Demeter, harvest goddess. Demeter's sadness and devastation affect the earth, that ceases to be fertile. Worrying that the sterility of the earth will have negative consequences for humankind, Hades reaches an agreement with Demeter: Persephone will spend a few months a year in the underworld with him and the rest of the year with her mother. When she is with Demeter, nature is in bloom; when she is with Hades, nature stops blossoming (2009, 66–67). According to Cavarero, Demeter's devastation over the loss of her daughter signifies the impossibility, for mothers and daughters, to be separated. This interpretation challenges traditional views, according to which the daughter needs to detach from the mother in order to realise herself as an individual (Hirsch 1989). Cavarero instead claims that the separation is only temporal and is always followed by a phase of reunion, where the bond between mother and daughter is restored. This view seems to be confirmed by Michelut's narration of her relationship with her mother. Initially, she must separate from her mother, in order to escape sociocultural pressure and gendered expectations. However, after realising her full potential as an individual, she can rethink the mother-daughter relationship and eventually return to it. Mother and daughter are not opposite poles, that only exist without each other. On the contrary, their constant detachment and bonding is essential to their existence.

The redefinition of the mother-daughter relationship functions as a starting point for a reconfiguration of the relationship with her native language(s), and enacts a return to the Friulian/Italian mother tongue. The breaking of the biological bond opens up new linguistic belongings and connections. Free from 'the original emotional servitude' (Beaujour 1989, 170), she can finally return to the Italian mother tongue. To this end, she spends five years in Florence to study Italian at the University of Florence. A parallelism can be drawn between her return home and her return to Italian. Both processes respond to a need to reconnect with one's origins; a quest that, according to Saidero, always involves 'a search for the mother and the maternal which is symbolically a quest for connection, language and creativity' (2021, 77). Saidero's words highlight the connection between the mother and the mother (tongue, land), revealing how reconnecting with both is essential to individuals' self-knowledge and formation.

Nonetheless, both returns are destined to fail because they are based on false and misleading grounds. Michelut realises how poor her knowledge of Italian is, as Italian seems 'to be another language altogether' (*Coming to Terms with the Mother Tongue* 1989, 65). She finds herself in the paradoxical condition of having to learn her L1 as if it were her L2 (i.e., the second language). As her years in Florence go by, though, Italian gains space, to the detriment of English: 'I suspected that my English had become insufficient so I went back to university in Toronto searching specifically for courses similar to those I had taken in Italy' (*Coming to Terms with the Mother Tongue* 1989, 66). Once again, linguistic relations and dynamics are overturned. Michelut must constantly rebuild her linguistic competence in all the systems, in a continual movement where neither language can be identified as maternal and intimate as it undergoes multiple processes of othering. She experiences the mother tongue as 'inescapably uncanny, rather than familiar, as the paradigm would have it' (Yildiz 2012, 35). She continuously attempts to refamiliarise herself with it, and to redefine its position with respect to the other linguistic systems.

The monolingual paradigm is therefore replaced by a multilingual one. The latter contemplates the coexistence and co-expression of her multiple mother tongues. Against this backdrop, Michelut resorts to linguistic means to create a space of connection and encounter among her languages and to translate her existential transmigration into a literary one. She initially resorts to bilingual writing, which, nonetheless, makes her feel like 'two different sets of cards shuffled together, each deck playing its own game with its own rules' (*Coming to Terms with the Mother Tongue* 1989, 66). The same happens with translation, perceived as 'a puny effort in such a struggle; something always seemed betrayed' (*Coming to Terms with the Mother Tongue* 1989, 66). Both writing and translating fail because they cannot offer her simultaneity of existence and expression: 'It was as if the languages had been amazingly attracted and yet unable to touch and penetrate [...] Feeling their exclusiveness, I could commit myself fully to neither' (*Coming to Terms with the Mother Tongue* 1989, 66). Both practices make her feel a lack of coincidence between what she lives and what she narrates. They also reinforce the distance between her linguistic systems, which seem unable to translate or narrate the experience lived in the other one. Through bilingual writing and translating, the language of narration is split, which results in the splitting of the experience as well: 'What was lived in Italian stayed in Italian, belonged to it completely. And vice versa' (*Coming to Terms with the Mother Tongue* 1989, 67).

68　　　　　　　　VOICES OF WOMEN WRITERS

Eventually, Michelut resorts to self-translation, which puts her languages in a reciprocal relation, thus allowing both 'to see each other' within her (*Coming to Terms with the Mother Tongue* 1989, 67). Through self-translation, she manages to bring her linguistic systems and her life experiences together. The fragmentation of the individual is overcome because self-translation breaks the split between existence and narration. The experience lived in one language is not nullified or annihilated by the other; on the contrary, as it is told in both systems, it is eventually multiplied. The possibility to develop her works in parallel grants her the possibility to achieve unity, simultaneity and continuity:

> Mine was a process of self-translation: I spanned the languages within my awareness simultaneously while each experienced the other in a "felt" relation. I was generating a dialectical experience that was relative to both languages, and yet, at the same time, I was beyond them both [...] By translating myself into myself, by spinning a fine line in-between states of reality, I transcended the paralysis of being either inside or outside form (*Coming to Terms with the Mother Tongue* 1989, 67–68).

Self-translation puts not only her linguistic systems but also her multiple selves in a dialogical relationship. Together with her multilingual writing, it can be seen as an attempt to establish connections to several mother tongues. Given that Michelut is not complete in one language only, she can achieve unity only by combining her languages. To exist in both worlds, she must be able to express herself in both linguistic systems, that is, to translate her multiple existences into multiple languages.[8]

3.3 Writing One's Cultural and Linguistic Otherness

What does the relationship with her mother tongue(s) entail on a linguistic level, and how does it affect her performance in writing and self-translating? How does she articulate the movement towards her multiple mother tongues on the page? To answer these questions, the collection of poems *Ouroboros: The Book That Ate Me* will be analysed. This collection has been selected because it presents a high degree of multilingualism. There are many self-translated poems and several examples of CS.

Ouroboros was published in 1990 by Éditions Trois. It is a collection of poems in various genres. The author scatters around several reflections on life and human relations, politics, identity and language. The poems are quite enigmatic and surreal and seem to be the result of a spontaneous and uncontrolled stream of consciousness and creativity. At the end of the book,

Michelut adds a few reflections about the creative process that led to the creation of *Ouroboros*. She specifically identifies a relationship between the act of writing and the act of dreaming: 'The first part of the book was poetry, the second, dream. Both sections rendered two complementary conscious states at work: one in wakefulness, one in sleep' (1990, 132). She claims the inextricability of writing and dreaming, both processes that ground in the individual's selfhood and thus contribute to redrawing the borders of identity and existence. Both acts intertwine in a process where dreaming discloses more levels of the narration, and vice versa. Through this interaction and exchange, the boundaries between writing and dreaming blur and disappear. Each one constitutes a reflection of the other, as they contribute together to the construction of the identitarian narrative of the author as well as of her storytelling.

Michelut also explains the reason behind the title, which refers to the cannibalistic nature of the book. An ouroboros is the snake that bites its own tail, so she cannibalises herself through writing and self-translating, 'relentlessly demanding, from the page, nothing less than life itself' (1990, 141). Her words reinforce the relationship between living and writing and support the ontological dimension of her literary activity. She redefines and renegotiates herself through the process of telling her story. She ascribes the cannibalising dimension of her writing and self-translating to her gender: 'I suspect that I struggled with the page to such an extent because I am female: my body has a womb, a certainty that it can generate life' (1990, 141). Through the image of the womb, she explores 'how language inhabits the body' (Saidero 2011, 33). Indeed, this image refers to a bodily and more intimate relationship between the subject and the activity of writing. It is a connection that goes back to origins and roots and therefore entails the total involvement of the subject in writing.

The poems in this collection constitute a perfect example of Michelut's experimental writing. The author plays with language on many levels, creating poems that are linguistically and thematically obscure and complex. The collection is also particularly interesting from the perspective of multilingual writing, as she scatters around poems in her three languages and makes wide use of CS.[9] The latter particularly emerges in relation to specific semantic domains, such as food and cultural references.

In Chapter 1, it was specified that CS in this volume is used as an overarching term to refer to diverse phenomena of language contact. In light of this definition, the cases where Michelut punctuates her narratives with entire poems or passages in the other language are investigated as examples of CS. For instance, the author often inserts poems entirely written in Italian, adds quotations in Italian, or gives Italian titles to poems written in English,

70 VOICES OF WOMEN WRITERS

like in 'Tu parti ed io'; 'Cappero in fiore'; 'Scirocco' (1990, 54; 64; 100). All these poems are dedicated to someone called Cesare. This dedication stresses the emotional connotation of the poems. Cesare is an Italian male name, which makes us suppose that he is Italian, or at least has some Italian origins. From this perspective, it is possible to assume that Michelut is using language to build a connection; by writing in the language of 'the other', she expresses her desire for closeness and understanding. This function becomes even more manifest in the poem 'Tu parti ed io' (p. 54), where she openly states that the need to write for Cesare is connected to her desire to bring him back: 'You leave and I restore you/wrestle words/ from that which like water/comes swirling/make you present'. Writing is connected to being. Words acquire existential power and are used to resist the absence of the other. Writing in Italian determines a connection, which gives presence and substance. At the same time, her use of English in the same poem conveys her will to bridge her Italian and Canadian worlds, finding a space where she can fully feel and express 'her self'. Writing in both Italian and English therefore acquires a cathartic function, as it helps her to resist both absences – of herself and the other – making it possible to exist and function in multiple territories. The two subjects in this poem are not defined and constricted by linguistic and physical borders. On the contrary, they are augmented and reinforced, as they manage to appropriate and embrace those boundaries.

On page 69 in the same collection, Michelut translates part of the song 'Caro amico ti scrivo', by the popular Italian singer Lucio Dalla. As the song was probably unknown to her Canadian readers, she engages herself and her audience with an act of cultural translation in a further attempt to bridge the Italian and Canadian worlds. The journey into the Italian culture continues in the poem 'The Worm Is Coming'. The following passage is particularly interesting: 'Everyone suddenly became Italian and I started singing *Terra Straniera*, a soppy, nostalgic Italian song. I surprised myself by remembering the words. It brought tears to everyone's eyes, so I was lifted out of the water to sing *Fratelli d'Italia*, the national anthem' (1990, 97). The song *Terra Straniera* was sung by Claudio Villa, a famous Italian singer. It is about a migrant who feels nostalgic for his native land. The reference to the songs achieves a twofold effect. On the one hand, it inscribes the Canadian reader in an Italian cultural space, connecting Michelut and her audience on an emotional level as well. Immersed in an Italian atmosphere, the reader ends up being part of Michelut's experience of estrangement and uprooting, as expressed by the author's statement that her song 'brought tears to everyone's eyes'. On the other hand, singing helps Michelut connect with her Italian origins, expressing both a feeling of nostalgia – with *Terra Straniera* – and a sense of pride and belonging – with the national anthem. The act of singing Italian songs, exactly like the act of writing and self-translating, is a strategy of re-grounding.

The same process of cultural translation emerges in the insertion of the following lines from the *Divine Comedy*, by Dante Alighieri (1990, 65):

Guido, i' vorrei che tu e Lapo e io fossimo presi per incantamento e messi in un vassel, ch'ad ogni vento per mar andasse a voler vostro e mio	Guido, would that you and Lapo and I be taken by enchantment to a vessel where every wind on the sea would yield to your will and mine

The choice of this specific passage seems connected to Michelut's desire to physically navigate between Italy and Canada. To some extent, her vessel is represented by her writing and self-translating, activities that, exactly like a vessel navigating the sea, allow her to move from one linguistic and cultural shore to another.

Other striking examples of her use of CS are constituted by spelling and grammar 'mistakes'. They function as markers of a process of interference and contact between two linguistic systems, as well as authentic expressions of her hybrid personality. The poem 'A Baldin/For Baldin' presents an interesting example (1990, 98). In line 12, the Italian word 'Curdi' is misspelt as 'Kurdi', demonstrating the influence of the English term 'Kurds'. In the poem on page 114, of the same collection, the probable spelling mistake 'culture' instead of the Italian 'cultura' unconsciously suggests a further connection and combination between Italian and English, that appear on the page even beyond the writer's conscious decision.[10] These terms show that English is the language Michelut masters better, as its influence is stronger than the one exercised by Italian. However, her 'mistakes' show that both languages are activated when bilingual people communicate and how this interaction affects the writing and creative process. Even if the author is expressing herself in one language, the presence of the other one becomes tangible, evident and concrete. These 'mistakes' indicate her attempts at forging a hybrid identity that results from the interaction between her multiple languages.

If pragmatics is 'the study of language from the point of view of users' (Crystal 1985, 240), then a study of CS cannot neglect the personal motivations behind a speaker/writer's decision to codeswitch. If 'the language user is the centre of attention in pragmatics, and his/her point of view is the point of departure' (Mey 2001, 5), drawing on the psycholinguistic tradition of research into CS can illuminate how authors perceive the switch, not only with respect to the text, but also with respect to the broader context of their transmigrant experience. In light of this, the present analysis of CS will not consider exclusively textual factors but will also be informed by extra-textual elements relating to the public and private spheres of the author, such as specific life events and experiences. This approach to CS justifies the decision to investigate as CS also what can be perceived as unmarked (Callahan 2005, 19) or meaningless (Alvarez-Cáccamo 1998, 29) CS. Some of the examples provided in this section seem to overlap with other phenomena, such as naming and borrowing. Nevertheless, CS in this volume is used as an umbrella term, including all forms of language contact. Secondly, the emphasis on the user establishes his/her understanding of the switch as the basis for a recognition of what constitutes or does not constitute CS. Basically, the examples provided here are interpreted as CS on the basis that 'the juxtaposition of two languages is perceived and interpreted as a locally meaningful event by participants' (Auer 1999, 1). This point is even more pertinent in the case of written CS which Pfaff defines as 'conscious', because every language alternation is intentional and purposeful (1979, 295). Lipski also stresses the conscious connotation of written CS, when he claims that, in writing, CS 'is not the result of confusion or inability to separate the languages, but rather stems from a conscious desire to juxtapose the two codes to achieve some particular literary effect' (1982, 191). Likewise, Weston and Gardner-Chloros recognise that, while 'a partial overlap between the functions of CS in speech and in literature' has to be acknowledged, one cannot neglect that 'the written language has to be more explicit, and code-switching in this modality is therefore more "conscious"' (2015, 187). Bearing this in mind, let us consider the following example, where CS is used as an instrument of linguistic re-grounding:

> when I went back to Florence in '85, after a five-year absence, the city seemed strangely sharp and clear and small. I shut my eyes in Via Nazionale, where I knew even the cracks on the walls, then, I walked. When I felt the time had come, I opened my eyes, expecting to be in Piazza Indipendenza – but I had walked almost an extra block ('August, 1988' 1990, 83).

Michelut spent some time in Florence in order to study Italian at the local university. The city that was so familiar and reassuring appears different when, a few years later, she goes back. The image of her losing her sense of direction and getting lost conveys her sense of dismay and contributes to shaping her relationship with the city as fictitious. Her idealised vision of home is destroyed by her failed return journey, as Florence becomes an 'imaginary homeland' (Rushdie 1991). The personal dimension of CS is particularly useful in analysing this paragraph. Talking about CS here might seem problematic. One could argue that it would be more appropriate to talk about naming. Michelut is simply naming places that belong to the toponymy of Italian cities and, therefore, it would make no sense to translate them into English. Yet, the significance of these codes becomes evident if we take into consideration some conversation-external knowledge and analyse the switch in relation to a biographical component. In this specific case, we have to consider the author's relationship with Florence and what value such a relationship acquires in the context of her displacement. Against this backdrop, these Italian names scattered in the English text constitute instruments to explore the notion of home through language. By using Italian, Michelut is trying to deny the loss of the familiar place and defeat her physical un-belonging by establishing a form of linguistic belonging. By recreating contact with the Italian mother tongue, she attempts to reshape her bond with the Italian mother land as well. Within the context of her migration, codeswitching to Italian is therefore an instrument to articulate a movement back to Italy. Like mentioned already, the idea of a metaphorical return to the Italian motherland in the writings of Italian-Canadian authors has been explored by both Nannavecchia (2014) and Baldo (2013). They have specifically analysed how language (through CS and translation) can compensate for the authors' failed return home, granting them a form of connection despite the impossibility of being physically reinscribed in an Italian territory. Michelut's use of CS in this example has to be analysed against the same backdrop. As stated by Auer (1999, 1), CS is interpreted as meaningful by the person who codeswitches. On these grounds, these urban names constitute effective examples of CS. What makes them function as CS is the meaning and function they acquire for Michelut, in the context of her physical displacement. In fact, they help both the writer and the reader to articulate a backward movement. Such a purpose, nevertheless, emerges only within the context of mobility; outside this context, their role vanishes and their presence can be classified as mere naming. This provides evidence that CS must be rooted in the transmigrant experience of the writer. The practice of writing back (in Italian) and writing forward (in English) helps Michelut articulate her relationship with both her origin and host land and find a space where she can eventually fit. By doing so, she transmigrates on a linguistic and textual level; writing back constitutes a journey back to her roots, while writing forward represents a movement towards new routes. In inserting Italian or English words in a mainly monolingual text, she articulates a linguistic exchange, which helps her to overcome the tension generated by the experience of being displaced. CS, therefore, constitutes a strategy of re-appropriation of both spaces, which allows her to revise the meaning of displacement and deracination. This aspect is particularly evident in the poem 'A Matter of Faith', on page 35. Here, Michelut moves in a liminal space, which exists across Italy and Canada. This is made clear

74 VOICES OF WOMEN WRITERS

from the very first line, as the poem begins with the image of her 'rummaging through my duffel bag in the foyer of a library that was a cross between La Biblioteca Nazionale in Florence and Robarts in Toronto'. The library is presented as 'a cross' between her two countries; therefore, mentioning two specific libraries in Florence and Toronto helps her to ground herself in those places, claiming her possibility to belong to, and exist in, both simultaneously. The fact that the act of bridging takes place in a library is not surprising at all. Libraries are places that contain books and, as such, they refer to the act of writing. Basically, Michelut uses the image of the library to reinforce her belief in the unifying power of her literary activity.

The poems in *Ouroboros* also show a pattern that will be thoroughly examined and described in the analysis of *Loyalty to the Hunt*. For now, it suffices to say that Michelut's style is more figurative in Italian and Friulian, while being more rational and concrete in English. An example of this is offered by the poem that appears on page 17, which is written in both Friulian and English. Michelut narrates a bad event experienced by her mother, who used to work for a guy who used to harass the young girls who worked for him. In talking about the guy in Friulian, she uses more metaphors and idiomatic expressions, as well as bad words:

ere grant come un ors (he was as big as a bear)	was twice my size
Tocjis un cjavêli dal cjâf di me fie	if you ruin my daughter
Bastart di un bastart	Omitted in the English text

The use of a bad word in the Friulian text seems to refer to the studies conducted by Dewaele in *Psychological and Sociodemographic correlates of communicative anxiety in L2 and L3 production* (2002) and *Blistering Barnacles! What language do multilinguals Swear in?* (2004). He analysed the use of swearwords and found that the perception of the emotional force of the word is higher in the L1, as well as in contexts where the language acquisition occurs in a natural and uninstructed context. The higher emotional force perceived by Michelut in Friulian is clearly illustrated by the omission of the bad word in English. As stressed by Saidero, this specific language is also determined by the fact that 'the Friulian account reproduces the flavour of the peasants' oral speech pattern' (2011, 36–37). This stratagem recreates a Friulian locus for the Canadian reader, signalling where the action is taking place and contextualising the whole narration.

Michelut's poems also show many cases of stanza restructuring. The borders are completely fluid and, as such, totally dismantled and recreated in the passage from one language to the next. She plays with punctuation and metrics, altering the rhythm and the pace of reading. Let us pay attention

DÔRE MICHELUT

to the following poem on page 47, where the change in tense also acquires a highly metaphorical meaning:

Ti tengo dentro la mia mente per intero.	You are fully inside my mind. Without that,
Senza quello, non sarei niente.	I am nothing

There are two important things to notice in these lines. Firstly, the passage from Italian to English seems to coincide with a loss of agency. While in the Italian version her mind is actively involved in the process of containing someone else, in the English version her mind passively contains, showing no involvement, willingness and influence. In English, Michelut's agency is compromised, as she seems to adjust to an action that is externally imposed, not internally enacted. This lack of agency and identity is further reinforced with the movement from the conditional tense 'sarei' to the present 'I am'. Using different tenses, Michelut changes the perspective from which the events are narrated. Like conventionally understood, the present tense indicates acts and events that are currently occurring. As such, they possess a connotation of certainty and stability. On the contrary, the conditional indicates something that might happen or not. It is used to speculate, and as such, it vehiculates uncertainty and incertitude. In English, the present tense expresses that Michelut is completely dependent on the other, to the point that, without it, her identity is broken and she becomes nothing. In Italian, instead, she claims stronger agency and autonomy. Her identity is not dependent on the other, as the choice of the conditional puts the events in a dimension of uncertainty, hinting at the possibility that they may not happen. Her willingness in Italian is preserved. Such a choice acquires a metaphorical meaning, that must be analysed in correlation to the moment of migration. In the English version, Michelut is more overtly referring to her life in Canada, stressing the uncertainty and instability that were connected to it – at least initially. The movement to Canada determined a loss of identity and agency, that is revoked and expressed in the English version through specific syntactical and grammatical choices.

3.4 The Importance of Self-translating in *Loyalty to the Hunt*

Dôre Michelut engaged with self-translation throughout her entire life. Her self-translated poems are gathered in two collections: *Loyalty to the Hunt* and *Ouroboros: The Book That Ate Me*. In this paragraph, the focus will be on the second collection, which contains interesting cases of self-translation. As a matter of fact, some of the self-translations contained in *Ouroboros* have already been analysed in the paragraph about codeswitching.

76 VOICES OF WOMEN WRITERS

Loyalty to the Hunt was published in 1986 by Guernica Editions. The collection is divided into four sections: 'About Flight', 'Loyalty to the Hunt', 'Double Bind' and 'Letters'. Each one explores different themes; for instance, the last section, 'Letters', is made up of four poems dedicated to her family members. In this paragraph, I will analyse the third section, 'Double Bind', consisting of self-translated poems.[11] This section can be read as a metalinguistic reflection. Michelut explores the relationship between her three linguistic systems: Italian, English and Friulian. The decision to self-translate seems to emanate rightly from the nature of the text itself. The linguistic means contribute to putting forward and expressing a specific discourse. In her case, this hybrid language is used to recreate and represent her movement towards a multilingual paradigm.

No information about the chronological precedence of either the English or Italian version and the directionality of the translation has been retrieved. Therefore, all the comments derive exclusively from the analysis of the parallel versions in the collection. The three poems in this section can be read as 'language memoirs'. In each one, the author engages in metalinguistic reflections on her relationship to her linguistic systems. Through the poems, it is therefore possible to reconstruct her linguistic trajectory and highlight the different phases of the process leading to the emergence of a multilingual paradigm. This analysis begins with the first poem in the section, 'Tra l'incudine e il martello/Double Bind' (1896, 32–33). Here and in the following examples, the texts will be reproduced using the same graphic and formatting style that appears in the book:

Tra l'incudine e il martello	Double Bind
Il mattino di Bloor Street spaventa i miei sogni. Di giorno riemergono, campane che osservano il dimenticare. Mantengo il passo. Materia grigia. Pezzi di carne truciolata e grigliata. Scola il sangue, voglio salsa rubra.	Bloor Street mornings frighten my dreams. By day, they return like bells to observe the forgetting. I keep the pace. Matter is grey. Pieces of meat get ground and grilled. Drain the blood. I want ketchup.
L'arancione di Firenze mi penetra. Faccio all'amore e la notte si spiega dall'utero di mia nonna, mi lega, aggroviglia nomi e tempo, è la mia voce, urla il dolore di donne dilaniate che si vestono l'anima di carne.	In Florence, orange light arouses me. I make love and the night unfurls from my grandmother's womb. It binds me. It tangles names and time, is my voice, howls the pain of lascerated [sic] women that dress their souls in flesh.

The title anticipates the main topic of the poem: the torment of the individual who is pulled between two linguistic, cultural and geographical contexts that, in this specific case, are constituted by Italy and Canada, Italian and English.[12] At this stage, Michelut's relationship to her languages is still shaped by the monolingual paradigm. She perceives the relation between these languages according to a dialectical framework that makes it impossible for her to establish a dialogic relation between them. This fracture is recreated in the poem, which is built around different levels of opposition. From a visual perspective, its structure is articulated into two big and separated blocks, thus reproducing and conveying this idea of being caught in between different push-and-pull factors. A physical opposition also marks the linguistic opposition between Italian and English. Michelut refers to and narrates experiences that took place in two different geographical sites: on the one hand, she mentions Bloor Street, in Toronto; on the other hand, she recalls the famous Italian city, Florence.

This poem demonstrates well how, in her linguistic trajectory, the redefinition of a mother tongue in terms of mother tongues entails the recognition and acceptance that her linguistic systems occupy different spaces in her personal and literary spheres. She conceives of her Friulian, Italian and English languages as separate entities that contribute to her identitarian narrative in different ways and to varying degrees. This aspect is expressed rightly through the revisional changes, which are clear examples of how her subjectivity is shaped and expressed differently in each language. This distinction emerges clearly in 'Tra l'incudine e il martello/Double Bind'. In the title, the movement from Italian to English corresponds with a movement from the metaphorical and abstract, towards the rational and concrete. In Italian, Michelut opts for an idiomatic expression: tra l'incudine e il martello. In rendering this sentence in English, however, she decides to use a less figurative image: a double bind.[13] Figurative language is particularly useful in communicating and describing emotional states and experiences: 'the subjective nature of emotional experiences appears to lend itself to figurative expression' (Fussell and Moss 2008, 1). As such, Michelut's choice of a metaphorical language when writing in Italian suggests a stronger and deeper emotional attachment to it. This assumption seems to confirm the monolingual belief that the mother tongue is the language of emotions.[14] The relationship between languages and emotions is a widely investigated area of research concerned with bilingualism. Several studies (Dewaele 2002; Altarriba 2003; Wierzbicka 2004; Pavlenko 2005, 2008; Evans 2001; Opitz and Degner 2012; Ożańska-Ponikwia 2013) have investigated the perception and expression of emotions in both L1 and L2; that is, whether individuals perceive, express and convey emotions in different ways depending on whether they express them in the L1, or the L2. As Wierzbicka claims:

> Different languages are linked with different ways of thinking as well as different ways of feeling; they are linked with different attitudes, different ways of relating to people, different ways of expressing one's feelings (2004, 98).

The studies mentioned above all point out that the second language is normally perceived as less emotional than the first one.[15] This aspect has been explained in different ways and attributed to distinct factors. For instance, the time of acquisition of the L2 is believed to affect its emotional connotation. Pavlenko (2005) claims, for example, that individuals establish affective ties with languages they learn first. L2, therefore, is perceived as less emotional. Altarriba (2003) states that differences in the linguistic expression of emotions are correlated with cultural differences. As such, an individual's different linguistic expression of emotions is a reflection of different cultural practices. Some scholars have expanded upon this point, affirming that different languages not only determine different ways of expressing emotions but also establish different ways of perceiving them (Hull 1987; Wierzbicka 2004; Pavlenko 2006). For instance, Wierzbicka (2004, 99) claims that people perceive themselves as different when using different languages.[16] The context of language acquisition is also considered important. The acquisition of a language in a formal context is believed to prevent the development of emotional ties and connections between the individual and that language (Altarriba 2003). For instance, in his study of swearwords, Dewaele (2004) found that the perception of the emotional force of the word is higher in the L1 as well as in contexts where the language acquisition occurs in a natural and uninstructed context.

In 'Tra l'incudine e il martello/Double Bind', the emotional connotation of Italian is clearly expressed through other linguistic devices. For instance, the Italian verb 'penetrare', that is, 'to penetrate', which is opposed to the English 'to arouse', seems to hint at a deeper and more intimate connection between Michelut and the Italian space. Such a connection is further reinforced by the image of the 'womb'. The latter is to be understood in relation to the figure of the 'grandmother'. Since the womb refers to concepts of motherhood and giving birth, it inserts the Italian language into a discourse about origins and roots. The womb conveys the idea of a physical and biological linkage, as if the language was directly emanating from the individual. This connotation is reinforced through the image of the grandmother. In Italian families, the grandmother plays a very important role, as she represents the original ancestor.[17] Through these references, Michelut attempts to express the connection between the Italian language and the family unit, further expanding the concept of origins and reinforcing the connotation of Italian as the familiar language.

She also employs syntax in a way that embeds the two texts with different emotional charges. In English, the structure of the sentence follows a linear and simple subject-verb-object syntax: 'Matter is grey. Pieces of meat get ground and grilled'. In Italian, by contrast, the verb is often omitted and

DÔRE MICHELUT

nominal constructs are preferred: 'Materia grigia. Pezzi di carne truciolata e grigliata'. Such a syntactical choice creates a less linear and neutral tone that, in turn, achieves a greater poetic effect. Like Saidero claims, 'the Italian seems […] to convey the voice of an educated adult learner whose knowledge and experience of the language is mostly academic' (2011, 34), which reminds of the time Michelut spent in Florence to study Italian at the university. Also consider the following lines:

Di giorno riemergono, campane che osservano il dimenticare.	By day, they return like bells to observe the forgetting.
Faccio all'amore e la notte si spiega dall'utero di mia nonna, mi lega, aggroviglia nomi e tempo, è la mia voce	I make love and the night unfurls from my grandmother's womb. It binds me. It tangles names and times, is my voice

The omission of the conjunction 'like', together with the change in punctuation through the shift in the position of the comma, further contributes to creating a suffocating and pressing tone. The English text appears more systematic and structured than the Italian one, whose syntactical organisation conveys a feeling of anxiety and pressure that seems to overwhelm the reader. This specific use of syntax can be better understood in relation to Michelut's linguistic biography. As she declares in *Coming to Terms with the Mother Tongue*, after some time in Canada, she stopped speaking both Friulian and Italian. Her rediscovery of Italian came at a later stage, coinciding with her decision to study it in Florence. Against this backdrop, the more pressing rhythm of the Italian text seems to convey her anxiety and pressure to retrieve and express her silenced Italian voice.

This point also explains her different use of punctuation. Psycholinguistic research 'shows punctuation to be a […] locus of translational control, the place where translators assert the most authority' (May 1994, 6). On these grounds, analysing the role of punctuation can give interesting insights into how the author uses punctuation to exert her agency. By playing with punctuation, Michelut aims to dictate the reader's pace, thus managing to convey and express a specific sense of existence. In English, the extensive use of the full stop breaks the rhythm and gives the poem a more regular structure. In Italian, instead, words and sentences flow all together. As such, punctuation indicates when and where the reader should breathe. In Italian, the comma allows readers to pause for a shorter time before moving on to the following sentence. Thus, readers experience a sustained rhythm which seems to reproduce Michelut's uninterrupted movement between her multiple linguistic spaces.

The analysis of this poem, in conclusion, has revealed that, in the English text, Michelut follows a specific linguistic pattern that is described as 'rationalisation'

80 VOICES OF WOMEN WRITERS

by Antoine Berman (1992, 288–289). As he explains, this tendency affects features such as sentence structure, order, punctuation, avoidance of figurative language and tendency to generalisation. These grammatical, lexical and syntactical choices aim to make the text clear and more organised. Going back to the assumption that the self-translation of the text coincides with the translation of the self, it follows that, in rationalising the English text, she is translating and transposing her English identity on the page. The second poem in the collection is 'La terza voce diventa madre/The Third Voice Gives Birth' (1986, 34–35):

Ricerco categorie per dar voce al preciso agro	I research categories to give voice to
del diospero. L'inglese impazzisce: borbotta,	the exact bitterness of the persimmon.
mi spinge verso strade desolate, ordite di	English goes mad. It mutters. It pushes
teste di amori mai avuti o perduti in quel	me towards desolate roads, strung with
posto dove le cosce non si riscaldano mai;	heads of lovers that never were, or that got
dove stormi di uccelli neri ancora afflitti	lost in the place where thighs never get
da languori vespertini farfallano, prigionieri	warm, where swarms of black birds still
di un quadro di de Chirico. Sento l'odore di	afflicted with the languors of vespers
sogno morto. O Susanna tal biel cjastiel	flutter, prisoners of a de Chirico painting.
di Udin with the tanti pesciolini e i fiori	I can smell the dead dream. *O Susanna tal*
di lillà don't you cry for the deer and	*biel cjastiel di Udin with the tanti pesciolini e i*
the dead buffalo…	*fiori di lillà don't you cry for the deer and the dead*
"*Per questo sei scappata?*"	*buffalo…*
"*Per questo. Per ciò che era scritto. Come*	"Was it for this you ran away?"
Corto Maltese cambiai il mio destino.	"For this. For what was written. Like Corto
Con una lametta, ne ritagliai un altro."	Maltese, I changed my fate, with a blade,
"*Allora riposiamoci. Il diospero*	I cut in another."
s' addolcirà."	"Then we can rest. The persimmon will
	sweeten."

The third voice is represented by her Friulian, whose maternal connotation derives from the fact that Michelut received this language directly from her mother. It also originates from Friulian's rooting connotation, that is, from its capacity to establish an alternative linguistic family romance that also includes Italian and English. At the beginning of this poem, Michelut is still caught in-between Italian and English. The metaphor of her researching categories, 'to give voice to the exact bitterness of the persimmon', refers directly to this point. Her English tongue 'goes mad' and 'mutters', in the attempt to express a sensory and intimate experience that brings her back to her life in Italy. In this existential and linguistic struggle, her Friulian voice suddenly erupts on the page and allows her to find routes to the other two languages as well. The following lines illustrate this point well: 'O Susanna tal biel cjastiel di Udin with the tanti pesciolini e i fiori di lillà don't you cry for the deer and the dead buffalo…'. Combination is achieved on two levels: on the one hand, through the actual presence of the three linguistic systems on the same page. On the other hand, through the juxtaposition of three folk songs: the famous American song 'Oh Susanna', itself a mixture of a variety of musical traditions. The banjo, which is mentioned in the opening lines of the song, is an instrument normally used in folk and country music. The rhythm of the song, however, is a polka. The Italian song is 'La casetta in Canadà', which tells the story of a man building a house in Canada. The latter is a song belonging to the Friulian musical repertoire. As stated by Saidero, 'The juxtaposition of lines from three well-known folk texts functions, in fact, to recover a polyphonic dimension, that incorporates intercultural and interlinguistic elements' (2011, 35). In defining Friulian as 'the third voice which gives birth', Michelut identifies it as the purely maternal mother tongue, from which the others emanate. Friulian constitutes the language that allows her to find a common ground between her two acquired languages, Italian and English. The latter eventually manage to 'touch and penetrate' because they both 'can happen in the light of Furlan and, when possible, vice versa' (*Coming to Terms with the mother Tongue* 1989, 64–66). The combination of her three linguistic systems guarantees Michelut a simultaneity of existence and expression that, in turn, gives continuity to her identitarian narrative. The image of the sweetened persimmon represents the fact that she is finally able to perceive and exploit the advantage of her linguistic hybridity: 'I find that when a poem or a story has passed through the sieve, gone from English to Furlan and back, from Furlan to Italian or Italian to English and back, each language still speaks me differently, because it must, but each speaks me more fully' (*Coming to Terms with the Mother Tongue* 1989, 71).

This specific recognition of Friulian as the first mother tongue is pointed out in the last poem of the section, which is self-translated between English and Friulian. Its title is 'Ne storie/A Story'. In this poem, which will not be reproduced here, the author describes her re-conjunction with her dialectal mother tongue. This re-conjunction is narrated through the image of the prodigal son. Michelut imagines a dialogue with her Friulian mother tongue that celebrates the return of her prodigal daughter: 'I shudder as this suffering history greets me with kisses, tells me I've been bad, says: 'Where have you been? We'll settle this at home' (1986, 36–37).[18] This relationship ascribes an affective dimension to Friulian, defining the relationship as one of affection and love between parents and sons. The re-conjunction with Friulian unearths the fallacy of the monolingual paradigm, showing that the relation with the mother tongue is not eternal and unbreakable; exposed to alternative multilingual practices, Michelut initially detaches from Friulian, relegating it to a past time and place. Furthermore, the maternal language is not exclusive. Going back to her Friulian mother tongue does not imply the exclusion of the other languages. Michelut claims her belonging and connection to all of them and attempts to make them constantly present in her personal and

82 VOICES OF WOMEN WRITERS

professional activities. The return to Friulian as the primary mother tongue recurs in the following poem as well:

Tornarès a cjase	I would come home
par la puarte	by the door
che tu mi tègnis viârte	you keep open
dome par la viròcs	if only to hunt snails
di bunore tal miluzâr	in the orchard
dongje il sumitèrei	by the cemetery
quant ch'a la tiare	at dawn
luzinte	when the wet earth
a respire ploe	shines

Michelut identifies a connection between returning home and returning to Friulian. In this poem, home refers clearly to her hometown in Italy, as it emerges from the childhood memories she describes. She moves on both a temporal and physical level as she re-grounds in a past time and place. The connection between Friulian and Sella di Rivignano becomes even stronger because she uses the Friulian mother tongue to re-ground herself in the Friulian mother land, bringing back past experiences and moments. Returning to Friulian nevertheless does not mean moving away from Italian and English. Her linguistic trajectory does not comply with the monolingual paradigm. This is evident in the poem above, where the connection between her multiple languages emerges in the juxtaposition of the same text in Friulian and English. By putting one poem next to the other, Michelut makes each version intelligible to her readers, who can almost read them simultaneously and therefore infer their meaning based on this correlation. The result is a hybrid text whose meaning and essence only result from the combination of both versions. In doing so, the author suggests to the reader that the gap between both languages and cultures can be bridged, as translation helps to defeat the opacity inherent in each language. The unfamiliar Friulian acquires some level of familiarity thanks to the juxtaposition with English, and vice versa. Rather than being excluded because of the impossibility of reading in the other language, readers experience the text in new forms, in a process that prompts and reinforces their metalinguistic awareness.

Including the English version in this text about her relationship with Friulian therefore constitutes a way to further reinforce her movement towards the multilingual paradigm. Michelut is not returning to Friulian to settle into it; her personal and professional lives still maintain and guarantee places for her other mother tongues. This coexistence is the foundation of her linguistic and stylistic inventiveness. Her stories and poems ground themselves in a linguistic, cultural and historical heritage with no exact boundaries.

DÔRE MICHELUT

Notes

* Chapter 3 is also available as an article in an academic journal, 'Italian Canadiana'.

1 Michelut uses the term Furlan; nevertheless, I will be using Friulian, thus adopting the conventionally accepted English version, which is also used by scholars of Italian-Canadian literature, such as Saidero in 'Plurilinguismo e autotraduzione' (2008), 'Self-Translation as Transcultural' (2011) and 'Self-Translation as Translingual and Transcultural Transcreation' (2020).

2 See "Dôre Michelut," English-Canadian Writers, Athabasca University, http://canadian writers.athabascau.ca/english/writers/dmichelut/dmichelut.php.

3 To expand upon this point, please see Auer, *Italien in Toronto* (1991); Haller, *Varieties, Use, and Attitudes* (2011).

4 The letter 'H' signifies standard variety, the one that is usually used in official settings.

5 When talking about Italian, then, I do not refer to the fixed and literary idiom, but to the heterogeneous and mutable variety that is spoken across the peninsula.

6 To expand upon this point, refer to Clivio and Danesi, The *Sounds, Forms, and Uses of Italian* (2000).

7 The metaphor of the mother that represents the mother tongue is quite common among bilingual writers.

8 Part of this analysis has been used in my article 'Italian Mothers and Italian-Canadian Daughters: Using Language to Negotiate the Politics of Gender' (2019).

9 I wish to specify that I have a basic knowledge of Friulian. However, in my analysis of the poems in Friulian, I relied on the help of a Friulian friend.

10 This poem has no title.

11 The poems in *Ouroboros* and *Loyalty to the Hunt* have also been analysed by Saidero, in her article 'Self-translation as Trasncultural Re-Inscription of Identity in Dôre Michelut and Gianna Patriarca' (2011).

12 I wish to specify that in this analysis I refer to Italian and do not include Friulian because she overtly refers to Florence, the city where she lived and studied Italian.

13 Alternative idiomatic expressions would be 'between a rock and a hard place'; 'between the hammer and the anvil'; 'between the devil and the deep blue sea'; 'have the wolf by the ear'.

14 Ortony (1975) and Ekmand and Davison (1994) claim that metaphors and idioms are often chosen to talk about feelings and emotions because they add intensity and completeness to the message that one wants to transmit.

15 As Opitz and Degner point out, the same perception is reported 'even by highly proficient bilinguals, not just beginning learners or poor speakers of a second language' (2012: 1961).

16 The study by Ożańska-Ponikwia offers a very interesting and original perspective on this topic, as she introduces the concept of personality as one of the factors to consider when analysing individuals' response to emotions in both L1 and L2. I do not take this factor into account here, because it would require a deeper investigation into biographical aspects of these authors' life, which is not part of this research.

17 For an account of the role of the grandmother in Italian families, see Jo Bona, *Claiming a Tradition Italian American Women Writers* (1999).

18 The reference to such an image reinforces the parallel between mother and mother tongue.

CHAPTER 4

LICIA CANTON: REWRITING THE ITALIAN MOTHER (TONGUE, LAND)'S LEGACY IN SELF-TRANSLATION

4.1 Growing Up in a Cavarzeran Community in Montréal

Licia Canton is another representative of the Italian-Canadian literary movement. Her story retraces the steps followed by Gianna Patriarca and Dôre Michelut, and it echoes the stories of many other Italian-Canadian migrants. She was born in Cavarzere, a small town in the province of Venice. In 1967, when she was four years old, she moved to Montréal with her family. Being forced to leave her native land and start a new life in a new territory was a painful and distressing experience, which has thenceforth marked her personal and professional lives. In the essay 'Writing Canadian Narratives with Italian Accents: The Pink House and Other Stories', she writes that, while she used to be a talkative child in Italy, in Canada she became shy and did not speak much (2019, 60). The experience of being voiceless, which is common among Italian-Canadian authors, especially female ones, triggered her need and desire to retrieve her voice, which subsequently inclined her to write. Indeed, in the same essay, she declares that she was able to find her voice only when she began writing (2019, 60).

Canton shows a great interest in migration and minority literature, with a sharp focus on Italian-Canadian literature. She has explored this theme in both critical and creative writing. Among the critical texts are *Writing Our Way Home* (2013), *Conspicuous Accents* (2014), *Writing Cultural Difference* (2015), and *Writing Beyond History: an Anthology of Prose and Poetry* (2006). These anthologies collect the literary creations (both prose and poetry) of several Italian-Canadian authors. Among the literary texts that investigate migration from a less academic perspective is *Almond Wine and Fertility* (2008), where the author portrays the encounter between Italian and Canadian culture, and *The Pink House and Other Stories*, a collection of 15 short stories.

Among her many achievements, Canton was the recipient of the *Premio Italia nel Mondo*, that celebrates Italian excellence in the world. This award

86 VOICES OF WOMEN WRITERS

started in New York in 1994, when the famous Italian tenor Luciano Pavarotti was awarded. In 2018, the celebration took place in Toronto, and four Italian-Canadians were awarded, including Licia Canton. She has also served on the board of directors of the Quebec Writers' Federation (QWF) and is past president of the 'Associazione Scrittori/ Scrittrici Italo-Canadesi', 'una comunità di scrittori, critici, accademici e artisti di altre discipline che promuovono la letteratura e la cultura italo-canadese'. In 2019, she was Visiting Professor and Writer-in-Residence at the University of Calabria, and she is currently an Honorary Fellow in Translation at the University of Hull.[1] Moreover, she is the editor-in-chief of *Accenti*, an online magazine which promotes and propagates Italian culture and traditions on the Canadian territory.[2] The magazine is written in English, but it deals with Italian topics. Indeed, on its official website, *Accenti* is presented as 'the magazine with an Italian accent'.

The desire to bridge and combine, therefore, appears central to Canton's personal and professional experience. Her life and work crisscross between multiple linguistic, cultural and physical spaces, articulating hybridity in contraposition to purity and essentialism.[3] Like she claims, she lives 'dans une zone de traduction continuelle, une alternance linguistique' (2015, 87). Her personal pluralism intersects with the national pluralism of Canada, thus making life in multiple languages both a choice and a necessity: 'For Italian-Canadian authors living in Montreal, the activity of self-translation is not limited to a writing practice but can become an everyday necessity' (Pivato 2020, 18). Her career as a writer and editor is also animated by the desire to promote and support Italian-Canadian literature, highlighting its influence on, and contributions to, Canada. Like written in the Introduction to *Writing Cultural Difference*, 'whereas the first generation worked to build the urban skyline of Canadian cities, their descendants work to shape the artistic and literary landscape of the country' (2015, 14). These words acknowledge the role played by second and third generations in contributing to the cultural and artistic world of Canada. They become even more meaningful if we consider that the book was born in response to Pivato's essay *Nothing Left to Say: Italian Canadian Literature* (1990). The essay itself was written in defiance of those within the academic world who believed that Italian-Canadian literature had run out of topics, themes and meanings. Relegating the Italian-Canadian experience to the past, it was argued that these authors' stories did not speak to, or resonate with, the contemporary world and its main actors. Against this backdrop, Canton's professional path can be seen as a mission, complying with her need to give a voice to 'her self', as well as to the other Italian-Canadian writers, claiming their literary and existential space: 'We are all writers. We are Canadian. We are the writers and the Canadians that we are because we share roots elsewhere. That's what brings us together; that's what keeps us writing' (2015, 16). These words highlight the connection between migration and writing. Mobility offers new inputs and new visions, new experiences and stories, which enrich literary performance and further develop individuals' innate creativity and sensibility. The strength and importance of Italian-Canadian authors' literary productions lie exactly in the experience of migration, whose universal connotation validates their voices across time and space. Hence, also Canton's writing and self-translating performances derive from an existential need; the 'literary I' coincides with the 'factual I', and both voices are reinforced and substantiated in this *ensemble*. This is also the reason why her short stories often feature common people, the voiceless ones, who are unheard and invisible. She tells of their daily struggles, their hopes and fears, their successes and failures. Her use of writing as an instrument to give voice becomes even more evident if we consider that several stories focus on abuse, entrapment and alienation. Her characters seem unable to speak and act on their own terms. Against this backdrop, the written page gives them a space where they can finally be heard and seen. Canton tells their stories because, in the act of writing, lies the possibility of existence.

As mentioned before, she is originally from the region of Veneto. In her hometown, Cavarzeran was the 'official language'. In fact, as it was clarified in Chapter 1, while Italian is the standard language in Italy, each region has a different dialect, which is predominantly spoken by local people in their daily communication (Sobrero 1993, 101–102). In moving to Canada, Canton's family settled down in an area where there was a strong community from the same town.[4] Within this community, Cavarzeran continued to be the language of daily communication, which guaranteed some sort of linguistic continuity:

> Sono nata a Cavarzere (in provincia di Venezia) dove tutti parlavano el cavarzeran; [...] Nei primi anni a Montréal ero circondata da amici di famiglia, pochi, ma quasi tutti di Cavarzere o dintorni.

This passage illustrates the role played by the Cavarzeran dialect in building and reinforcing a bond among Italian migrants, who found closeness and harmony in the possibility of speaking the same language. Against their physical, linguistic and cultural displacement, the familiar language offered a way to re-ground. Even after migrating, Cavarzeran continued to occupy spaces in Canton's life. At the same time, moving to Québec (an officially bilingual area) put her in contact with both French and English. She started experiencing life in other languages as well, which led her to reconsider her relation to language and recognise

88   VOICES OF WOMEN WRITERS

'her self' as embedded in multiple linguistic systems. However, for a long time, Italian never really entered her world and kept representing only a distant and background sound. The relationship with the Italian mother tongue changed only when she became a mother and decided to teach her children Italian. This decision overtly refers to the relation between the mother and the mother tongue; when she becomes a mother, Canton wants her children to learn the mother's tongue: 'Ma è proprio quando sono diventata mamma che mi sono dedicata a trovare libri in italiano per poterlo insegnare ai miei figli. Leggendo ai miei bimbi, ho imparato e continuo ad imparare tuttora'. In teaching her children the language of the mother, she chooses Italian rather than Cavarzeran, as might be expected. The reason is mainly pragmatic: she chooses the language that is more influential and useful, from a political, professional and cultural perspective. However, her choice is important for what it signifies with respect to the monolingual paradigm. Her decision entails a movement of Italian from a background to a foreground position. Canton's relationship with Italian goes beyond the temporal dimension, undermining the monolingual assumption that the mother tongue necessarily and exclusively coincides with the language we learn first. As she declares, Italian and English are now the languages she uses the most:

> Oggi l'italiano è una grande componente della mia vita quotidiana. Ma non è sempre stato così. Oggi parlo l'italiano con i miei figli. È una scelta importante, alla quale tengo molto, ma non è una cosa naturale: mi sembra di nuotare controcorrente.

Although Italian is not the language Canton learned from, and spoke with, her mother, she reconfigures it as 'the mother's tongue' when she adopts it to communicate with her children. '*Andare controcorrente*', that is, 'to swim against the tide', refers rightly to this specific configuration. It expresses the tension lying in the rupture between what her real relationship with Italian is and what the monolingual framework would expect it to be. This idea seems to adhere to a conventional notion of a mother tongue. Nonetheless, Canton's choice to teach her children Italian as 'the mother's tongue' opens up a rethinking of the native language as temporally, biologically and geographically determined. She destabilises the rooting connotation of Cavarzeran by opening up routes to other languages. Her movement beyond the mother tongue consists exactly in this: recognising each language as responsible for adding to her 'identitarian narrative'; accepting that what we call 'the maternal voice' is simply the result of the reciprocal and simultaneous communication of several voices.[5] This step paves the way for developing a notion of mother tongues, which includes all the linguistic systems her life has been lived and expressed in. She moves beyond the idea of a single mother tongue and eventually establishes relationships with multiple mother tongues: 'La persona che sono oggi è la somma totale delle lingue (e delle culture) che mi hanno influenzato: ossia, in ordine cronologico, il cavarzerano, il francese, l'inglese, l'italiano, il tedesco, lo spagnolo'. Canton recognises all her languages as mother tongues because, in different ways and to varying degrees, they all influence her life and contribute to her multilingual makeup. She finds a way to make sense of her linguistic and existential fragmentation, by creating spaces where her multiple languages can co-exist. This is manifest in her personal and professional choices, which reflect this movement towards a multilingual paradigm:

> Alla scuola Marie Clarac ho imparato il francese. Ma la mia istruzione è avvenuta in maggioranza in inglese. Al CEGEP e all'Università tentai di portare avanti l'inglese e il francese. Non è una contraddizione che abbia studiato il francese all'Università McGill, e scritto una tesi di dottorato in inglese all'Università di Montréal. Nel mio lavoro e nella mia vita quotidiana, ora l'inglese e l'italiano predominano.

As the previous paragraph illustrates, Canton actively attempts to break the boundary between languages and to adopt and apply a constant hybrid perspective. This attempt to negotiate and mediate is well represented by her decision to study French at McGill University, one of the three English-language universities in Québec. Conversely, she does her PhD in English at the University of Montréal, where French is the main language. This tendency can be read as her strategy to work through the transmigrant experience. She demonstrates that the different linguistic components of her life can be bridged and combined, in a process where everything is constantly hybridised. She re-grounds her identitarian narrative rightly in this capacity to move beyond borders and create linguistic, cultural and existential contact zones. Indeed, she claims: 'I have a deep connection to my Italian roots *and* I am Canadian' (2019, 60). The conjunction 'and' indicates connection and coexistence. Her Italian roots and her Canadian upbringing are not mutually exclusive but constitute essential components of her identity.

In the following paragraph, it will be illustrated how this attempt to bridge also emerges in her narratives, on both a thematic and a linguistic level. From a thematic perspective, the characters in her stories operate in a hybrid space, in-between Italy and Canada; they are Canadians who have spent some time in Italy, are married to an Italian partner, or have relatives and friends living in Italy. Travelling is a common condition for them, as they are always about to leave, or to arrive somewhere. Like the protagonists of *Coincidenza*, a short story in *Almond Wine and Fertility*. Luana, a Canadian woman with Italian origins who works as a writer – a coincidence that makes us think of her as the author's *alter ego* – is visiting Rome and meeting an old friend (or maybe old lover, the author does not specify it), an Italian architect who lived in Canada for a while. Their life experiences overlap and mirror each other in a liminal space between Italy and Canada, past and present.

Canton's characters operate in a constant condition of transmigration, both physical and metaphorical. Their experiences redefine concepts of 'home' and 'belonging'; for instance, many stories rethink 'home', through an open condemnation of Italian patriarchal society, especially in contraposition to Canadian culture. These narratives depict Canadian women who are married to Italian men, who abuse and mistreat them. Alternatively, they represent spoiled and immature male characters. This is the case with Frank, whose story is narrated in *Le rose rosse*. Frank lives with his parents, who cook for him, iron his shirts and tidy up his room. Despite earning more than his female partner, he does not want to buy a house together and keeps postponing their marriage. Basically, he refuses to engage in a series of actions that would inevitably mark his passage into adult life. He grew up in Canada, but his parents are Italian, a literary stratagem that serves the purpose of ascribing the character's flaws to his Italian origins, and to explore how the Italian heritage still manifests itself across generations. Through Frank and his parents, Canton is criticising the Italian system of values, highlighting the negative impacts it has on both men and women, old and new generations. The overwhelming presence of Frank's family interferes with his relationship as well. As we keep reading the story, we find out that his girlfriend has often attempted to break up with him, only to encounter his family's resistance and interference. Eventually, she finds a way to end their relationship. She sends him a letter in which she communicates her decision to him. She grants the end of their story to the written page, perfectly complying with the function fulfilled by writing in Canton's experience. The act of writing validates the woman's decision and grants her autonomy.

From a linguistic perspective, Canton also makes extensive use of CS. Like the analysis of *Almond Wine and Fertility/Vino alla mandorla e fertilità* will illustrate, CS in her book is interconnected with her condemnation of Italian society and acts as an instrument of resistance to patriarchy. Italian heritage seems almost a burden to the author, who is simultaneously frightened and intrigued by it. Like claimed by Pivato, 'Licia Canton share[s] the love-hate relationship with Italy that is evident in the work of many other Italian-Canadian writers' (2020, 25). She cannot but dissect and analyse this culture in her narratives, thus granting the creative act a cathartic function.

Writing allows Canton to come to terms with her Italian heritage, unveiling a model of Italianness which, in most cases, seems uncomfortable and almost disturbing. By exposing the flaws and shortfalls of this sociocultural system, she repositions 'her self' as simultaneously connected and disconnected to it. Furthermore, in her stories, CS indexes a specific sociocultural context against which a correct understanding of the narration must be sketched. To this end, Canton specifically uses Italian words and sentences, which are imbued with strong cultural references and which overtly refer to a specific system of values. CS to Italian helps the Canadian reader to understand why and how the characters in the story interact, to locate their actions in a specific context, and to appreciate to what extent and in what ways individuals and their lives are the products of their legacy. Culture and language are interlinked, and this link is expressed and articulated through CS. Indeed, she uses CS to perform a cultural translation, translating the Italian context to her Canadian readership.

Canton's stories are written in a simple but never banal way. Their communicative strength lies exactly in this. The author depicts characters that represent all of us; she narrates stories that echo everyone's memories. They are individual stories, yet surprisingly universal. Her simple writing style complies rightly with this purpose: speaking to the people, and for the people.

4.2 Italian-Canadian Spaces and Narratives of (Up)rooting

In the chapter about Patriarca, the concept of 'not being home' was introduced. This notion was developed by the scholars Martin and Mohanty to refer to a process through which migrants realise the misleading and dangerous potential of 'home'. The physical distance from the motherland triggers an emotional and cultural detachment from its sociocultural legacy. This detachment gives migrants an external perspective, which allows them to develop a form of criticism towards values and habits of their origin country. Exposed to new ways of thinking and operating, migrants learn to challenge taken-for-granted beliefs and traditions in a process that leads them to reconfigure both their personal and social identities. For Patriarca, 'not being home' meant to point out and condemn gender dynamics and inequalities within the Italian migrant community. The same attitude emerges in Canton's narratives. For her, rethinking home is necessarily connected to a condemnation of Italian society. She openly addresses politics of coercion and abuse, aiming to highlight the effects of the Italian cultural heritage, thus challenging and dismantling a system of values that she perceives as inherently sexist and unsafe for women. To do so, she takes the image of home, intended as a physical place, as a starting point to engage with a rethinking of home,

92 VOICES OF WOMEN WRITERS

metaphorically understood as a sociocultural space. The politics of home are reassessed and reimagined through this concrete image, as Canton stresses power dynamics, which are enacted in the space of the house. She attempts to alter the personal significance of domesticity by redefining private identities that are tied to the specific politics of home. Many women in her stories are trapped inside the domestic space. This is the case of the main character in the short story 'From the Sixth Floor' (*Almond Wine and Fertility*; 2008: 41–47). Here, Canton introduces us to a Canadian woman who has moved to Italy after marrying an Italian man. Her husband abuses her both psychologically and physically. This abuse is visually represented through the image of the home: 'He begins his tirade of verbal abuse when I am in a confined space, when I am trapped' (2008, 45). The woman is physically confined and is unable to leave the domestic space. Her only contact with the external world is provided by a small window, from where she often looks out. The window seems to offer her an escape from her situation, and it works as a reminder of the life she could have. Nevertheless, the window also acquires an ambiguous and controversial connotation; her husband keeps telling her to throw herself, exactly like another woman in the same building did years ago. The woman's status of confinement becomes very polarised and radical when he starts threatening to lock her up in a mental asylum, which represents the ultimate enclosed space: 'I will have you committed, he threatens' (2008, 46).

The woman is surrounded by people who tell her that she cannot leave and abandon her husband: 'You cannot leave, they say. [...] You must not leave. You should not have such thoughts' (2008, 45). These words reiterate the belief that a woman's place is in the house. Leaving is considered a form of guilt that cannot be forgiven. Even suicide is portrayed as a more acceptable alternative. The imperative to stay and endure also conforms to the belief that everything must be hidden because *'i panni sporchi si lavano in casa'*.[6] People must repress their feelings and needs in order to preserve appearance and make everything look perfect to the eye of the external society: 'No, you can't leave. That would be a disgrace to my family and to yours' (p. 44). Leaving means to expose the internal world to the external eye, breaking the norms and rules that conventionally regulate this relationship. It means to debunk the illusory representation of home, revealing the corrupt mechanisms that determine people's allegiance to it.

In the story, the woman's entrapment also acquires a metaphorical value, as it refers to the impossibility of realising her potential outside the domestic space. She often refers to her education and the professional ambitions that she could not fulfil. On her arrival in Italy, she was offered a job as a secretary in the family company. She nonetheless refused the job, as she would have preferred something related to what she had studied. By looking for a

LICIA CANTON

different job, she is also seeking independence and attempting to overcome mechanisms of power. However, her attempt is ridiculed and criticised because her goals and aspirations do not match traditional models of femininity. Within this patriarchal and conservative world, her existence is only defined by borders. She can only express and realise herself within them, not beyond. Her subjectivity is nothing more than a social and familial construct in which there is no space for her individuality. Unable to speak and be heard, the woman offers her voice to the written page: 'Maybe if I send a page of my diary to someone and let my thoughts speak for me?' (2008, 46). The diary conveys the existential power of writing; writing means to exist, and vice versa. Writing legitimises and validates an existence that is otherwise denied and dismissed.

Eventually, she finds the courage to leave her husband. The story ends with an image of her leaving home: 'I sit on the train pulling out of Termini Station. I don't know where I will go, but I am leaving' (2008, 47). As Canton depicts the woman leaving for the station, she presents movement as a 'metaphor of liberation', not only from the abusive and dangerous space of 'home', but also from a system of values that, in Canton's literary world, shapes and regulates the relationships between Canadian women and Italian men.

The same story is reiterated in 'The Courtyard' (p. 89). At the beginning of the narration, the author does not overtly specify it, but it is impossible not to notice a number of similarities and convergences between the two stories. Only towards the end of the narration Canton specifies that the woman lives on the sixth floor, thus making the overlap more overt. Indeed, the protagonist is also a woman who is trapped at home, abused by her husband and his family. Reading the first pages, we find out that she lives in one of those big modern buildings, with lots of flats, where people barely know who lives next door. This image intensifies her invisibility. Like she says, almost no one knows she lives there. Furthermore, the voices of the children playing in the courtyard and the noises of the traffic jam cover her voice and further contribute to her invisibility. This aspect is made even more evident when we learn that she is simply occupying the flat, almost like a lifeless object. As a matter of fact, the author compares her to *un segnalibro nella pagina sbagliata* (p. 148), a bookmark on the wrong page (p. 93). Another similarity between the two stories is offered by the window, essential and overarching presence in both narratives. In 'The Courtyard', the narration begins exactly with the woman looking out of the window. She spends hours observing and feeding the pigeons, that constitute the only contact she has with the external world. This image also acquires a metaphorical value, as the pigeons clearly refer to an idea of freedom. The whole narration revolves around the window, which represents simultaneously an instrument of liberation and death.

94 VOICES OF WOMEN WRITERS

Like the woman states, she is at the same time attracted to and scared of it. She looks out of the window, looking for an escape but also contemplating and fantasising her suicide.

A constant trope in Canton's narratives is represented by what the author calls *la bella figura*, an Italian expression meaning to make a good impression and project a positive image of oneself. It is a concept that includes appearance, good manners and a general sense of dignity and decorum. Canton's characters operate according to this concept. They are constantly observed and judged by the world outside, which forces them to play a role. Adhering to this concept is another form of entrapment; it prevents people from living life on their own terms and obliges them to deal with external interferences and intrusions. Indeed, Canton's characters seem unable to escape society's pressures and expectations. For instance, they are surrounded by relatives and friends telling them to continue in their married life, even if they are unhappy. This happens in 'Espresso Cup' (p. 49). The male character announces to his mum that he wants to leave his wife. As she stubbornly tries to change his mind, their dialogue is continuously interspersed by her questions, 'Are you sure about this?' (p. 49), 'There must be something that can be done' (p. 49), 'Maybe you should think about it some more?' (p. 49), 'Couldn't you make it work' (p. 50) and so on. In this society infused with religion and strict morality, the sacred bond of marriage cannot be broken. Both men and women have to endure because what appears externally is more important than what happens internally. This conduct is necessary for the sake of appearances, regardless of how painful and complex keeping with them might be.

This story seems to continue in 'Self-Made Man' (p. 67), where the situation is told and explored from the perspective of the man. Here, the male character appears completely different. Depicted as a respectable and clever man in 'Espresso Cup', he now reveals himself to be arrogant and self-centred. His narcissistic attitude prevents him from understanding his wife's needs and rights, as he is only preoccupied with escaping from this unhappy marriage as the successful party and with preserving his appearance. His words display no love or affection for his wife, as he continues to belittle her and her achievements in life, comparing them with his own successes and accomplishments. From his words, the woman emerges as a weak character who has given up on everything for him and their children and whose only purpose in life was to be a wife and a mother. At first, then, she seems to perfectly represent a specific idea of femininity, whose core essence revolves around the concept of motherhood. Nevertheless, the author counteracts this narrative by revealing that the male character's contempt for his wife derives from the impossibility of moulding her and imposing his own view of life. This aspect emerges clearly in the conversation between the man and his father. Their words revolve around the necessity to shape women according to a specific model of femininity:

> My father warned me years ago. "Such a woman is not for you", he'd said. "She is quiet and gentle, but her eyes are intelligent". He knew the type. She would revolt. "Find a woman that you can mold into the wife *you* need. This is not the right woman for *you*," he'd said. When I think about it, I want to puke. What a mistake. I lowered my standards by marrying a woman with expectations. Wants to be loved. Listened to (2008, 70).

The woman's intelligence represents a threat to the harmony in the family, as it goes against her husband's desire to dominate her. This negative connotation is made even more evident through the juxtaposition of the verb 'revolt', which literally refers to breaking the rules and threatening the social order. The wife will not obey, and thus she will destabilise the peace and quietness in the family unit. Her behaviour disrupts the husband's framework of reference and dismantles power dynamics that are associated with a specific model of femininity. She therefore represents alternative models of both womanhood and motherhood. The man's narcissistic attitude is further reinforced through the stratagem of the italics, which is used to highlight the fact that he is exclusively focused on himself: *you*. His view of marriage revolves around a dichotomy: him against her. In this view, there is no space for cooperation and understanding between men and women. The social and familiar order is established and preserved by a power game, not sustained by love and affection.

In the story, the woman's personality is depicted in contraposition to the male character's mother: 'My mother ... now there's a real woman' (p. 71). This 'real woman' represents what Rorato calls 'a patriarchal notion of motherhood' (2018, 75). She listens but does not speak, unless consulted. She always looks elegant and well-groomed. She is patient and submissive. These qualities comply with moral and cultural norms that regulate womanhood, aiming to control both women's bodies and minds. Women are not only told how to behave but also how to look. The man's mother is reduced to her nurturing function and ends up representing what Recalcati calls 'la madre del seno', that is, the mother whose essence revolves around satisfying the requests and needs of her children (2015, 47–56). This maternal figure is common in patriarchal societies, where mothers are not perceived as human beings but simply represent 'a product of the child's imagination', a fantasy 'that often lasts into adulthood' (Rorato 2018, 79). This is well expressed by the character's perception of his mother; despite being an adult, he cannot detach himself from his childish and stereotypical view of motherhood.[7] In comparison, his wife instead emerges as a disrupting character whose behaviour and appearance reconfigure established norms and codes. Podnieks and O'Reilly claim that female authors writing about motherhood create 'maternal texts', whose function is to challenge traditional concepts of motherhood (2010, 1). This aspect is evident in the narrative above, where Canton uses the woman's story to celebrate alternative ways of being mother and wife, specifically counteracting conventional ideas of self-abnegation and denial.

The narration 'In the Stacks' appears in *Writing Our Way Home* (2013: 129).[8] It can be seen as a sort of meta-narration. The female character shows traits and features that partially overlap with those displayed by the author. Furthermore, the story is about two Italian-Canadians (Rita and Massimiliano) who meet in a library as they both research about Italian migration in Canada. The narrative is a reflection on roots as Canton rethinks traditional discourses of identity and belonging. The characters' conversation offers her the opportunity to investigate and remap the terrains of identity and belonging for first and second generations of Italian migrants. Rita and Massimiliano continuously attempt to label each other, assessing themselves through stereotyped views of Italianness and Canadianness. Concepts such as the accent and the name are evoked in order to mark their otherness as Italian-Canadians, thus establishing both a private and a collective sense of self. On these grounds, the story offers interesting insights into how Canton rethinks concepts of otherness and sameness from her transmigrant position.

According to social identity theory (Tajfel and Turner 1986), an individual's sense of self is socially constructed, that is, based on the relations and interactions with the surrounding environment. Identity 'depends upon the presence of others' because who we are appears uniquely and distinctly only to others (Cavarero 2000, 21). In the context of migration, individuals' otherness becomes more evident and therefore highly noticed. Migrants must redefine their identity within a new community, whose members show social, linguistic, cultural and even physical features that differ from those displayed in the origin society. In 'In the Stacks', the characters express their sense of self through two main features: the body and the name. These features function as 'regulator[s] of the individual's visibility as a migrant' (Burns 2013, 13): as markers of his/her alterity. The body and the name serve as metaphors for how migrants negotiate border-crossings, and how their subjectivity is transformed through, and by, the movement to a different community.

In this analysis, the word 'body' constitutes an umbrella term referring to physical features in general. The body plays an important role in shaping migrants' encounters with locals. Sara Ahmed claims that familiar bodies are

LICIA CANTON 97

usually 'incorporated through a sense of community [...] while strange bodies are expelled from bodily space – moving apart as unlike bodies' (2000, 50). This means that perceptions of bodily otherness or sameness can affect migrants' inclusion or exclusion from the host society. For this reason, the body becomes a site of observation, transformation and negotiation: 'migration narratives often figure the migrant as constantly under surveillance. Migrants monitor themselves, and are monitored by the host community' (Burns 2013, 25).

Rita and Massimiliano monitor each other, looking for signs of Italianness and Canadianness. When Massimiliano recognises her as an Italian, Rita's reaction is surprised and slightly annoyed. At first, she refuses this label and what she perceives as a simplistic classificatory act by claiming her non-Italian looking body: 'She didn't look Italian, she'd been told. Red hair and freckles' (p. 131). Immediately after, though, she claims her Italian origins by denying and challenging this stereotype that revolves around a specific image of the Italian body: 'Do you know that not every Italian has dark hair and an olive complexion? Some are blond and have blue eyes or green eyes, and some have red hair like me' (p. 131). Thus, she is building her sense of identity both in relation to and in contrast to dominant representations of Italianness. Massimiliano reacts by intensifying his labelling act, this time switching the focus to the accent: 'You don't look Italian [...] but I can tell by your accent' (p. 131). For several migrants, accent is a site that makes questions of identity and belonging evident. It is another mark of otherness and sameness, which puts them in a position of visibility. Aiming to gain control over the conversation and to reposition herself, both within Canadian society and in the eyes of her interlocutor, Rita claims a hybrid and multiple identity:

I'm a Montrealer. Born in Italy. Raised in an Italian family in the east end. Went to English school. Studied French at Marie Clarac. Spanish in college. Germany in German. I speak a Venetian dialect with my parents. Yes, I have an accent. Everyone does (p. 131).

Her words overtly defy the monolingual paradigm. While Massimiliano is trying to ascribe her to a unique and specific linguistic and physical space, she claims an identity that grounds itself in, and is made by, multiple languages and cultures.

Despite refusing Massimiliano's act of labelling, Rita ends up reiterating the same approach in looking at him, as it emerges when they talk about his name. Names serve two main functions. Firstly, they are strong personal identity markers, expressing one's singularity and uniqueness. When 'the subject is interpellated, called into being, by using its name' (Nyman 2009, 103), he is identified as a specific individual and distinguished from others.

98   VOICES OF WOMEN WRITERS

Names also have a social connotation, as they can foreground and signal individuals' affiliation with a specific group. We perceive some names as being typical of certain communities and distinguish names that sound like Italian, English, Polish and so on: 'Names serve the purpose of situating people in social space, connecting them to family, lineage, ethnic group, and such' (Palsson 2014, 621). In the context of migration, the 'practice of naming, [...] is not simply a classificatory exercise' (Palsson 2014, 621). Names work as coordinating factors, as they indicate migrants' position in the host society, identifying them as insiders or outsiders. For this reason, migrants might have the tendency to change or adjust their names when they sound too foreign. By doing so, they attempt to disguise those traits and features that mark their otherness, thus encouraging locals' acceptance and welcoming. The necessity of adopting a different name is often related to the fact that names can convey specific cultural and social associations, be perceived in dismissive terms and thus arouse prejudices and stereotypes. This specific connotation ties migrants to a forced backward movement: as the host society continuously recognises and portrays them as outsiders, they have no other place to re-ground than the origin community. For instance, Italian names abroad often aroused feelings of distrust because of the widespread idea that Italians were all corrupted and criminals (La Gumina 1973, 291). Many Italian migrants in Canada therefore decided to change their names, adjusting them to the phonetic and graphic North-American system. Rejecting their Italian-sounding names was a way to escape the 'stereotype threat' (Steele and Aronson 1995) that such names aroused, hiding the otherness which their foreign-sounding names embodied. Name changing constituted a purposeful act, through which they wished to gain a new social identity, thus undermining a relation that was based on unequal power dynamics. Nevertheless, an individual's uniqueness 'lies rather in the paradoxical fact that everyone responds immediately to the question "who are you?" by pronouncing the proper name' (Cavarero 2000, 18). Therefore, by adopting another name, migrants confront themselves with an extreme form of otherness: as they accept an identity, which is imposed on them by other people, they end up being 'other, stranger' to themselves primarily. The following passage shows the opposite attitude:

> ' "My name is Massimiliano". His pronunciation was perfect [...] but he put the accent on the o, as a francophone would. He looked québécois, he sounded québécois, but his name – a very long Italian name – was not a common one. This man was not a Tony, Frank or Joe. [...] he was not a Réal or Jean-Guy either'
> 'So what do your friends call you? she asked.

Massimiliano, he said again with the accent on the o.
I mean your francophone friends.
[...] They call me Massimiliano. Everyone does.
Not Max or Maxime? she insisted.
No. [...] Why would I change my name? My name is Massimiliano.
I like it.' (p. 131).

Massimiliano claims his right to be called by his proper name, as the latter constitutes a marker of his identity . He reacts to a 'narrative of homogeneity' (Parati 2005, 24), thus reinventing himself as an agent of change rather than an object. In preserving his foreign-sounding name, he asserts his agency and introduces otherness into the host society. By doing so, he activates a transformative process that undermines the conservative discourse at work in multilingual and multicultural Canada. This is a process of internal othering through which the host society comes to terms with the presence of 'the other' within its territory.

Rita and Massimiliano show different attitudes towards languages and cultures. On the one hand, he fully operates within a monolingual paradigm. Despite being immersed in a multilingual and multicultural environment, he shows a monolingual attitude. He is comfortable in his exclusively French-speaking dimension: he lives in Quebec, his friends speak French and his work is in French. For him, there is no need to step outside this monolingual condition, to the point that he even refuses to speak English.[9] His attitude shows an essentialist position, which focuses on differences rather than commonalities. Despite his mixed origins, he has not developed a hybrid potential. He is trapped in a dichotomous view and portrays reality according to a 'we/they dialectics'. In his world, differences function as agents of marginalisation (Parati 2005, 88), which tie him to a single space (origin or destination) and to a single directionality (backwards or forwards). On the other hand, Rita seems to perfectly comply with a multilingual paradigm. She is perfectly comfortable with her hybrid condition. She displays an accommodating attitude and expresses an identity that can simultaneously relate to several contexts, positively engaging with approaches and practices that span across languages and cultures.

4.3 Juggling Two Cultural Heritages through Code-switching

In Canton's stories, CS is used to reinforce her critical approach to issues of gender and patriarchal conventions. The codeswitched terms work as acts of derogation, as she uses them to criticise specific aspects and values of Italian

100 VOICES OF WOMEN WRITERS

society, in contrast to the culture of the Anglophone world. This function particularly emerges with formulaic expressions, such as greetings, exclamations and imperatives. When analysing these formulas, it is even more important to consider the distinction between oral and written CS that was pointed out in Chapter 1. The latter has been defined as artificial because it does not constitute the real CS of everyday communication (Callahan 2002, 2). Yet, this ignores the fact that written CS can mimic oral CS, for instance, to recreate real dialogues. This mimetic function is evident in the following passage, where CS is used to enhance the realism of the scene. It fulfils three main functions: it suggests that the setting is in Italy, that the scene is taking place in Italian, and that the content of the scene must be read against the sociocultural Italian background. The extract appears in 'Twenty-Four Hour Conversation', one of the short stories in *Almond Wine and Fertility* (2008, 55–60):

'One day soon', I say, 'I will come here with my four children'.
'Magari', he says smiling. 'That would please me enormously…and bring your husband, too'. He looks at me intently.
'Of course, I say'.
'You should come in the summer. I'll take the kids to the beach and you can spend some time with your husband'. He is searching again. 'I don't think the two of you spend enough time alone'.
I wince, but I don't say anything.

This is a dialogue between an old man living in a rural town in Italy and a young Canadian woman with Italian origins. She travels to Italy on a business trip and decides to visit him. The relationship between the two is not specified, but they might be relatives, as the tone and topic of their conversation are private and confidential. The entire narrative is based on an intergenerational conflict, as the two characters represent two contrasting views of family and relationships. The entire conversation between them is articulated around their binary position, with the old man constantly telling off the young woman for the way she is running her family. Their contrasting positions are expressed through the code-witched term 'magari'. This word is an exclamation used to refer to something we would like to happen, but is unlikely to. It expresses both feelings of hope and nostalgia. The old man utters the word 'magari', whose meaning and function can be completely understood only within the context of mobility. The man and the woman are not only temporally distant, as they belong to two different generations, but also physically distant as they belong to two distinct countries: Italy and Canada. They also represent diverse social and cultural systems. Within this scenario, the word 'magari' signals the man's awareness that the woman's promise will likely never come true. Likewise, her loss of words indicates her inability to conform to his system of values. It signifies a deep estrangement from the culture he represents. On these grounds, the dialogue between them sounds fake and superficial, as many things are unsaid or implied, while others are said only out of social pressure and conformity.

CS therefore focuses readers' attention on the Italian system of values, and it builds the cultural and social frame through which they should read the story. It operates like a contextualisation cue (Gumperz 1982): through it, the reader infers the old man's perspective and evokes the Italian system against which the conversation and understanding (or lack thereof) between the two characters are sketched. CS also creates an emotional and cultural gap between the characters and a conversational gap between the old man and the Canadian reader. Through CS, therefore, Canton voices her Canadian half and implicitly suggests that her perspective diverges from the man's vision, which represents and voices Italian society. The conjunction 'but', which follows the activity of wincing, is indicative of the woman's disagreement with the man. CS also refers to the possibility of reshaping the relationship between the two characters, shortening the 'distance' that migration has created. 'Magari' is a way to establish a new sense of belonging, and to remind the young woman of her Italian heritage. Its presence in the text manifests a need for reconciliation: between the characters in the story, between diverse generations and different cultural identities.

This story is reiterated in 'Refuge in the Vineyard' (2016), where Canton writes about a woman who tries to cope with her Italian heritage.[10] Like she claims, 'it's a story about love and frustration. It explores intergenerational relationships and difficult family dynamics' (2019, 62). This struggle is represented through the complicated relationship between the female character and her father. The story begins with the woman's return home. This return is neither happy nor desired, but the result of an imposed choice. This theme emerges in the opening line, where she wonders: 'Why had she come back?'. The woman asks herself this question several times throughout the story. This feeling of unfamiliarity and unease is also expressed in the title of the novel. In fact, the word 'refuge' is used in an ambiguous way. While it would seem to refer to the fact that one's home is a refuge, the term reveals its ambiguity when the author clarifies that the woman in the novel is looking for a refuge from her origin 'home'. The use of Italian, which often appears in scattered terms and sentences, is mostly justified by the fact that the story takes place in Italy. For instance, the insertion of entire sentences quotes the dialogue with her father. As stated with respect to 'Twenty-Four

102 VOICES OF WOMEN WRITERS

Hour Conversation', the presence of Italian also suggests to readers that, to fully understand the story and the relationship between the two characters, they have to consider the Italian cultural and social context. As a matter of fact, Canton often uses CS to express a negative attitude towards the Italian context:

- Silenzio
- Dolore
- Freddo
- Cattivo

The words *dolore* and *cattivo* possess an inherent negative connotation. In the other cases, the negative connotation emerges from the context. For instance, in the following example, the term 'freddo' acquires a negative connotation because the main character identifies it as the reason why her parents decided to leave Canada after decades spent there. The word 'freddo' also symbolises the fact that her parents never really felt at home in Canada, hence their return to Italy. Canton therefore uses references to the weather in a way that is conventionally used in migrant narratives:[11]

> "Fa troppo freddo qui." Her parents moved back because of the weather. That's what they said. The weather. The cold. Il freddo. Is that a good reason to move back?

The weight of the woman's Italian heritage mainly emerges in the dialogue with her father. This dialogue is written in English, but some Italian sentences appear. Canton made this linguistic choice not only to indicate to the reader that the dialogue is taking place in Italian, but principally because Italian is the language that can better express the sociocultural pressure she feels. Indeed, in analysing the same story, Pivato states that 'these Italian words seem to be emotional triggers that emphasize the tension between the young mother and her unhappy father' (2020, 23). Writing in Italian conveys not only the voice of her culture, but also the voice of her father. Therefore it hints at a specific patriarchal culture. As a matter of fact, she claims that 'Her father was still the same. Still the patriarch'.

References to elements and factors, which belong to the historic, social, cultural, literary and artistic Italian heritage play an essential role in articulating and prompting that process of translation, mediation and negotiation between different systems that Canton attempts to enact. They constitute a privileged channel of encounter and interaction, giving precious insights into the author's perception of both countries.

In order to analyse this point, let us consider the following example, which appears in *Almond Wine and Fertility* (2014, 71):

> It was *my* mother – not hers – who took the time to train her in the beginning. *My* mother taught her how to iron a shirt correctly. First the sleeve, then the other sleeve, then the back, and the front of the shirt LAST because that's what people will see. *La bella figura*. That's the right way.

The use of CS is related to the plot. It helps Canton to create the Italian setting, which is at the root of the reader's understanding of the narration, and of the relationship between the two characters. Essentially, Canton uses a different language to reflect a different reality, that is, the Italian one; in doing so, she voices her Canadian stance and translates a stereotyped idea of Italian society, as one that gives importance to appearance and good looks. This point is also stressed by Baldo (2013, 212); in her analysis of the Italian translations of Italian-Canadian works, she claims that most translations 'seem to stress [...] the Italian roots of the authors and a stereotypical notion of italianità centred on fashion, good food'. The reference to the *bella figura* also has a gender-based connotation. The man is complaining about his wife, who does not seem able to accomplish all the duties and tasks of a 'good wife'. Consequently, her incapacity makes him fail his attempt at achieving a 'bella figura', that is, perfectly fitting in society. Within this scenario, CS is therefore used as a subversive element; it foregrounds negative aspects of Italian society, attempting to dismantle them. The linguistic device of CS adds emphasis to the expression 'bella figura' and highlights its foreignness within the English text. This linguistic foreignness stresses the contrast between the Italian and the Canadian system of values. As Jonsson claims, CS can be used 'to mark closeness, familiarity, to emphasize bonds, and to include or, on the contrary, to mark distance, break bonds and exclude' (2010, 1296). In this example, Canton uses it to signal and emphasise her estrangement and detachment from the Italian cultural system. She reveals a sort of irony and criticism towards a system of values that she has not internalised. Nevertheless, she knows that she is partially embedded in this cultural system due to her Italian origins. Writing against these codes therefore becomes a form of empowerment and emancipation, as she highlights her distance and refusal of such rules. In underlining the emotional and conversational gap between her, the readers and the host society, she uses CS as an element which contributes to the construction of the plot. It signals how difficult her process of understanding is. Although these words are mostly recognisable to Canadian readers, their appearance within the English text creates a subtle disharmony and clashing, which at a textual level represents Canton's difficulty accepting her Italian heritage.

104 VOICES OF WOMEN WRITERS

4.4 A Model of Collaborative Self-translation in *Almond Wine and Fertility/Vino alla mandorla e fertilità*

Canton's first book was originally written in English and published in 2008. Like already explained, it is a collection of short stories that are set in a hybrid space in-between Italy and Canada. Through the characters in her stories, Canton stresses the differences but also the similarities between the two worlds. They meet and overlap, intermingle and disconnect, in a process which is mediated and modulated by the author.

The Italian version, which is entitled *Vino alla mandorla e fertilità*, appeared in 2015, positioning it as a delayed or consecutive self-translation. Yet, the book is also a transparent and collaborative self-translation; in fact, credits are given to the translators who helped her in the process of self-translating the stories.[12] Their names are reported on the front page. Furthermore, in the introduction to the Italian version, it is stated that:

> l'idea di tradurre i racconti di Licia Canton nasce da un incontro con l'autrice presso il Centro Siena-Toronto nell'aprile 2011. Un piccolo gruppo che tra i partecipanti portò alla conversazione con l'autrice il proprio generoso contributo, ha poi continuato a 'dialogare' con la sua opera nell'intento di renderla in Italiano (2015, 3).

As the description on the back cover states, given that it is a collection of short stories, it seemed 'il libro perfetto per un esperimento di traduzione a più mani, traduzioni che si confrontano le une con le altre, si confrontano con l'autrice (che collabora come traduttrice di se stessa) con il testo'. The book is a polyphony: the multiple voices of its characters emerge, and with their individuality contribute to the overall design of the collection. The dialogic nature of the book emerges both in the writing and translating performance. A *continuum* is established by the ongoing interaction between the characters in the narratives; Canton and her co-translators; the characters and the readers; as well as Italian and English. Establishing continuity seems to be at the core of *Almond Wine and Fertility*, as well as of Canton's literary activity in general.

In this analysis of the self-translated version of *Almond Wine and Fertility*, the focus is on whether and how the translations managed to preserve and express the author's criticism of Italian society; to identify whether and how, in the process of collaboratively translating the English text, the author's voice was tamed or was instead free to express itself. To this end, it is necessary to specify that I do not know how the author intervened in the translation of the stories.[13] She could have just supervised the final version, granting the translators the freedom to shape the Italian text. Alternatively, she could have more deeply cooperated with them, influencing their choices and decisions. However, one aspect of the translations seems to lean towards the first possibility. The translators must have mainly worked on their own, subsequently submitting their translations to the author for proofreading. This statement is based on the fact that, in many translations, the translator's voice seems to be dominant over the author's voice. Each translation shows specific features and adopts a different approach, especially when it comes to conveying the author's point of view. Some of the translations are more literal and tend to reproduce Canton's voice more faithfully, while others move away from the source text, reshaping her voice against the backdrop of the target context and reader. These translations display a less critical position, in the attempt not to overtly criticise and write off values and traditions of the Italian culture, thus facilitating the book's reception in the target context. Since the receiving culture is imbued with the values and beliefs the author criticises, the translator decides to tone down the author's criticism. To illustrate this point, the present analysis refers to Seccia's investigation into the Italian translations of D'alfonso's works (2018). Combining literary criticism and linguistic analysis, the scholar illustrates why misunderstanding the literary world of an author can lead to incorrect translation strategies. Likewise, I will demonstrate that some of the translators fail to grasp the main themes of Canton's works, which results in questionable translation choices. To this end, let us consider the following example, contained in the short story 'Twentyfour hour conversation'. Like described in the section about CS, the story describes a conversation between an old Italian man and a Canadian woman of Italian origins. Their conversation revolves around the woman's management of her family and her relationship with her husband. Their words echo the contrast between the man's stance, which represents the Italian system of values, and the woman's point of view, which instead reflects her Canadian upbringing. This story overtly allows Canton an analysis and criticism of Italian culture, especially with respect to the relations between men and women. In the English version, the author does not hide her criticism of the man and the culture he represents. Her criticism emerges in the use of specific sentences and words. However, the Italian translation slightly diverts from the author's critical position, softening and tempering its disapproving and condemning traits. This tendency is evident in the following lines:

'Dipendeva da *lui*' (p. 80);
'It was *his* fault' (p.55).

The main character is referring to the fact that the old man and his wife did not have any children because of a not specified issue within the couple, which apparently was connected to him. In the English version, her words

106 VOICES OF WOMEN WRITERS

have an accusatory tone. The term 'fault' is quite strong, and it is used to reinforce the author's negative view of the man. On the contrary, the Italian translation shows a more empathetic and less severe attitude towards him. By removing the reference to the concept of fault, the reproving tone of the main character is toned down. While the man's agency is not questioned, the guilty nature of his behaviour is, however, tamed. This strategy reduces the reader's negative perception of the male character in the story. The same approach is adopted in the following example:

'Non è la persona alla quale dire queste cose' (p. 85);
'He is the wrong man to say this to' (p. 59).

In English, the gendered connotation is reinforced, as the man's lack of understanding and empathy is ascribed to his gender. He is not able to understand because of his upbringing as a man, which, especially in a patriarchal culture, does not favour and encourage such feelings for men. The Italian translation again attempts to minimise this contentious stance by replacing the gendered connoted term 'man' with the more neutral 'persona'. In doing so, the translation does not convey the author's distrust of men. In Italian, the patriarchal substratum of the man's words is weakened, and the author's gendered assumptions are silenced.

Canton often depicts the relationship between men and women in Italy as based on power dynamics. Men control and belittle women, perceiving them only in relation to a specific model of femininity, which represents women as fragile, dependent and delicate. This aspect is evident in the following example, contained in the story 'The Vespa Ride'. Here, the man's patriarchal voice is expressed in the way he addresses the woman:

'Oh yea of little faith' (p.12)
'Donnina di poca fede' (p.11).

The word 'donnina', literally 'little woman', embodies the patriarchal culture the man belongs to. It also shows his intention to put himself in a position of superiority, thus enhancing his paternalistic attitude. 'Donnina' therefore has a performative power: it belittles the woman, minimising her ability and importance. The relationship between the man and the woman is centred on power, and the man's addressing the woman as 'donnina' clearly conveys his intention and desire to control her. Indeed, 'donnina' also refers to what is represented as a common perception of women in a patriarchal society. The term has a defective connotation and expresses women's position of inferiority.

It is interesting to notice that, in this case, the Italian translation contains a more overt reference to the patriarchal dynamics between the two characters. The English version instead lacks the gendered connotation in the dialogue between the man and the woman. Nevertheless, the Italian translator takes as a starting point the critical stance of the author, which emerges more clearly in other stories, to add another level to the present narration. Her translation choice perfectly resonates with the criticism which is part of Canton's literary production in general. In this case, I would say that the Italian translator has perfectly understood and voiced the author's subjectivity; an aspect which seems to lack in other translations, which more overtly suit the ST to the new context than to the author's intention and message. This perfect communication and cooperation between the author's and the translator's voices also emerges in the following example, where both the author and the translator express a condemnation of a traditional view of motherhood, which sees it as the most natural and fulfilling condition for women. The example is an extract from 'Call Me Mamma':

'Sono la governante per eccellenza' (p. 123);
'I am the "primary caregiver"' (p. 79).

Canton uses irony to subvert and counter traditional concepts of motherhood.[14] She intentionally downplays the importance of the mother within the family, challenging the way mothers are perceived by their husbands and children. In English, the inverted commas overthrow the importance and connotation of the maternal role, which is expressed by 'primary'. In Italian, this function is expressed through the word 'governante', which carries a slightly negative connotation. Moreover, such a word lacks the reference to feelings of care and affection, which are expressed by a caregiver, who generally does not just satisfy someone's practical needs, but also fulfils emotional ones. The 'governante', instead, is somebody external to the family unit, who carries out exclusively practical tasks, and whose role lacks any emotional connotations. Furthermore, the word 'governante' seems to refer to the overload of Italian mothers, who deals with every aspect of the family management, and do not seem to be always appreciated and supported as they should be. Canton's narration therefore seems an explicit condemnation of the 'mother-breast' (Recalcati 2015, 47–56), who sacrifices herself to satisfy the needs of the other family members. The Italian version effectively preserves and conveys this original message, embracing the author's condemnation of the role of men and women within the family unit. The woman's status within the house is questioned, and Canton exposes how 'the patriarchal notion of motherhood [...] rather than empowering women, [...] can contribute to their subordination' (Rorato 2018, 75).

The following example offers interesting insights into how the translators deal with the presence of religion in the book. Religion plays an important role in Italian society, to the point that it shapes and intervenes in most aspects of people's lives. On the contrary, in Canadian society religious influence in public life is weak.[15] This aspect is even more important for Italian-Canadian migrants, who 'brought their religious traditions, customs and rituals with them to Canada. Here the Roman Catholic religion acts both as an identifying marker of Italian-Canadian ethnicity and as a key factor of social interaction and cultural belonging' (Saidero 2018, 108).[16] Religion particularly shaped the lives of Italian women, on both a personal and a social level. Canton's criticism of the influence of religion on Italian society often emerges in her stories. This is evident in the following example:

'E per quelli che credono' (p. 119);
'And for those who "*believe*"' (p. 78).

She is targeting specific religious traditions, such as spending Christmas and Easter Day with the family, regardless of the fact that, during the rest of the year, the same people could be quite oblivious to each other and hardly spend any time together. In doing so, Canton engages in 'an ironic exposure of how certain tenets of the Catholic religion have been used to implement faulty social norms' (Saidero 2018, 107). Like Saidero claims, in most Italian-Canadian narratives, there is not a total dismissal of the Christian values. This attitude also emerges in Canton's story. Her character is still willing to follow and accept these rules. Despite acknowledging the falsity of these familiar gatherings, she is ready to attend. However, while her actions show some sort of allegiance to tradition, her words display an ironic and controversial relationship with it.[17] Her irony emerges in the use of italics, which signals that the girl in the story is engaging in 'a parodic dialogue with the religious culture of the old country' (Saidero 2018, 107).

Canton openly targets the hegemony of religion in Italy, by criticising those rituals and traditions that are part of the religious agenda. Nevertheless, the Italian translator is probably aware that such a criticism of religion would not work for the target reader, and therefore decides to tone down this aspect. For this reason, in Italian, the italics is removed, subsequently eliminating the ironic connotation of the sentence. The Italian translator probably decided to avoid the original meaning, in order to cater to the target context. Indeed, in a religious society like the Italian one, the irony of the ST constitutes a challenging aspect. Nevertheless, this translation strategy obtains an effect, which is opposite to the original one; it intensifies and emphasises the importance of religion for Italian society, reclaiming its role in shaping people's lives and relationships. The Italian reader is therefore not invited to embrace the author's criticism.

In conclusion, this analysis has investigated the translation choices in *Vino alla mandorla e fertilità*, aiming to examine whether and how the Italian translators managed to effectively communicate with the author, establishing or instead breaking the continuity between the Italian and the English versions; between their voices and the voice of Licia Canton. The analysis has revealed that most translations respect and preserve the author's critical view of Italian society and culture. Nonetheless, in the collection, there are also a number of translations that instead chose to cater to the target reader rather than the author. This approach has emerged mainly with respect to the patriarchal and religious components of the stories. Considering them as essential elements of Italian society and possibly foreseeing a friction between the author and her readers, the translators decided to operate as cultural mediators, taming the author's criticism. In doing so, nonetheless, the translators fail to vehiculate Canton's message, and end up toning down elements, which are essential to understand the stories she narrates. Referring back to Seccia's paper (2018), it is possible to ascribe this failing translation strategy to a bad combination of literary criticism and linguistic analysis. With respect to the translation of D'Alfonso's books by Lombardi, Seccia claims that they lack 'a previous critical reading of the source text' (2018, 169). The same can be said about some of the translations contained in *Vino alla mandorla e fertilità*; failing to critically read and understand the literary world of Canton, the translators also fail to convey and transfer her message from English into Italian. Thus, the Italian reader is not able to fully comprehend and embrace Canton's perspective and positioning between Italian and Canadian systems. This analysis has therefore further demonstrated the importance of combining literary criticism, translation and linguistic analysis, a point that has sustained the examination conducted in this volume.

Notes

1 I met her at a conference in Italian Studies at the University of Hull.
2 http://www.accenti.ca/: this is the official website.
3 https://www.writersunion.ca/member/licia-canton.
4 This phenomenon is called 'chain migration'. To expand upon this point, please see William M. DeMarco *Ethnics and Enclaves: Boston's Italian North End* (1981).
5 All the extracts can be found here: www.bibliosofia.net/files/belpaese.htm.
6 Do not air your dirty laundry in public.
7 In *Writing Mothers and Daughters: Renegotiating the Mother in Western European Narratives by Women*, Giorgio states that 'Within the Holy Family [...] the Mother is subordinate to the Son. This pattern was reproduced in the secular family, where women's position reflected the changes in the cult of the Madonna' (2002, 119–120).

110   VOICES OF WOMEN WRITERS

8   This story also appears in the collection *The Pink House and Other Stories* (2018).

9   In 'Writing Canadian Narratives with Italian Accents: The Pink House and Other Stories', Canton states that the dialogue between Rita and Massimiliano takes place in French (2019, 64).

10   The story can be found here: https://canadianliteraryfare.org/2016/08/05/refuge-in-the-vineyard/.

11   The role of weather in migrant narratives has been stressed also by Gardner, in *Age, Narrative, Migration. The Life Course and Life Histories of Bengali Elders in London* (2002), and McCarthy, in *Personal Narrative of Irish and Scottish Migration, 1921–65: 'For Spirit and Adventure'* (2007).

12   They are: Giulia De Gasperi, Gabriella Iacobucci, Filippo Mariano, Isabella Martini, Moira Mini, Marta Romanini, Tiziana Tampellini.

13   In the paper 'Self-Translation as Problem for Italian-Canadian Authors', Pivato explains that 'Canton self-translated the title story and the other stories were translated by Italian graduate students and academics (2020, 25). However, I believe that more information is needed to know to what extent, and in what ways, Canton engaged with the translators.

14   In her article 'Women and Religion in Italian-Canadian Narratives' (2018), Saidero examines how contemporary female Italian-Canadian authors use irony and parody to counter stereotypical notions of womanhood and motherhood, that revolve around the role of religion.

15   https://www.pewresearch.org/fact-tank/2019/07/01/5-facts-about-religion-in-canada/.

16   To expand upon the role played by religion in Italian-Canadian community, please see the books *Sacro o Profano? A Consideration of four Italian-Canadian Religious Festivals* (Giuliano 1976), and *Leaving Christianity: Changing Allegiances in Canada since 1945*, by Brian Clark and Stuart Macdonald (2017).

17   This partial dismissal is explained by Saidero in this way: 'Since religion has more to do with social dynamics than with individual spirituality, any attempt to distance oneself from Catholicism may well be perceived as a rejection of the ethnic community. In their narratives Italian-Canadian writers, thus, acknowledge the need to retain some of the traditional religious-cultural values that are part of their distinctive ethnic identity while criticizing others that impede acculturation into the new world society' (2018, 108).

CHAPTER 5

FRANCESCA DURANTI: 'TRANS-WRITING' THE SELF THROUGH ACTS OF NARRATION AND ACTS OF LIVING

5.1 The Link between Author, Character and Narrator in the Autofictional Novel

Francesca Duranti is the pseudonym of Maria Francesca Rossi. She is a popular Italian writer who has published fourteen books, such as *La casa sul lago della luna* (1984), *Come quando fuori piove* (2006) and *Un anno senza canzoni* (2009). She has won several literary prizes, such as the famous Premio Campiello, or Premio letterario nazionale per la donna scrittrice.[1] She is also well-known abroad, and her novels have been translated into eighteen languages. Her books explore the connection between life and art, illustrating fiction as a reflection of life and vice versa. For instance, in *Effetti personali* (1988), the protagonist Valentina is a translator who looks for 'her self' through writing and translating. Her lack of 'personal effects' becomes clear to Valentina when, in leaving her, her husband removes the name plate from the front door of what used to be their apartment. This moment marks the beginning of her quest, as she embarks on a professional journey, which is nonetheless deeply connected to a personal need and purpose. In *Un anno senza canzoni*, the protagonist is a young girl; in the background, Duranti depicts a solitary and empty Milan, abandoned by people on holidays. Alone in her room, the young girl starts writing a diary in order to reflect on her life. In this novel as well, the exploration into life is therefore interwoven with the act of writing, which Duranti sees as two different yet indissoluble moments of one's existence. The stratagem of the diary makes this interconnection even stronger, as the girl is literally transposing her life into a narration. Alongside her career as a writer, Duranti is a prolific translator who has also engaged herself in an experiment of self-translation.[2] This unique episode in her literary career will be the focus of this chapter, which investigates the bond between living, writing and self-translating in *Sogni mancini/Left-Handed Dreams*.

112 VOICES OF WOMEN WRITERS

Duranti was born into a rich Italian family, where she grew up bilingual and learned, simultaneously, to speak Italian and German. Moreover, as a child, she also learned English and French (Dagnino 2021).[3] This means that she grew up 'with two or more languages from the beginning' and never knew 'a purely monolingual state' (Yildiz 2012, 121). Nonetheless, she rejected the German language, as she linked it to a traumatic experience. She was taught German by private teachers; as a child, she believed their main mission was to keep her busy and thus prevent her from bothering her mother (Wilson 2009, 188). Her rejection of German is therefore linked to the experience of being separated from her mother. This separation acquires a double meaning, as the mother can be perceived not only in the physical sense of a 'person who gives birth to you', but also in the linguistic sense of a 'native language'. As both definitions refer to the concept of a mother as something that sets and defines one's relation to his/her origins, learning German (that is, acquiring a second language) means to break the connection with the mother (tongue) and with one's 'identitarian' past; essentially, to become rootless. Within the context of her family dynamics, Duranti therefore experiences German as an element of disruption and estrangement.

Her process of re-grounding, though, does not imply rejecting German and speaking only Italian. Monolingualism is not the solution to her uprooting. On the contrary, she chooses to have two mother tongues: one is Italian, the language which was given to her by her mother; the other is English, a language that she consciously and freely chooses to adopt, both in her life and profession.[4] Thus, she moves beyond the monolingual paradigm and its assumption that individuals possess only one language. This aspect emerges in her activity as a translator, and even more in her self-translating experience, which allow her to continuously transfer herself from one linguistic and cultural system to another. At the same time, her decision to spend six months in Gattaiola (Lucca) and six months in New York works to physically transfer her from one place to another. By deconstructing the binary opposition between source and target languages, as well as between points of departure and arrival, Duranti relocates herself, linguistically and geographically, in an in-between space of connection and interaction, that produces a fluid movement beyond oppositional and essentialist categories defining the world.

The need to move beyond dichotomies and binary oppositions seems to be the essential spark that nourishes both her poetics and her attitude towards life. She continuously attempts to break the dichotomy between the author and the character; most of her novels are overtly autobiographical or draw inspiration from her life. For instance, *La bambina* (1976) recalls her childhood and her difficult relationship with her mother.[5] In *Sogni mancini* (1996), the protagonist is Martina Satriano, an Italian woman who moved from Tuscany to New York, to teach at the local university. Such similarities are suggestive of Martina being understood as Duranti's *alter ego*. The story is also told in the first person, thus further reducing the distance between narrator and character, and reinforcing the overlap between Duranti and Martina. In this novel, the author moves one step further. As she writes the story in Italian and self-translates it into English, she also deconstructs the binary opposition between author and translator; these two conventionally distinct figures are assimilated into her own persona. This deconstruction is also reinforced by the fact that *Sogni mancini* and *Left-Handed Dreams* represent a form of simultaneous self-translation; they were created almost simultaneously in both Italian and English. This near-simultaneous creation further disrupts the traditional separation between original and translation. The Italian version can be identified as the original only on a chronological basis. From a textual perspective, both versions hold the same importance.

Duranti's literary experience therefore seems like an attempt to mend the breach between life and writing, as well as between writing and translating; a way to look for 'a fluid and dynamic "third way", a convergence of opposites and a totally novel concept that transcends the notion of oppositions rooted in the established cultural praxis' (*Left-Handed Dreams* 2000: viii). Her narrative can be seen as a counter-narrative, aiming to go against oppositional and absolute concepts and notions in an attempt to redefine and represent the hybrid and varied nature of the self. From this perspective, it is no surprise that Duranti began writing in order to satisfy 'un'esigenza liberatoria, quasi volesse in tal modo psicanalizzare se stessa'.[6] The autobiographical elements of her novels help her to reflect on her own experience, and redefine 'her self' through writing:

> Dal momento che non si può: né scrivere; né vivere; né stare a metà strada tra scrivere e vivere: che fare? (*Ultima stesura* 1991: 10–11).

This impasse can be solved only by establishing a connection between the act of narration and the act of living through 'the translation of life into writing and vice versa' (Wilson 2009, 187). The connection between writing and living is well expressed by the philosopher Adriana Cavarero, in her *Relating Narratives: Storytelling and Selfhood* (2000), a text that has been previously mentioned. Cavarero focuses on the relation between the self and the act of narration, and looks at individuals as 'unique existents', who long to narrate and reveal the uniqueness of their identity and life story. Duranti's decision to write and self-translate can be linked to her need to affirm the uniqueness of her transmigrant experience. Nonetheless, Cavarero states that we cannot tell our own story, but we need someone else to tell it: 'the story can only

114 VOICES OF WOMEN WRITERS

be narrated from the [...] perspective of someone who does not participate in the events' (2000, 2). In order to avoid this problem and be able to tell her own story, in *Sogni mancini/Left-Handed Dreams* Duranti uses the literary device of the *alter ego*. Thus, she creates a novel that can be identified as autofiction, that is, a literary genre blending fiction and autobiography. The story which is narrated is fictional, but it draws inspiration from the author's life (Doubrovsky 1977, Gasparini 2008). The choice of this specific genre helps her to simultaneously locate herself inside and outside the narration, giving the impression of having her own story told by others. The creation of an autofictional novel allows her an act of 'self translation', through which she builds a link between her existential and her authorial voice: 'what she narrates' coincides with 'what she lives'.

The main themes and topics of her literary world are perfectly encapsulated and illustrated in *Sogni mancini/Left-Handed Dreams*, where she explores the concepts of identity and belonging, questioning their meaning within contemporary society and illuminating alternative views. The deconstruction of identity as a unitary and fixed entity is symbolically entrusted to Martina. While playing her solitary morning bridge, she notices that she cannot read the numbers on the deck as she is holding her cards as if she were left-handed. This apparently insignificant aspect enacts a process of redefinition of identity in Martina, who convinces herself of being corrected left-handed and therefore having another, alternative identity: 'And now if I were to discover that I'm a correct lefty, everything would have to be multiplied by two' (2000, 74).[7] This belief leads her to question and deconstruct the traditional view of the self as a finished and coherent unity. This idea is expressed through the dicotyledonous theory:

A dicotyledon, for example a bean or a pea, has a double nature. The seed is divided in two halves and the baby plant, as soon as it sprouts, bears two identical little leaves. Let's say that human identity is like a dicotyledonous plant. One of the little leaves dominates, the other is dominated but is there, like in an invisible mirror... (2000, 39).

The image of the dicotyledon helps to think of identity as fragmented and multifaceted; even if only one part can emerge, the other one remains under the surface, thus enacting a dialectical process between both of them. The fact that Martina often refers to herself in the third person also creates a continuous shift, which conveys the dialogic relation between her identities. Determined to prove her assumption and to give voice to 'all the other contiguous entities, hitherto suffocated and overshadowed' (*Left-Handed Dreams* 2000, x), that is, to the potential possibilities of her selfhood, she starts registering her dreams with the help of the Machine. Her aim is to demonstrate that dreams constitute a parallel reality where these potential possibilities can be represented and expressed. Life, exactly like identity, can be multiple and varied. It is not limited within spatial, temporal or even linguistic borders. Every morning, the Machine wakes up Martina with the following formula: 'You're Italian but you live in New York. You're forty-two years old. This is my voice: yours. Tell me your dream' (2000, 25). She then starts recounting her dreams, which are recorded and re-narrated by the device. The act of narration gives them a tangible presence and allows them to escape the risk of forgettability. Thus, dreams are given recognition and enter the sphere of existence.

Martina's aim to demonstrate the weakness of the traditional view of the self is nourished by her belief that such a discovery could help fight against intolerance. Rethinking and rewriting the notion of otherness as something that does not exist only outside, but also inside the single individual, questions and deconstructs all the ideas and beliefs that racism and prejudice are built on. This ideological mission can therefore be seen in relation to Duranti's use of writing as a tool to redefine the self; the narratable self (Cavarero 2000, 33) longs to tell his/her story as a unique, and therefore diverse, individual. From this perspective, Duranti's writing and self-translating can be seen as a form of 'trans-writing', that is, as an instrument to transport the self beyond oppositional and unitary concepts and to rewrite it within numerous linguistic spaces. This trans-writing becomes what Nikolau defines as a 'textual journey of self-discovery' (2006, 30); in being continuously transferred from one linguistic dimension to the other, the self is rewritten not as a stable and fixed entity but as a dynamic one, which is constantly 'in divenire'. Identity is a matter of becoming, not of being, something that emerges in the interspace between constant uprootings and re-groundings:

> Call me Robinson. Given that in life we go from one shipwreck to the other, losing most or all of our possessions, each time forced to give up most or all of our privileges, habits, affections, and so on, I take some consolation – in both the small and big shipwrecks of life – in examining what I have left and seeing what can be made of it (2000, 14).

As the anthropologists Arjun Appadurai and Carol Breckenridge claim, every displacement possesses a series of collective memories 'whose archaeology is fractured' (1989, i). Duranti resorts to self-translation and multilingual writing as powerful instruments that help her make sense of such fragmentation and perceive it positively. Source and target languages, in merging with one another, contribute together not only to the creation of the text but also to the redefinition of her subjectivity, which is inscribed in multiple linguistic

116   VOICES OF WOMEN WRITERS

and cultural contexts. At the end of the novel, the Dream Machine is broken by a dog that Martina finds in the building where she lives and decides to keep with her. One day, the dog puts his paws on the tape deck's keyboard and deletes all the recorded material. The breaking down of the Machine can be read as a metaphor, which represents Martina's acceptance of her hybrid identity:

> Here the two halves can stop spying on each other. But they shouldn't be reunited, though, heaven forbid. [...] Side by side in harmonious coexistence. That way they could be somewhat at peace, but please, not too much so. Not the sepulchral peace of Absolute Truth, of unlimited self-importance, of unshakeable opinions. Stand by me, my left-handed twin, and laugh at me if I begin to take myself too seriously (2000, 116).

Duranti's exploration of 'her self' through English and Italian is located rightly against this backdrop. She engages in a dialogue between two voices, a constant movement between languages: that is, in a continuous condition of (self)translation. Living, writing and translating in Italian and English guarantee her simultaneity, which is essential to the transmigrant feature of her mobility. In producing the same text simultaneously in two languages and in inserting foreign words within the monolingual text, she produces a back-and-forth movement between Italian and English, which mirrors her physical movement between Tuscany and America. Thus, 'her self' is detached from exclusive identifications with specific linguistic, cultural, or geographical spaces. Her movement beyond the mother tongue consists exactly in overcoming and destabilising its specific conceptualisation as exclusive, predetermined and irreplaceable. Duranti does so by ascribing a route that leads her to establish several connections to several languages, attributing to each of them a different space in her personal and literary sphere.

5.2 Remembering or not Remembering, That is the Question

The trope of memory occupies a prominent position in the novel. Through it, Duranti adds multiple layers to the storyline and further explores matters of identity and belonging. If memories form a 'frame of reference we all use to meaningfully interpret our past and present experiences and orient ourselves towards the future' (Stock 2010, 24), the characters in the novel constantly move between remembering and forgetting, in the attempt to rearticulate their positioning between past and present, old and new, here and there.

FRANCESCA DURANTI

In investigating the trope of broad memory in this chapter,[8] I draw on Mieke Bal's distinction between narrative and habitual memories.[9] This distinction takes into account the role played by emotions. Habitual memories are flat, almost like chronicles, for they simply record the occurred events in a chronological way, positioning them within a historical moment; they 'remain buried in routine', with 'no events that stand out' (1999, viii). Bal suggests the act of avoiding stepping into a puddle as an example of habitual memory, to illustrate that they are 'automatic' (1999, vii), 'a behavioural tic' (1999, viii). On the contrary, narrative memories 'are affectively colored, surrounded by an emotional aura that, precisely, makes them memorable' (1999, viii). While habitual memories recall aspects of the past in a way that makes them ordinary, narrative memories give them a meaningful interpretation and provide an analytical framework, because they are pervaded by the emotions of the individual; in this case, events stand out because they have a special value. Bal claims that the difference between habitual and narrative memories also lies in the fact that the agency of the subject is implicated only in the second case: the 'narrator's sudden response to them', in fact, turns 'unnoticed memories' into 'affectively colored [memories]' (1999, viii). Habitual memories, instead, are unreflective and do not constitute conscious decisions (1999, vii).

In this section, the focus will be on narrative memories because they offer the chance to examine migrant subjects' conscious decision to remember or forget, how the subjects doing the remembering (or the forgetting) react to their memories and how this reaction shapes their movement across multiple spaces. Within the context of mobility, migrants move between past and present memories; rearticulating their position with respect to the 'there and then' corresponds to reimagining their position between origin and host society, too. Their choice to forget or remember shapes their relationship with the native country and with the receiving one. For some migrants, the act of remembering becomes very important, as it helps them to cope with what I call the 'fear of forgetting', understood as the fear of losing what constitutes their narrative of belonging and identification with the country of origin. Because of this fear, they need to maintain a form of continuity with the native land. This sense of continuity, which is built and reinforced through their memories, is reassuring for them, because it gives them the feeling that what they have left behind will always stay the same, thus making their return home always possible. This form of remembering makes migrants move backwards on a temporal level, thus making up for the impossibility of inscribing a physical backward movement.

118   VOICES OF WOMEN WRITERS

Remembering is important for Martina, the main character in *Sogni mancini/Left-Handed Dreams*. She appreciates her past memories and struggles to maintain a relationship of continuity with her origins: 'I was a year old when we left Potenza – and yet I don't feel I'd be myself without the memories of Lucania that my mother had passed on to me' (2000, 7). She acknowledges the constitutive power of memory and accepts that her identity is the result of the exchange between past and present. Her attachment to objects also conveys her desire to remember. In going back to New York from Nugola, Martina packs up 'the only thing that had a shadow of a memory about it, a terracotta jar with two small opposing handles' (2000, 12). Material objects effectively engage migrants with the act of remembering; they establish forms of continuity with 'home', as they can materialise abstract feelings and emotions. Like Bartoloni claims, objects are 'vehicles of humans' meanings' and 'active partners of meaningful engagements' (2016, 2). Within this scenario, Martina decides to take away with her the terracotta jar, because it objectifies concepts, beliefs and values that pertain to her personal and social sphere. It is therefore a tangible narrative of her identity, as it reinforces and keeps alive her bond with specific places, events and people.

At the same time, the novel features many characters who feel what I call the 'fear of remembering'. For them, it is necessary to move away from 'there and then', to invest 'here and now'. In order to re-ground, it is first necessary to be uprooted, as cutting ties with their past means investing in the present, laying the foundations for a complete and total integration within the new context. Forgetting therefore represents a movement forward, which brings them closer to the host society, in an attempt to assimilate them. Martina's sister, Carmelina, shows this attitude, as she seems unable to remember their life in Nugola:

> I tried to remind her of the Elephants' Ballroom, the mushrooms, the bee-eaters. But I understood perfectly that she only pretended to remember [...] with the death of our mother, even the memory of Nugola [...] had become a cumbersome link to a past she no longer needed. [...] That's how she is. Some people have to forget in order to move on (2000, 6–7).

Likewise, Costantino, Martina's first love, changes his name and burns bridges with everyone after he moves to America:

> I had cut loose from the old days and didn't want to meet up with you. I had succeeded in distancing myself from sad memories, I didn't want anything to attach me to the past again (2000, 90–91).

FRANCESCA DURANTI

For Costantino and Carmelina, every step towards the host country constitutes a step away from the origin country. For them, memory becomes a 'cumbersome link' to an overwhelming past and forgetting is seen as the necessary premise 'to mov[ing] on'. Forgetting means fighting the desire and the need to live in the past, in another time and space, which do not coincide with those where one is currently operating; to overcome the 'homing desire' (Nasta 2002) and thus fully exploit and appreciate the present. The need to forget becomes even stronger when the relation to the past is problematic and characterised by conflict. This aspect emerges in Costantino's words:

> You know, I'm not the only one in America who wants to forget. The misery, the discrimination. Things here are easy for Roman princesses, for the Milanese fashion designers. Much less, believe me, for a guy that lands in this country penniless from southern Italy (2000, 91).

In this case, remembering coincides with 'the painful resurfacing of events of a traumatic nature' (Bal 1999, viii), such as the miserable conditions that migrants had to face at their arrival in the host country. For this reason, the mobile subject feels the need to forget. Costantino's words also include a clear condemnation of the terrible conditions experienced by the first wave of Italian migrants in the US. His bitter words highlight how social and economic differences would affect one's position within the host country, acting as factors of inclusion or exclusion. Despite referring to past migration, his words sound tremendously contemporary and work as an invitation to reflect upon current migratory flows.

In the novel, it is also possible to identify a third tendency, which consists in preserving the sentimental reminiscences of the native land while at the same time constructing new memories, which are associated with the host country. This tendency is an overt manifestation of transmigrants' need to build links and affiliations with both locations. It lies in the awareness that memories have a constitutive nature: the act of remembering is intimately connected to the making of one's identity. Martina displays this attitude:

> Then there are the memories of Tuscany, the Tuscan colours of Treasure Island, the cafeteria at the Stanic refinery, the sea cliffs of Calafuria, the University of Pisa, and lastly the memories of New York when I had just arrived – when helicopters used to land on the roof of the Pan Am Building [...] (2000, 7).

Her Italian memories resonate with the American ones. She preserves spaces for the original land to survive and express itself. Concurrently, she does not reject her host country but finds points of contact with it, thus establishing a continuity, from which she gains a sense of unity and harmony. This interconnection is also displayed in her dreams. Here, she operates within a liminal site, where she constantly mixes places and people belonging both to Italy and America:

> I reviewed the dream in my mind, the dirt road winding dizzily down the cliff. The stormy sea was obviously Italian. That smell in the crisp salt air – so pungent – can only be felt near a smaller sea, worn out and condensed by a long history. The road, on the contrary, couldn't be in Italy. [...] The road resembled rather the dusty ribbon which uncoils from Arizona down to Monument Valley, the most typical American landscape [...] (2000, 30).

In *Memory*, a collection of essays curated by Patricia Fara and Karalyn Patterson, and dedicated to the theme of collective memory, Richard Sennett investigates the repression and reconstruction of disturbing memories. He claims that dreams have a therapeutic role because 'the act of dreaming sets people free to create incidents and forge connections between events which they could not do in a waking state' (1998, 14). This connection is evident in Martina's dreams. Her present is so deeply intertwined with her past that, on a subconscious level, one cannot exist without the other. The act of dreaming brings together her different experiences and life events, thus creating a coherent and complete narrative of 'her self'. Indeed, 'these unforgotten presences represent the links between past and present, as well as the possibility of interacting with the past in order to create the future' (Caporale-Bizzini 2018, 72). Narratives of the past are incorporated into the present and can thus inform the way the future is constructed. For Martina, the act of remembering constitutes a dynamic process based on the ongoing exchange between past and present. Through this exchange, she reconciles and reconnects her narrative and existential voices. This dynamic process forges connections and articulates multiple movements backwards and forwards, which locate her in a relation of continuity. This continuity undermines the traditional opposition between here and there, now and then. By using the movement metaphor, a transmigrant attitude can be described as the condition of someone who moves forward while simultaneously looking back. Exactly like the redefinition of home nullified the physical distance, the redefinition of memory in a transmigrant context nullifies the temporal distance, as past and present continue to operate in the territory of the other. Bal uses the definition 'presentness of memory' to refer to the process through which 'the past is "adopted" as part of the present' and highlights how it 'raises

FRANCESCA DURANTI

the question of agency, of the active involvement of subjects [...] who "do" the remembering' (1999, xv). Transmigrants intentionally perform this form of memory because it gives them a temporal continuity, as well as the possibility to control the recalling and how this recalling impacts the redefinition of the self. Through the 'narrating structure of memory' (Cavarero 2000, 34), the subject can redefine itself across temporal connections and associations, unfolding itself through time.

5.2.1 Rebuilding Memories of Home and Belonging

In *Sogni mancini/Left-Handed Dreams*, Duranti also rethinks and rewrites the traditional concept of 'home' from her transmigrant perspective. In the novel, 'home' does not represent a physically and linguistically bounded place; home is a mental attitude, a location of the mind, which emerges through the individual's personal and emotional connections. The author sets the rupture of the family union as the starting point for this rethinking of home, as the book begins with Martina's return to Italy for her mother's funeral. The reference to the mother-daughter relationship hints at the continuity with one's origins, which is symbolically represented and secured exactly by this relationship. Hence, the death of the mother anticipates Martina's questioning of her bond with the past and lays the foundations for redefining her identity. In the book, she wonders: 'Why let me get there just as she departed, she who had probably been the start of it all?' (2000, 4). This aspect emerges even more strongly in the following passage. Here, she indulges in an idyllic recalling of home, which is again recreated through a list of people, practices and objects. This recollection signals the power of objects to recreate home (Burns 2020).[10] From the very first line, though, she makes it clear that the place she is describing now exists only in her dreams. In reality, she is confronted by her return to an unfamiliar place:

> I fell into a sleep filled with the jumbled images of Nugola as it was: the jars of artichoke hearts in oil lined up on the shelves I built for Mamma's pantry, the mulberry trees in the church square, the village doctor's house (2000, 15).

In the passage below, the image of her childhood bedroom, which is compared to a common hotel room, reinforces Martina's feeling of estrangement as it overtly dismantles the familiar connotation of the domestic space. Her disaffection with the place is also reinforced by the image of the unpacked suitcase, which defines her presence there as temporary and transitory.

122 VOICES OF WOMEN WRITERS

The discrepancy between 'what she sees' and 'what she remembers' exacerbates these feelings, as Duranti plays with the image of the failed return home:

> I didn't even unpack the small bag I had brought with me. It was there sitting on a chair, as if I were staying in a hotel. From the window I couldn't see the country I remembered, but only the dismal suburbs that were gradually cementing together the beautiful old Tuscan cities and villages (2000, 10).

The solution to Martina's impossible return home lies in a re-conceptualisation of home itself. As these examples demonstrate, what used to be a familiar site now shows elements of unfamiliarity. On the contrary, the foreign place has acquired a certain level of intimacy, as her decision to return early to New York demonstrates. In the following paragraph, the emergence of this emotional connection is evident in the repetitive use of the verb 'to miss'. Here, Martina is tracing a forward movement:

> I missed my New York apartment. I even missed all of you. I missed the Machine that was waiting for me on its cart next to my bed. There was nothing left for me to do in Nugola. I had arrived too late to hold my mother's hand while she was dying. It was too late for everything. I called Alitalia to change to an earlier flight to New York (2000, 10).

As her experience demonstrates, migrants can feel at home in the host country, and experience estrangement within their country of origin. In transmigrant discourses, home emerges through multiple backward and forward movements, where no place can be identified as origin or host. As they move from one geographical location to another, from one point in time to another, these mobile subjects reconceptualise a notion of 'home' that, devoid of any physical, temporal or linguistic connotation, can be constantly destabilised and recreated. For instance, in the story narrated by Duranti, Martina's constant backward and forward movement is expressed through her indecision about accepting a job offer and going back to Italy or continuing in her American life. Even if, at the end of the novel, she chooses to stay in New York, her metaphorical movement backward is articulated through Costantino, her lover, who, after years spent in America, decides to return to Italy. Their relationship establishes a form of rooting in the other country as well. Despite living somewhere else, their sense of home is continuously reinvented in relation to someone else. The sentimental connection between Martina and Costantino is fundamental to generating their emotional

FRANCESCA DURANTI

attachment to both Italy and the USA. The end of the novel therefore exhibits an idea of home, which does not imply the replacement of one place with another, but which is based on the possibility, for both places, to coexist and be connected.

Martina's rethinking of 'home' as an allegedly familiar and intimate space also becomes manifest in her constant feelings of belonging and unbelonging to both American and Italian societies. Though a proud Italian, she identifies specific cultural, social and political traits of Italian society that pushed her to leave and which make it impossible for her to return 'home'. Throughout the narration, she often remembers how she could never really fit in Italian society, thus offering an image of home as a place that was never really perceived as such: 'Listen, I've tried in Italy. And I didn't make it' (2000, 31). At the same time, she shows a mixed disposition towards the American community. On the one hand, she is ready to adapt and conform to its rules: 'I conformed to the strict American code, I didn't sigh, I didn't raise my eyes to heaven, I didn't keep looking at my watch' (2000, 54–55). On the other hand, her desire to conform does not overstep a specific point. This attitude is manifest in the homeless episode. One day, going back home, Martina stumbles into the body of a tramp. Her first reaction is to adapt to the American custom of ignoring him and passing by. Later on, though, she decides to help him, thus creating disconcertment and embarrassment in people around her:

> I was embarrassing everybody. I was a foreigner not going by the rules [...] There was a limit to my willingness to adapt to the local etiquette. My zeal to conform didn't go beyond a certain point (2000, 82–83).

By referring to herself as a 'foreigner', Martina articulates a backward movement, positioning her belonging to the host society as partial. Nonetheless, she makes it clear that this partial belonging is not an externally imposed condition but a conscious and autonomous choice: 'my willingness', 'my zeal'. She is not subjected to an external and complete act of assimilation into the new society. Instead, she enacts a process of self-translation through which she manages to ground herself 'in the here and now', simultaneously investing these spaces with a revisionary and revolutionary intervention. In this in-between space, she can fully exploit and express her hybrid potential. She thus preserves her subjectivity by simply reframing it according to the American context. Her words, at the end of the novel, openly claim her hybrid position: 'But this country – this city rather – is mine too, by now. It's true I don't understand it, but I know it. I've learned its essential etiquette' (2000, 117). Martina presents New York as her city.

124   VOICES OF WOMEN WRITERS

Nevertheless, the admission that she does not completely understand it and that she had to learn its etiquette exhibits the conflicting nature of this relationship. Not understanding something, but knowing it, reveals a perspective that is internal and external at the same time. 'Learning the essential etiquette' of the city refers to Martina's belonging there as something that she has to perform, and which results from processing and internalising her experiences there.

Her conflicting sense of belonging to the host society is also expressed by her complicated relationship with the Statue of Liberty. As she candidly confesses, she keeps postponing her visit to the monument because of what it represented and still represents for people moving to America. As she admits to herself, the monument reminds her of the fact that she does not fully belong to America. She is a welcomed guest, but still a guest:

> To tell the truth, just the thought made me panic. I knew that if I had arrived in America two generations earlier, there would have been the anguish of the break from home, the fear of the unknown, the humiliation of Ellis Island, the leap into the hostile void of an unknown language. That towering woman with the upraised hand would have meant more of a threat than a welcome to me [...] I thought if I'd kept the puppy, I would have moved to an apartment in the West Village [...] I too would have walked my dog on the pier before going to work [...] I would have had the usual plastic bag in my pocket, ready to obey the rule about cleaning up after your dog [...] If I didn't do it better than the others, the statue would have turned on me, and accused me. I saw you, you dirty wop. Yes, that's the way you all are (2000, 68).[11]

This passage represents Martina's shifting perceptions of her position in America, and her multiple backward and forward movements. In the first lines, the reference to the Statue of Liberty arouses the memory of Ellis Island and of the first Italian migration. This sudden shift 'there and then' projects her backwards in time, and it makes her question her presence 'here and now'. Immediately after, though, she performs a mental process of assimilation. As she imagines herself involved in activities and a daily routine that she perceives as typically American, she makes a forward movement, through which she envisions a potential total integration. Nevertheless, the illusion of this total integration is broken soon, when she reveals a sort of performance anxiety, that is, the anxiety of confirming and reinforcing, with her behaviour, a negative view of Italians, here specifically described as people who do not observe the rules. At this stage, she recognises that her inclusion in the host society is only partial. Within this scenario, her use of the term 'wop' to refer to herself is provocative. This word serves as a direct and overt manifestation of a stereotyped view, according to which all Italians were violent and cocky. The term derives from the Neapolitan word '*guappo*', that indicates a boy with an arrogant and almost aggressive attitude. Martina intentionally uses this derogatory word, in order to stress her outsider condition and identify herself with other Italian migrants. The term is used to signal and emphasise estrangement and detachment, and it therefore acquires an ironic connotation; she uses the language of 'the other' to represent herself as 'the other'. Through this process of projection and identification, she inscribes again a backward movement, which re-grounds her in her society of origin.

5.3 Multilingualism as an Authorial and Existential Imperative

From a linguistic perspective, Duranti's novel offers extremely interesting insights. Being a self-translated book, it provides a good example of a crisscrossed encounter, where different readers (Italian and American) are put in touch with two diverse cultural contexts at the same time. As Duranti belongs to both cultural systems, her self-translation offers a unique interpretation and rendition of cultural references. Furthermore, examining how she deals with these differences illuminates how she positions herself with respect to both systems. For instance, in the Italian version, she adopts a highly foreignising approach: the text is full of English words that are not explained, even when Italian readers might not be so familiar with them (basement, tenement house, dill, neatly, dean, sunken living room and spare room). The Italian version is also full of English sentences and expressions. They are mostly simple and basic sentences, which should not cause too many problems to an Italian reader: 'Welcome home, deary' (p. 42), 'Have a good day' (p. 49), 'Are you Ok?' (p. 157). Nonetheless, Duranti often inserts more complicated phrases: 'Black puppy, cute and loving, needs a family' (p. 117), or 'Why did you pretend you didn't know me?' (p. 172). In doing so, she engages Italian readers in an autonomous process of translation, as they must infer the meaning of the word from the wider context in which it appears. On the contrary, in the English version, Italian terms which might be too culture-specific are replaced by more accessible ones.[12] Two reasons for this different approach can be identified. Firstly, she is aware that Italians speak English and know English words with a greater frequency than English speakers know Italian words or speak the language. Secondly, she might also increase the foreignising effect of the Italian version because she does not perceive specific American items as destabilising. Her insider gaze prevents her from perceiving the foreignness

126 VOICES OF WOMEN WRITERS

of the American things she is talking about. It makes it difficult for her to filter them through her Italian point of view.[13] The way she treats CS with respect to these cultural references, then, marks a shift in perspective, as she adopts a stance, which is internal to American society and external to the Italian one. An example of the domesticating approach in the English text is shown in the following lines, where Martina remembers when her mother bought her first car:

'Le conserve, che aveva continuato a preparare ogni estate, venivano caricate sulla **Uno**' (p. 21)	'The preserves she had continued to make every summer were loaded into the **Fiat**' (p. 9)
'Poi la mamma poté comprarsi una **Cinquecento** e imparò alla meglio a guidarla' (p. 31)	'Then, when Mamma could afford it, she bought a small **Fiat** and learned how to drive it' (p. 15)

Duranti replaces both words 'Uno' and 'Cinquecento' with the hypernym 'Fiat', thus acting as a cultural mediator and helping the American reader to access the text and the Italian cultural world. Consider the following example, too:

'Mi preparai le tagliatelle con il pesto e le portai in salotto assieme a un bicchiere di **pigato**' (p. 46)	'I made myself the tagliatelle with pesto and took it along with a glass of **red wine** to the living room' (p. 23)

Pigato is an Italian white wine, which is produced in the region of Liguria. This wine is not very well-known in America, and for this reason, the author opts for a more general reference to a red wine. Thus, she avoids the communicative and cultural gap with American readers and facilitates their reading process. We can think of Duranti's cultural mediation as a backward movement (to Italy) and forward (to America). Domestication implies a motion back to her country of origin, while foreignisation entails one towards the host society. In moving from the Italian to the English version, she opts for a movement forward, as she locates herself closer to the American than to the Italian reader. The motivation behind this linguistic choice may also be to represent and voice Martina's conflictual relationship with Italy, a country that she never perceived as fully and entirely familiar. Martina's partial belonging to Italy is reproduced linguistically, by resorting to a linguistic code that causes attrition and makes communication with the Italian reader more complicated.[14] Likewise, the frequent use of English words and sentences in the Italian text indicates her attempt to linguistically re-ground in 'the territory of the other', by using rightly 'the language of the other'.

Duranti's use of language therefore grounds in her personal experience, as illustrated in the following passage: the use of the Italian word 'naturalezza', to which she opposes the English word 'naturalness', is used to refer to the Italian social and cultural context in which she is writing, and acts as a reminder of this context's influence on her persona. Basically, she is using the Italian language to express her relationship to her Italian cultural heritage:

> The problem is how to succeed at being unnatural with sufficient *naturalezza*. I can only express my meaning in Italian, because the word 'naturalness' I found in the dictionary a few days ago has for me such an unnatural ring. 'Naturalness' does really translate *'naturalezza'*, a word that means a way of being, of behaving, living or feeling. [...] I wonder (2000, 117).[15]

The author decides to maintain and incorporate the Italian word in the English text. The American reader can easily infer the meaning of the word as it appears in combination with its English equivalent. Furthermore, the word is repeated many times throughout the same passage. Its continuous and repeated presence helps the American reader to become familiar with it and stop perceiving its otherness or feeling the tension created by the linguistic clashing of Italian and English. In doing so, Duranti demonstrates that it is possible to bring two different languages together, as languages do not constitute self-contained and independent systems, and despite their differences, they can be intelligible to each other. The way she uses such a term is particularly important because it makes explicit the connection between a specific behaviour and her Italian upbringing. For Martina, behaving with 'naturalezza' means adhering to an Italian form of sociability and behaviour. The impossible linguistic assimilation, therefore, mirrors her impossible cultural assimilation. CS, in this case, triggers a backward movement, as she uses the code-switched term to distance herself from American society and re-ground within the Italian community.

Like mentioned before, the Italian version of the novel exhibits a high degree of multilingualism, with English words and sentences often scattered around the whole text. For example, CS is often used in the semantic domain of food. The latter occupies a prominent position in shaping belonging in the novel, which makes Duranti's use of CS in this specific domain particularly interesting and illuminating. As Spunta points out, Duranti 'uses the central metaphor of "international" cuisine to explore the protagonist's split identity between her native Italy and her new home in New York, and to discuss the question of tolerance and social integration' (1999, 228). The use of CS further contributes to this exploration, as her linguistic choices intend to validate her existential

128   VOICES OF WOMEN WRITERS

choices as well. If food making and eating are 'performative politics of one's subjectivity' (Longhurst et al. 2009, 342), then cooking for Martina is a way to voice and bring to life her left-handed identity. She often wonders whether, had this left-handed identity prevailed over the right-handed one, she would have become a chef, rather than a lecturer.

The events narrated in the novel span an entire week. Each day is associated with a specific recipe; for example, Saturday is matched with the Italian recipe 'risotto alla milanese' (2000, 3), while on Tuesday Duranti chooses a French recipe, the 'lobster Armoricaine' (2000, 25).[16] Moreover, references to recipes and dishes appear throughout the novel, as the main character enjoys cooking. Apart from the Italian culinary tradition, Duranti inserts several recipes belonging to other cuisines, such as French and American: tarte tatin, upside-down pie, casserole and bagel. Thus, she makes her character establish a transnational and hybrid relationship with her cooking habits; cooking becomes a metaphor for Martina of border-crossing and mixing. It constitutes an instrument with which to mediate and accommodate her multiple belongings and positions. She negotiates the survival of her Italian upbringing through cooking and simultaneously connects it with her transnational and multicultural identity. As it emerges in the following paragraph, food memories forge her emotional bond with Italy. In the following passage, she specifically refers to 'customs and kitchen utensils', thus confirming the idea put forward by Chianese that 'objects signifying Italianness are most often found in the kitchen, contributing to the idea of cooking as an activity that Italians carry out with almost religious devotion' (2022, 7):

> that special air that my parents had brought with them from Lucania and that permeated our house. It wasn't just the southern accent that they both retained until they died, it was more the Christmas and Easter customs, the food, certain kitchen utensils, the way bread and preserves were made (2000, 4).[17]

Likewise, Martina expresses her intimate connection to New York through her reference to the smell of food. Food memories redefine New York as a homely space:

> I'm so used to the smell of New York that I almost don't sense it anymore. But I find it again and so keenly every time I come back from Italy [...] The ethnic cuisines, with their own special spices [...] And garlic, pepperoni, hamburger, French fries [...] Powerful, more than any other smell, is broccoli (2000, 18).

The historian Cruz Miguel Ortíz Cuadra talks about the intersection of food and senses in his book *Eating Puerto Rico: A History of Food, Culture, and Identity*. He proposes the concept of 'palate memory' to refer to the sensory dimension of food, which can arouse memories of specific places, people and experiences (2013, 2). In the passage above, Martina refers to the sensory dimension of food experience and describes how this dimension is essential to her construction of a sense of place.[18] New York's homely connotation unfolds through its smells and flavours, which she is able to recognise and 'keenly' rediscover every time she returns from her trips to Italy. Her relationship with the smells of New York city depicts the latter as 'home'.[19]

As mentioned earlier, food manipulation and creation also mirror Martina's process of forging and rebuilding her subjectivity. For her, blending different food traditions means blending her different identities:

> In the subway I jotted down the menu: Cajun jumbalaya, artichokes *alla giudia, gateau des adieux*. The shrimps I would buy downtown at the Chinese fish market where I always shop. For the artichokes I'd have to stop at Dean & De Luca, the only store in New York that has artichokes comparable to the Italian ones (2000, 103).

The passage above is fully representative of the transcultural potential of food in the novel. Martina refers to different culinary traditions; the Italian one is represented by the artichokes *alla giudia*, a recipe, which is traditional of Rome, while the *gateau* refers to French cuisine, and *jambalaya* is a traditional dish of Louisiana, with African, Spanish and French influences.[20] Furthermore, she shops at a Chinese market. Retaining her Italian culinary tradition is a way to reclaim her Italian origins. At the same time, the introduction of foreign recipes is a statement about her willingness to absorb other systems and her faith in the possibility of combining them. This is encapsulated in the metaphor of the American shop selling food as good as the one she used to eat in Italy. Experimenting with different cuisines becomes a way to come to terms with the experience of displacement, and to forge and exploit the different possibilities that come from it. The Italian recipe links her to her original roots, while the 'foreign' ones connect her to new possibilities and forms of being. Her experience indicates rightly the possibility of living in a liminal space, where linguistic and cultural differences are not perceived as a threat to the personal and social identity of the individual. Contrarily, they constitute an enrichment, as they define a subject that is not constrained by limitations and borders but that can thrive in the space beyond them.

5.4 *Sogni mancini* and *Left-Handed Dreams*: Why and How to Self-translate

The plot of Duranti's novel has been amply described throughout this chapter. Briefly, it tells the story of Martina Satriano, an Italian woman who lives in New York, where she teaches at a local university. As stated in the introduction to the English version of the novel, the nature of the book itself almost imposed the choice to self-translate on Duranti:

> Such an operation [...] was almost imposed by the nature of the novel itself [...] By narrating such a story in English as well, the author [...] intended to give as authentic a voice as possible to the experiences of the protagonist, emphasising the impact and effects of the North American society in which she has settled, and how they sedimented on, and reacted with, the substratum of values, memories and culture which are the patrimony carried forward from her native Italy (2000, v).

Duranti's words confirm that, for her, the practice of writing and self-translating exists in conjunction with the experience of living. Her decision to write Martina's story in two languages originates from the fact that this story is first and foremost lived in both an Italian and a North American context. Duranti is basically translating Martina's hybrid existence into a hybrid language. This link between living, writing and self-translating becomes even more overt when we consider that, to date, *Sogni mancini*/*Left-Handed Dreams* represents the only episode of self-translation in her literary career.

Concerning the self-translating process, it is important to focus on the time span between the two versions. Grutman and Van Bolderen state that, while 'standard translators are generally expected to work on complete texts, self-translators can start transferring their text in another language while it is still in progress in the first language' (2014, 327). They label this form of self-translation as simultaneous.[21] By contrast, delayed or consecutive self-translations are 'prepared after completion and even publication of their other-language counterparts' (2014, 327). With respect to this point, Duranti's self-translation occupies a hybrid position, as it locates itself at the juncture between both types of processes. In the introduction to *Left-Handed Dreams*, it is stated that the novel 'has been conceived of and developed simultaneously in both Italian and English' (2000, v). Nevertheless, the 'English version has had a somewhat more extended process of evolution, and has undergone a number of revisions for over four years after the Italian edition [...] was published' (2000, v). In fact, the Italian edition was published in 1996, while the English version dates back to 2000. In the same introduction, it is further stated that the 'changes, made on various occasions [...] were intended to make *Left-Handed Dreams* read less as a translation and more as an autonomous text, a novel in its own right' (2000, v). Whether Duranti succeeded or not at this is not relevant here. However, despite her intention to make the English version look like an autonomous text, this version is overtly presented as a translation. In fact, great part of the introduction presents a detailed description of the self-translated process. Furthermore, it is specified that Duranti 'availed herself of the cooperation of an American friend', who helped her 'to "de-italianize" her English' (2000, v), a process that has an almost political connotation. Indeed, like Dagnino states, the author 'more or less consciously even manages to destabilize, although ever so slightly, the centrality of English as the dominant global language' (2021, 295). Duranti's self-translation, then, can be classified as a collaborative self-translation, that is, a translation that is carried out with the help of a second person other than the author. As she provides all this information about the English version, her performance can be classified as an 'autotraducción transparente'. It is a translation in which the para-textual elements inform readers that they are dealing with a text translated from another language (Dasilva 2013, 112). Dasilva specifies that this kind of information 'suelen aparecer consignadas fundamentalmente en los peritextos, como la cubierta, la portada interior, la página de créditos y la página de los títulos' (2013, 112).[22]

Duranti's self-translation is a perfect example of what I have defined as a *continuum*. Her authorial presence and voice resurface at different points in the novel. The relationship between both versions is not characterised by equivalence, but rather is inspired by an attempt at rethinking and rewriting. The author's dialogue with her mother tongues redefines both texts in novel ways, as she experiments with the creative potential of her multilingualism. An example of this approach to self-translating is offered by the style of the narration. For example, she displays a more metaphorical and figurative use of language in Italian. The table below shows some examples:

per trovare un buco dove mettere la macchina (p. 19)	to find a parking space (p. 8)
venirmi la fantasia di aiutare (p. 20)	be keen on helping (p. 9)
pensai con il cuore stretto (p. 21)	I thought that (p. 9).
di passare senza ore morte (p. 30)	to shift instantly (p. 14)
in quella specie di proiettile che è la cabina dell'ascensore (p. 38)	got into the elevator (p. 19)

132 VOICES OF WOMEN WRITERS

This point emerges clearly in the following passage, where the movement from an emotional to a rational language is in correlation with the emotional charge that Italian carries. Here, Martina talks about her flight to Italy:

Il pilota aveva girato sopra Roma per quasi un'ora cercando **un buco** nella tempesta autunnale che infuriava sulla città. Poi **riuscì a tuffarsi in una voragine nera** e a noi passeggeri sembrò di venir giù come un sasso dentro un pozzo. Quando le ruote toccarono terra lasciai andare i braccioli a cui mi ero aggrappata e guardai l'ora: le sette e mezza, appunto (p. 9)	The pilot had circled over Rome for almost an hour trying to find **his way** in the Autumn storm that was raging over the city. Eventually **he made his way through the clouds** and let the plane drop like a stone in a well. When the wheels touched the runway I let go of the armrests and looked at my watch: seven thirty, exactly (p. 3)

The changes in these passages are made to convey different emotional charges. Martina is returning home for her mother's funeral. The bad weather conditions seem to increase the negative connotation of her return home, which is caused by her mother's death. The Autumn storm also represents the storm of emotions inside her. In the Italian text, the figurative language reinforces the emotional weight of her return home. The pain of the loss of her mother is expressed through a specific use of what represents the actual language of the mother. Specific lexical choices such as 'buco' and 'voragine nera' reinforce the negative tone of the narration and give a bleak connotation to her return. In the Italian text, the word 'aggrappata', which is omitted in the English version, similarly strengthens her sense of estrangement. Without her mother, she feels rootless. The act of holding onto something is a reaction to this feeling, and it expresses her need to ground herself in the familiar space defined by the mother (tongue, land).

Duranti's different use of metaphorical and figurative language therefore aims to express and transmit how her emotions are conceptualised and framed in her linguistic systems. Given her perfect knowledge of English, her different tone and style in this language are not due to a weaker mastery of it. She is equally able to play with language, whether writing in Italian or English, but she consciously and intentionally decides to adopt two different styles. In some cases, the choice to polish and tone down her speech is related to the fact that she is addressing a different reader. The re-contextualisation of the text imposes on her the adoption of a different style. For instance, let us consider the following example:

La base è un aggeggio che si vende dappertutto – ce ne sono varie marche, la mia si chiama *Dream Machine*. Dovrebbe servire per addormentarsi dolcemente, per svegliarsi di buon umore… […] Più che altro è una delle tante invenzioni **acchiappa-scemi** (p. 62)	The main part is a device that's sold everywhere under various brand names, mine is called the Dream Machine. It's supposed to help you drop off to sleep and wake up in a good mood… […] More likely it's just one of those traps for **gadget-lovers** (p. 33)

Martina is talking about one of the devices she bought to build her Machine. Her tone sounds quite sarcastic in the Italian text, where her criticism is conveyed by the expression 'acchiappa-scemi', which is quite strong and can be perceived as offensive. In English, instead, she opts for a more neutral expression, 'gadget-lovers'. This different lexical choice is reader-oriented. She is aware that these objects are more popular in American society, and therefore tries to attenuate her words so as not to offend her American reader. However, she manages to preserve her thought but convey it in a more polite way, by replacing the Italian 'invenzioni' with the English 'traps'. Thus, she still maintains the main idea of the fraud behind these devices, but in English, the negative connotation is associated with the objects, not with the people. This translation choice is in line with the idea put forward by Arrula Ruiz (2017, p. 8) that, perhaps, 'the role-taking of the author changes when rewriting a text to target another community of speakers, […] aiming to attract a readership from a group or category that may be different from the initial one'. In self-translating this specific passage, Duranti is undoubtedly considering her new American readership.

Duranti also uses definite and indefinite articles to articulate her relationships with her origin and host country. With respect to this point, an interesting example is offered by the passage below:

Erano anni che non venivo a Nugola Vecchia […] Mi parve irriconoscibile, deturpato da un orribile agglomerato di case costruito sulla collina detta Poggio di Mezzo […] ebbi la stessa sensazione […] mentre cercavo di ricordare la duna com'era, **la** perfetta cupola alberata (pp. 13–14)	I hadn't been to Nugola Vecchia in years […] It was unrecognisable, defaced by an ugly bunch of houses that had been built on the hill called Poggio di Mezzo […] I actually had the same feeling myself as I tried to remember the dune as it was – **a** perfect dome covered with trees (pp. 5–6)

Martina is talking about her return home, more precisely, about her return to Nugola Vecchia. Her narration is built in accordance with the traditional trope of a failed return home. She realises that the ideal place in her memories does not correspond to the real one. When talking about Poggio di Mezzo, the hill that occupies a special place in her memories, she shifts from a definite

134 VOICES OF WOMEN WRITERS

article – in Italian – to an indefinite one – in English. As conventionally understood, definite articles are used to refer to a specific noun, while indefinite articles refer to non-specific nouns. No differences in such use can be identified between Italian and English. For this reason, one would expect these features to be preserved in the passage from one language to the other. The change in Duranti's text must, therefore, acquire a specific significance as part of this narrative of a failed return home. The use of the definite article in 'la perfetta cupola' suggests that Martina is referring to a specific place, which still exists in her memory of Italy. Essentially, it serves the purpose of reinforcing her connection with Italy. The shift also indicates a change in her attitude. While the Italian Martina still believes in the possibility of an authentic return home, the American one rethinks her relationship with the native place in a more realistic way and is ready to enact a process of redefinition of home. In English, the weakened relationship between Martina and Nugola is expressed linguistically with the indefinite article. In Italian, instead, she uses the language as an instrument to reinforce and claim belonging to Nugola. The definite article presents Poggio di Mezzo as a specific place she can always return to.

The analysis of pronominal markers in the novel should be considered against the same backdrop. They are also particularly important with respect to narrative construction. Writers can use them to convey and express different degrees of insideness, or outsideness; agency, or inaction; proximity, or distance, with respect to the events they narrate, or the states they refer to. The use of these devices is tied to specific communicative purposes, as well as to the stance writers take in reporting something. For instance, the following passages offer interesting insights into the writer's ability to consciously use the narrative voice to represent and transmit her protagonist's sense of displacement and to express her shift from a feeling of involvement to a feeling of detachment:

Prima il suono: rauco, né musica né rumore. Poi il sussurro: «Sei italiana ma vivi a New York. Hai quarantadue anni. Questa è la mia voce: la tua. Racconta il nostro sogno» (1996, 49)	First a rasping sound, neither music nor noise, then a whisper "You're Italian but you live in New York. You're forty-two years old. This is my voice: yours. Tell me your dream" (2000, 25)

In line four, the movement from Italian to English presents an interesting change in perspective, as 'il nostro sogno' becomes 'your dream'. The Machine is the instrument that Martina uses to connect both her dream-like dimension and the dimension of reality, as well as to bridge the gap between her right-handed and realised self and her self-handed and potential self. In the English

FRANCESCA DURANTI

version, the shift from the inclusive 'nostro' to the exclusive 'your' determines a change in perspective, which reinforces Martina's dualistic and fragmented sense of the self. Thus, she manages to illustrate her hybrid condition as an experience of continuous transit, which makes her continuously shift from an insider to an outsider perspective, from inclusion to exclusion.

Analysing Duranti's self-translation, another interesting aspect was identified. It concerns the presence, in the English text, of frequent omissions, additions and clarifications. These features might seem minor in the overall design of a text and therefore unimportant to understand the meaning of writing and translating practices in the literary production of a writer. Their extra-linguistic nature, however, is particularly illustrative of revisional changes. Additions, omissions and clarifications can, in fact, represent the authors' evolution towards greater detail and therefore manifest their intention to improve the text. Clarifications can also respond to authors' needs to correct inconsistencies they notice once they go back to the text to transpose it into another language; or to their need to clarify specific aspects for the target reader; or to reinforce and highlight topics and moments, which are essential to build the overall meaning of the story. Their presence in the text therefore seems to refer back to Wilson's idea of translation as a conscious activity, while writing is mainly unconscious. Omitting, adding and clarifying allow authors to consciously intervene on the text, re-enacting their voice in a less spontaneous and more controlled way, thus revising and editing potential inaccuracies or pitfalls of the writing process. This function emerges in the following example, which is found at the beginning of section 3, in the chapter entitled 'Tuesday: Lobster Armoricaine'. In section 2, Martina receives a phone call from Professor Cerignola, who invites her out for dinner, because he wants to offer her a job and, with it, the chance to return to Italy. Their conversation on the phone paves the way for a solitary dialogue that Martina has with herself, as she remembers as, during one of her lectures, she tried to explain to her students the concept of 'prossimo', that is, 'the closest'. This concept is the starting point for a broader reflection on the theme of identity and on the several potential identitarian possibilities for each individual:

> I just wanted to know who I would have been if the course of events hadn't been changed. [...] If I had a twin sister and had been separated from her, wouldn't it be logical that I would try to find her? And if that twin lived in my own body, isn't it even more justifiable wanting to know what happened to her? (2000, 29).

136   VOICES OF WOMEN WRITERS

In the English version, Martina refers back to these inner thoughts at the beginning of section 3, thereby establishing a connection between the two sections. This continuity is missing in the Italian version, where the sentence is completely omitted:

Mentre parlavo pensavo al mio appuntamento al Crystal Roofdeck (1996, 57)	**I would have liked to say this, but I didn't. I don't know exactly what I did say**, because while I spoke I was thinking about my appointment at the Crystal Room (2000, 30)

The addition of this sentence allows Duranti to reinforce the cohesion and coherence between the parts of the book. It also constitutes a stratagem contributing to the construction of the plot, through which she can further articulate and reinforce her discourse around what represents the most important theme of the book. The addition at the beginning of this chapter reopens the discourse about the deconstruction of identity as a unitary and fixed entity, thus engaging the reader again with reflections about life and identity.

In the following example, Martina visits her neighbour and friend Jerry Keleti, and asks him to help her locate her old lover Costantino, who is in America:

Non chiese spiegazioni. Ne fui lieta. Jerry è monolitico (1996, 126)	He didn't ask for explanations. I was glad about that. Jerry takes his dreams into reality and his reality into dreams in an uninterrupted time span, which is neither day nor night but a sort of uninterrupted twilight. He's the most monolithic creature I know (2000, 64)

This sentence must be analysed with respect to the role that Jerry plays in the novel. He works as a translator. His profession is particularly interesting with respect to one of the themes of the novel; exactly like Martina, he continuously moves in the interspace between multiple linguistic and cultural worlds. Nonetheless, his daily routine is quite unusual, as his temporal and physical spaces are constrained and limited. He rarely seems to leave the building where he lives, while he follows a strict schedule, eternally committing to the same activities and the same times. On the one hand, his profession connects him to Martina's transmigrant experience; on the other hand, while she attempts to exist in a multiple and fluid world, he perfectly functions in a circumscribed context, where everything is set and immutable. As Wilson states, Jerry can therefore be seen as Martina's 'double in the mirror'; while she attempts 'to map her multiple identities, he is self-sufficient in his liminal space' (2009, 194). Given this, Duranti's addition in the English version characterises Jerry more in detail, reinforcing the contraposition between him and Martina.

Duranti's self-translation offers another interesting aspect to analyse: the rendering of numbers. As Chesterman (1998, 93) claims, the rendering of numbers is generally not problematic in translation. Unless the source and target languages use two different systems of numerals, no change should be noticed in the passage from one language to another. To say it with his words, 'Trente francs has to be thirty francs, not twenty' (1998, 93). This assumption holds true for Italian and English. They use the same system of numerals, so no change is required in translation. In light of this, investigating the rendering of numbers can be particularly useful to explore the definition of self-translation as a *continuum* between writing and translating. As the rendering of numbers is generally not related to the re-contextualisation of the ST or linguistically determined, examining why Duranti, in the process of self-translating, decided to change the numerical references is useful to understand how and why her subjectivity interacts with the text. The side-to-side reading of *Sogni mancini* and its self-translated counterpart revealed many changes in the rendering of numbers:

tre gradi almeno (p. 33)	several degrees hotter (p. 16)
sei ore (p. 33)	for nine hours (p. 16)
la settimana seguente (p. 39)	in a couple of weeks (p. 19)
una cinquantina al giorno (p. 40)	about twenty a day (p. 20)
alle tre e mezza (p. 43)	at three (p. 21)
trenta secondi di silenzio (p. 49)	ninety seconds of silence (p. 25)
alle otto (p. 52)	at eight-thirty (p. 27)
a trecento dollari l'ora (p. 53)	at a hundred dollars an hour (p. 27)
sulla Trentaduesima (p. 62)	on 42nd street (p. 33)
di dieci o dodici anni (p. 78)	about six or seven years old (p. 42)
erano le due passate (p. 93)	it was two o'clock (p. 49)
inserii tre quarti di dollaro (p. 93)	put in five quarters (p. 49)
sono trascorsi i dieci minuti del ciclo della macchina (p. 94)	the dryer has run through its twenty-minute cycle (p. 50)
di dieci anni (p. 111)	five years older (p. 58–59)
la scelta fra due date (p. 129)	a choice of three dates (p. 66)

These examples effectively illustrate that it is wrong to assume that, in translation, numerals never change. This point was highlighted by Natalia Strelkova. In her book *Introduction to Russian-English Translation: Tactics and Techniques for the Translator*, she identifies a number of issues that translators might encounter when rendering numerals. As she states, in some cases,

138 VOICES OF WOMEN WRITERS

changing numerals is desirable due to stylistic, cultural and historical reasons (2012, 128–129). The rendering of numerals can pose some problems for translators, because numbers may represent and convey specific social and cultural differences, and express specific meanings. For instance, in the table above, some of the changes are deemed necessary by the re-contextualisation of the ST. With respect to this point, let us consider the following example:

E dove d'estate faceva un caldo infernale, **tre gradi almeno** più che a Nugola Vecchia, una differenza che si avvertiva benissimo: bastava fare un passo al di là della casa del dottore e in quei **sessanta centimetri** tutto cambiava	On that side it gets beastly hot in summer, **several degrees hotter** than in Nugola Vecchia, a difference that can be felt immediately on crossing the borderline. Just one step beyond the doctor's house, a matter of **two feet**, and everything changes – or used to change

In rendering this passage in English, Duranti converts her metric measurements into imperial, thus making them more accessible to her American reader. Italy and America employ different scales. For this reason, in Italian, she refers to the Celsius scale, while in English, she adopts the Fahrenheit scale. Besides the decision to adopt a system of numerals, which is more familiar to, and understandable by, her American reader, she is also trying to make the sentence more logical from an American perspective. She adopts another metric measurement to reflect the fact that, in switching from Italian into English, she is adopting another view of life as well. As she knows, her American reader would probably have not been impressed by a temperature which is three degrees hotter and therefore would not have been able to perceive her reference to the 'beastly hot'. The need to cater to a different reader might also explain the change in the following example. Martina is watching an American TV programme:

Mentre mi spogliavo accesi la Tv. Oh, mio Dio. Una bambina **di dieci o dodici anni**, in un pigiamino a orsetti bianchi su fondo rosa. Seduta sul suo letto. Non aveva né capelli né sopracciglia	I turned on the TV while I was undressing. Oh, my God! A girl, **about six or seven years old**, wearing pink pyjamas sprinkled with white teddy bears. Sitting on her bed. She didn't have any hair or eyebrows

The appearance of a little girl talking about her disease paves the way for a reflection on the different attitudes that Italian and American societies show towards death:

Is it really true that in this extraordinary country you've found a way to accept the idea of death? [...] There must be a trick that gives you

FRANCESCA DURANTI

so much courage. Otherwise how could you be so different from us? How do you explain why Italian men and women – strong, aggressive, used to driving fast, smoking, living life as a continuous gamble – are incapable of facing death with the same grit a child in teddybear pyjamas has? (2000, 42).

Duranti/Martina is adopting her outsider perspective, as made evident in her use of the pronouns 'you' and 'us'. She uses them to build the contraposition between Americans and Italians, to whom she recognises to belong. The girl's age in the Italian text reflects her Italian attitude towards death: even if of a few years only, Duranti acknowledges that, in the Italian text, the girl must be a bit older in order to help the Italian reader cope with her disease. In translating this passage into English, though, she does not seem so worried about the American reader, who, in her opinion, being more used to dealing with death, might more easily accept it, even when it involves a little girl.

In some cases, numerical differences are simply incidental. For instance, in the following passage, Duranti changes the street number, and there is no apparent reason for that. Such a change reinforces the assumption that self-translation is more the repetition of a process, rather than of a text (Wilson 2009, 187). The author is not simply recreating the same text in two languages; rather, she is actively repeating the same creative process in two languages. The repetition of the process accounts for these small modifications, which do not affect the general structure of the 'original':

'«È un attrezzo complicato» cominciai. «L'ho costruito con l'aiuto di un bravo tecnico elettronico turco, che ha un negozio sulla **Trentaduesima**	It's a complicated piece of equipment. I built it with the help of a very good Turkish technician who has a store on 42nd **Street**

In her text, nevertheless, there are several cases where the different rendering of the numbers is not incidental, or not deemed necessary by the re-contextualisation of the text. Analysing these examples gives interesting insights into the significance that Duranti gives to numbers in her book, and how they are part of the wider discourse she puts forward in the novel. For instance, let us consider the following extract, where Martina talks about her marriage to Cesare:

Era un gran raccontatore – alcuni lo giudicavano noioso, ma non io. Mi piaceva ascoltarlo. Era più vecchio di me di **dieci anni** – aveva studiato a Milano, alla Statale	He was a great story teller – some people thought he was boring, but I didn't. I liked listening to him. He was **five years** older than I – he'd studied in Milan at the Statale University

140 VOICES OF WOMEN WRITERS

The numeric change can be linked to Martina's perception of Cesare. Throughout the book, she often refers to her relationship with him. He is described as a social climber, who would impose on her a view of life that she could not accept. Describing him as ten years older, therefore, can be seen as a way to represent his patronising attitude, also linking it to the patriarchal system in Italy. Duranti is perhaps implying that, as an Italian woman, she was more willing to accept his control over her life. In the English version, the physical and cultural distance from Cesare weakens his control over Martina's life. His less overarching position is represented numerically, when Duranti describes him as younger in the English version. His age becomes a reflection of their relationship. For this reason, it is possible to state that the different use of numbers in this case has a personal meaning. The rendering of numerals fulfils a specific function in the following example as well:

Prima il suono: rauco, né musica né rumore. Poi il sussurro: «Sei italiana ma vivi a New York. Hai quarantadue anni. Questa è la mia voce: la tua. Racconta il nostro sogno» [...] Quando, avendo misurato **trenta secondi di silenzio**, la Macchina capì che non avevo più niente da dirle, smise di registrare	First a rasping sound, neither music nor noise, then a whisper "You're Italian but you live in New York. You're forty-two years old. This is my voice: yours. Tell me your dream". Without opening my eyes, still half-asleep, I began to speak. After **ninety seconds of silence** the Machine understood I had nothing more to say and stopped recording

In this passage, she switches from thirty to ninety seconds. Such a switch reflects Martina's perception of time in relation to specific moments and feelings. The more or less prolonged time indicates what she perceives as a more intense and important moment. In this scene, she is describing her morning ritual: the Machine awakes her with the formula above, and she starts narrating her dream, which is then recorded by the device. The aim of this ritual is to give voice to the other unvoiced existential possibilities of her life and identity. Recording them gives them a tangible presence, which makes them enter the sphere of existence. By referring to a more prolonged time in English, Duranti is telling us that the American Martina perceives this moment as more intense, possibly because this is a ritual and a project that belongs to her American life.

Notes

1 National literary prize for the female author.

2 In her article 'Self-Translation in Transcultural Mode: Francesca Duranti on how to Put 'a Scent of Basil' into One's Translations', Dagnino claims that, in an interview with the author, the latter claimed that she did not enjoy the process of self-translating, defining it as 'una faticaccia' (2021, 289).

FRANCESCA DURANTI

3 In Dagnino's article 'Self-Translation in Transcultural Mode: Francesca Duranti on how to Put 'a Scent of Basil' into One's Translations', Duranti claims to be a polylingual, that is, someone who speaks multiple languages. However, she rejects the label of bilingual, as she cannot recognise any of those languages as a second dominant one (2021, 290).

4 Italian and English, to date, constitute the languages she mainly uses in her daily life (as she lives in-between Italy and America) and in her career, as she writes and translates in both of them.

5 It was published again with *Rizzoli* in 1985.

6 'A liberating need, as if she wanted to psychoanalise herlself': this is what Duranti admits in the preface to her first novel, *La bambina*.

7 In some cultures, in the past, there was the habit of forcing left-handed people to use their right hand.

8 I use 'broad memory' to refer to memory in general, without taking into account differences between cultural, individual, or social memory.

9 In *Acts of Memory: Cultural Recall in the Present* (1999), Mieke Bal, Jonathan Crewe, and Leo Spitzer explore the different forms and meanings that remembering acquires in diverse diaphasic and diatopic contexts.

10 Burns states that 'not only the objects themselves, but the ways in which the participants presented and handled them, exposed powerfully the capacity of the objects to materialize connections and, at substantial distance, to signify immediately as 'things from home' (2020,183).

11 Martina finds a puppy in the building where she lives. Initially, she tries to find a potential owner. Eventually, though, she decides to keep the puppy.

12 For instance, an endnote explains the meaning of Lucania, Scavolini and tressette. In the Italian text, instead, there are no endnotes.

13 While the Italian version is full of English sentences, in the English version there is only one Italian sentence, which is spoken to Martina by a Greek woman, in order to stress the closeness of Italians and Greeks: 'Ciao [...] Una razza, una faccia' (2000' 53).

14 The role of CS in expressing a composite identity and even distance from the origin country on the behalf of migrant authors might only be perceived in the comparison between the two versions. In fact, by reading the Italian text alone, one might simply perceive it as a translation that does not particularly domesticate. Nevertheless, throughout the book, I have argued that, in the case of self-translation, both versions are related to one another and participate in a wider creative process. In light of this, it follows that, in order to reach a full understanding of the text, a side-by-side reading and analysis of the two versions must be conducted.

15 This aspect is connected to Marciano or Lahiri's book about the woman teaching American to live according to an Italian lifestyle.

16 For references in the whole book, I refer to the English version of the novel, unless otherwise specified.

17 In the article 'Remembering Kedgeree', Adrian Carton (2002, 83) claims that eating and cooking constitutes forms of remembering.

18 Longhurst et al. (2009) stressed the role played by smell and taste in recreating a sense of home.

19 In this respect, Ratnam states that 'senses of "home" (and place) can range from micro-level understandings within a household to the macro-level considerations of cities, institutions, nations and previous home(lands) (2018, 2).

20 It represents a hybrid dish itself.
21 'Simultaneous self-translations are significantly less frequent than consecutive self-translations. They mostly appear when the practice of self-translation is repeated to the point of becoming systematic, as it did for Beckett, Federman, Huston [...]' (Grutman and Van Bolderen 2014, 328).
22 'They normally appear in para-textual elements, such as the book cover, the front matter, the copyright page and the title page'.

CONCLUSION

The present book has explored the connection between migrating, writing and self-translating within transmigratory contexts, specifically investigating how transmigrant authors use language to negotiate and reframe their identity against the backdrop of the monolingual paradigm. Starting from the premise that writing and translating are not only linguistic and cultural processes but also self-reflexive practices, they have been examined in conjunction with a process of redefinition of the self.

To this end, I selected a corpus of four transmigrant authors of Italian origins, who moved to English-speaking countries. The aim was to work with a language pair, that to date, has been mainly neglected. Indeed, while the relation between English and Italian in writing and translating has been investigated in several articles, so far it has not been the focus of any specific volume. The decision to work with Italian and English was not only connected to a personal interest (as I am an Italian speaker who lives and works in the UK). The focus on Italian and English also allowed me to investigate the subversive power of the former and the role played by multilingual practices in reshaping the borders and dynamics between dominant and dominated languages. By juxtaposing Italian and English on the page, or writing in both, the authors in this volume rewrite the borders between linguistic systems, challenging the norms that dictate language dynamics and redefining whether and how languages assert themselves within the context of globalisation.

The choice to focus on Italian was also connected to its specific connotation with respect to the monolingual paradigm. Like mentioned in Chapter 1, the concept of a mother tongue acquires an interesting value within the Italian context, where dialects, standard and regional Italian coexist. Given this connotation, the Italian language perfectly allows an examination of multilingual practices as postmonolingual, a point that has been put forward in this volume. The writing and self-translating performances of the authors can be considered postomonolingual, 'as they survive, exist and emerge', against the monolingual paradigm. Indeed, all the writers in this corpus were never fully included in the monolingual paradigm, yet they conceived of themselves as monolinguals and attempted to establish relations with a unique mother tongue. However, the movement to a country speaking another language showed them the impossibility of the monolingual paradigm and made them reconsider their relationship with the mother tongue in terms of mother tongues. Acknowledging and accepting that their lives were lived in multiple languages, they rethought the role each language played in both their personal and professional experiences.

Finally, I decided to work exclusively with female authors. The gendered connotation of the corpus allowed me to analyse and understand the writers' need to express themselves against the backdrop of a patriarchal culture. Their experiences were analysed as examples of daughters' struggles to exist and express themselves beyond the mother (tongue), rewriting conventional concepts of womanhood. They write to assert their voice as women and to claim alternative identities and roles. In their texts, the Italian woman, who is traditionally seen only as a mother, wife, or daughter, is thus engaged with translational and transcultural forms of femininity.

For the transmigrant authors in this volume, writing and self-translating therefore become highly meaningful practices, which are intimately tied to the need to express a voice and obtain visibility, also as individuals who live beyond the borders defined by monolingual and monocultural configurations. Within this scenario, their use of language constitutes a political act; it shows that the alleged associations between language, place and identity do not work anymore, it enacts a reconfiguration of conventional ideas of ethnicity and nationhood, and it expands the borders of the literary canon. Indeed, their texts explore 'the role of language both in the formation of personal identities and in the reconfiguration of constructions of national identity and literary belonging' (Wilson 2019, 213). More specifically, these writers challenge the belief in a monolithic Italian identity, paving the way for the expression and recognition of the multiple facets and features that, in a transcultural and translingual world, represent what it means to be an Italian. In 'Landscapes of return: Italian-Canadian writing published in Italian by Cosmo Iannone', Michela Baldo claims that, within the Italian context, the increasing interest in the topic of migration has led to a political interest in their former migrants by Italian regions, that started to encourage their return (2013, 200). Baldo highlights that, from a literary perspective, this return home has been recreated by translating into Italian some of the works of Italian authors abroad, such as the Italian-Canadian ones. Their voices are brought back into the Italian context, thus contributing to new readings and understandings of the literary canon, that opens its borders and welcomes authors who write from outside the national frame. Their Italianness and the ways in which it can enrich and enhance Italian identity is therefore recognised and supported.

CONCLUSION

This point demonstrates that the landscape of the publishing field is starting to change, following the changes that are affecting the landscape of our society. However, it is not enough. The hope is that the inclusion of Italian authors abroad will positively affect the attitude of the publishing field towards migrant authors writing in Italian, shaping the direction and the future of what Gnisci called 'letteratura italiana della migrazione'.

One of the major aspects of this work was the interdisciplinary approach adopted in the analysis of the migrant narratives. Indeed, this study has demonstrated and promoted the necessity of combining literary criticism, translation and linguistic analysis, in order to enhance and gain a better understanding of the authors' literary world. This combination was articulated on three different levels: a thematic analysis, examining how traditional migrant tropes are rewritten from a transmigrant perspective; a linguistic analysis of code-switching; an examination of the self-translating performance. The assumption is that all these elements are connected and together shape the authors' message, their position in the literary system, and the meaning of their texts. By acknowledging the shared ground of these elements and examining them together, we will be able to fully listen to the voice of the author, and thus understand the deep connection between identity, writing and translating.

REFERENCES

Primary Sources

Canton, Licia. 2008. *Almond Wine and Fertility*. Montréal: Longbridge Books.
——— 2015. *Vino alla mandorla e fertilità*. Il Mio Libro Editore.
——— 2016. 'Refuge in the Vineyard'. *Canadian Literary Fare*, 5 August. Available at: https://canadianliteraryfare.org/2016/08/05/refuge-in-the-vineyard/.
Duranti, Francesca. 1996. *Sogni mancini*. Milan: Rizzoli.
——— 2000. *Left-Handed Dreams*. Leicester, UK: Troubador Publishing.
Michelut, Dôre. 1986. *Loyalty to the Hunt*. Montréal: Guernica Editions.
——— 1990. *Ourobouros: The Book that Ate Me*. Laval (Québec): Éditions Trois.
Patriarca, Gianna. 1994. *Italian Women and Other Tragedies*. Toronto: Guernica Editions.
——— 1997. *Daughters for Sale*. Toronto: Guernica Editions.
——— 1999. *Ciao, Baby*. Toronto: Guernica Editions.
——— 2005. *What My Arms Can Carry*. Toronto: Guernica Editions.
——— 2007. *My Etruscan Face*. Thornhill, ON: Quattro Books.
——— 2009. *Donne Italiane ed Altre Tragedie*. Toronto: Lyrical Myrical Press.

Secondary Sources

Ahmed, Sara. 2000. *Strange Encounters: Embodied Others in Post-coloniality*. London: Routledge.
Ahmed, Sara, Castañeda, Claudia, Fortier, Anne-Marie and Sheller, Mimi. 2003. 'Introduction'. In *Uprootings/Regroundings. Questions of Home and Migration*, edited by Sara Ahmed, Claudia Castañeda, Anne-Marie Fortier and Mimi Sheller. Oxford: Berg.
Alfonzetti, Giovanna. 1998. 'The Conversational Dimension in Code-switching between Italian and Dialect in Sicily'. In *Code-switching in Conversation*, edited by Peter Auer, 180–211. London – New York: Routledge.
Altarriba, Jeanette. 2003. 'Does *cariño* equal "liking"? A Theoretical Approach to Conceptual Nonequivalence between Languages'. *International Journal of Bilingualism* 7(3): 305–322.
Alvarez Cáccamo, Celso. 1998. 'From "switching code" to "code-switching": Towards a reconceptualisation of communicative codes'. In *Code-switching in Conversation*, edited by Peter Auer, 29–48. London – New York: Routledge.
Anselmi, Simona. 2012. *On Self-translation. An Exploration in Self-translators' Teloi and Strategies*. Milan: LED Edizioni Universitarie.
Appadurai, Arjun and Breckenridge, Carol. 1989. 'On Moving Targets'. *Public Culture* 2: i–iv.

148 VOICES OF WOMEN WRITERS

Arrula Ruiz, Garazi. 2017. 'What We Talk About When We Talk About Identity in Self-Translation'. *Ticontre. Teoria Testo Traduzione* 7: 1–21.

Atwood, Margaret. 1996. *Survival: A Thematic Guide to Canadian Literature.* Toronto: Anansi.

Auer, Peter. 1991. 'Italien in Toronto: A Preliminary Comparative Study on Language Use and Language Maintenance'. *Multilingua* 4: 403–440.

———— 1999. 'From Code-switching via Language Mixing to Fused Lects: Toward a Dynamic Typology of Bilingual Speech'. *International Journal of Bilingualism* 3(4): 1–27.

Bachmann-Medick, Doris, and Kugele, Jens. 2018. 'Introduction'. In *Migration: Changing Concepts, Critical Approaches,* edited by Doris Bachmann-Medick and Jens Kugele, 1–20. Berlin/Boston: De Gruyter.

Backus, Ad. 2001. 'The Role of Semantic Specificity in Insertional Codeswitching: Evidence from Dutch-Turkish'. In *Codeswitching World Wide II,* edited by Rodolfo Jacobson, 125–154. Berlin – New York: Mouton de Gruyter.

Bagnell, Kenneth. 1989. *Canadese: A Portrait of the Italian Canadians.* Toronto: Macmillan of Canada.

Bal, Mieke. 1999. 'Introduction'. In *Acts of Memory: Cultural Recall in the Present,* edited by Mieke Bal, Jonathan Creve and Leo Spitzer. Hanover: University Press of New England.

Baldo, Michela. 2013. 'Landscapes of Return: Italian-Canadian Writing Published in Italian by Cosmo Iannone Editore'. *Translation Studies* 6(2): 199–216.

———— 2019. *Italian-Canadian Narratives of Return: Analyzing Cultural Translation in Diasporic Writing.* London: Palgrave Macmillan.

Bandia, Paul. 2008. *Translation as Reparation: Writing and Translation in Postcolonial Africa.* Manchester: St. Jerome Publishing.

Bartoloni, Paolo. 2016. *Objects in Italian Life and Culture: Fiction, Migration, and Artificiality.* New York: Palgrave Macmillan.

Beaujour, Elizabeth Klosty. 1989. *Alien Tongues. Bilingual Russian Writers of the "First" Emigration.* Ithaca, NY: Cornell University Press.

Berman, Antoine. 1992. *The Experience of the Foreign. Culture and Translation in Romantic Germany.* Translated by S. Heyvaert. Albany: State University of New York Press.

Besemeres, Mary. 2000. 'Self-Translation in Vladimir Nabokov's Pnin'. *The Russian Review* 59(3): 390–407.

Bhabha, Homi. 1994. *The Location of Culture.* London/New York: Routledge.

Blom, Jan Petter, and Gumperz, John. 1972. 'Social Meaning in Linguistic Structures: Codeswitching in Norway'. *In Directions in Sociolinguistics: The Ethnography of Communication,* edited by John Gumperz and Dell Hymes, 407–434. New York: Holt, Rinehart and Winston.

Blunt, Alison. 2005. *Domicile and Diaspora.* Oxford: Blackwell Publishing.

Bond, Emma. 2014. 'Towards a Trans-national Turn in Italian Studies?'. *Italian Studies* 69(3), 415–24.

———— 2018. *Writing Migration through the Body.* London: Palgrave Macmillan.

Bonifazi, Corrado. 2009. 'Italy: The Italian Transition from an Emigration to Immigration Country'. *Idea Working Papers* 5: 1–91.

Burdett, Charles, Loredana Polezzi, and Barbara Spadaro. 2020. 'Introduction: Transcultural Italies'. In *Transcultural Italies: Mobility, Memory and Translation,* edited by Charles Burdett, Loredana Polezzi, and Barbara Spadaro, 1–22. Liverpool: Liverpool University Press.

Burns, Jennifer. 2013. *Migrant Imaginaries. Figures in Italian Migration Literature.* Oxford: Peter Lang.

REFERENCES   149

———— 2020. 'The Transnational Biography of 'British' Place: Local and Global Stories in the Built Environment'. In *Transcultural Italies: Mobility, Memory and Translation*, edited by Charles Burdett, Loredana Polezzi, and Barbara Spadaro, 23–46. Liverpool: Liverpool University Press.

Callahan, Laura. 2002. 'The Matrix Language Frame Model and Spanish/English Codeswitching in Fiction'. *Language and Communication* 22: 1–16.

———— 2005. *Spanish-English Codeswitching in a Written Corpus*. Amsterdam – Philadelphia: John Benjamins Publishing Company.

Camarca, Silvia. 2005. 'Code-switching and Textual Strategies in Nino Ricci's Trilogy'. *Semiotica* 154: 225–241.

Canagarajah, Suresh. 2013. *Translingual Practice: Global Englishes and Cosmopolitan Relations*. Abingdon: Routledge.

Caniffe, Eamonn. 2026. *The Politics of the Piazza: The History and Meaning of the Italian Square*. Abingdon: Routledge.

Canton, Licia, De Santis, Delia and Fazio, Venera. 2006. *Writing Beyond History: An Anthology of Prose and Poetry*. Montréal: Cusmano Communications.

Canton, Licia and Di Giovanni, Caroline Morgan. 2013. *Writing Our Way Home*. Toronto: Guernica Editions.

Canton, Licia 2015. *Writing Cultural Difference: Italian-Canadian Creative & Critical Works*. Toronto: Guernica Editions.

———— 2015. 'Se traduire au Quotidiane'. *Interfrancophonies* 6: 87–92.

———— 2018. 'Literary Women: Exploring the Voices of Delia De Santis and Venera Fazio'. *Italian Canadiana XXXII*: 79–91.

———— 2019. 'Writing Canadian Narratives with Italian Accents: The Pink House and Other Stories'. *Oltreoceano. Geografie e letterature: luoghi dell'emigrazione* 15: 59–65.

Caplan, Patd. 1997. *Food, Health, and Identity*. London: Psychology Press.

Caporale-Bizzini, Silvia. 2018. 'The Transcultural Reinterpretation of Italian Canadiana in the Writings of Michelle Alfano, Licia Canton and Terri Favro'. *Italian Canadiana* XXXII: 69–78.

Carton, Adrian. 2002. 'Remembering Kedgeree'. *Meanjin* 61(4): 82–85.

Casagranda, Mirko. 2008. 'Switching Identity in Multicultural Canadian Literature: Codeswitching as a Discursive Strategy and a Marker of Identity Construction'.

Cavarero, Adriana. 2000. *Relating Narratives, Storytelling and Selfhood*. Translated by Paul A. Kottman. Abingdon, Oxon: Routledge.

———— 2009 [1990]. *Nonostante Platone: Figure femminili nella filosofia antica*. Verona: Ombre Corte.

Chesterman, Andrew. 1998. 'Description, Explanation, Prediction: A Response to Gideon Toury and Theo Hermans'. *Current Issues in Language & Society* 5 (1&2): 91–98.

———— 2009. 'The Name and Nature of Translator Studies'. *Hermes, Journal of Language and Communication Studies* 42: 13–22.

Chianese, Francesco. 2022. 'Italian Items in Domestic Spaces. Representing Italianness through Objects in the Fiction of Helen Barolini and Chiara Barzini'. *The Journal of American Translation and Interpreting Studies* 1–20.

Clark, Brian, and Macdonald, Stuart. 2017. *Leaving Christianity: Changing Allegiances in Canada since 1945*. Kingston: McGill-Queen's University Press.

Clifford, James. 1997. *Routes. Travel and Translation in the Late Twentieth Century*. Harvard: Harvard University Press.

Clivio, Gianrenzo. and Danesi, Marcel. 2000. *The Sounds, Forms, and Uses of Italian: An Introduction to Italian linguistics*. Toronto: University of Toronto Press.

Cohen, Erik. 2000. 'Souvenir'. In *Encyclopedia of Tourism*, edited by Jafar Jafari, 547–548. London: Routledge.

Comberiati, Daniele. 2010. *Scrivere nella lingua dell'altro. La letteratura degli immigrati in Italia (1989–2007)*. Bruxelles: Peter Lang.

Comellini, Carla. 2004. 'Il cibo come tema e motivo nella letteratura canadese'. *Prospero. Rivista di Letterature Straniere, Comparatistica e Studi Culturali* XI: 101–115.

Conti, Christopher, and Gourley, James. 2014. *Literature as Translation/Translation as Literature*. Newcastle upon Tyne: Cambridge Scholars Publishing.

Cronin, Michael. 2006. *Translation and Identity*. Abingdon, Oxon: Routledge.

Crystal, David. 1985. *A Dictionary of Linguistics and Phonetics*. 2nd edn. Oxford: Blackwell.

Dagnino, Arianna. 2019. 'Breaking the Linguistic Minority Complex through Creative Writing and Self-Translation'. *Traduction, terminologie, rédaction*. 32(2), 107–129.

———— 2021. 'Self-Translation in Transcultural Mode: Francesca Duranti on How to Put 'a Scent of Basil' into One's Translations'. In *Narratives Crossing Borders: The Dynamics of Cultural Interaction*, edited by Herbert Jonsson, Lovisa Berg, Chatarina Edfeldt, and Bo G. Jansson, 275–305. Stockholm: Stockholm University Press.

Dasilva, Xosé Manuel. 2013. *Estudios sobre la autotraducción en el espacio ibérico*. Bern: Peter Lang.

de Certeau, Michel. 1997. *Culture in the Plural*. Minneapolis: University of Minnesota Press.

de Courtivron, Isabelle. 2003. *Lives in Translation: Bilingual Writers on Identity and Creativity*. New York: Palgrave Macmillan Press.

De Fina, Anna. 2007. 'Style and Stylization in the Construction of Identities in a Card-playing Club'. In *Social Identity and Communicative Styles: An Alternative Approach to Linguistic Heterogeneity*, edited by Peter Auer, 57–84. Berlin: Mouton de Gruyter.

Delabastita, Dirk, and Grutman, Rainier. 2005. 'Fictionalising Translation and Multilingualism', *Linguistica Antverpiensia, New Series: Themes in Translation Studies* 4: 11–34.

Deleuze, Gilles, and Félix Guattari. 1975. *Kafka: Pour une littérature mineure*. Paris: Éditions de Minuit.

De Luca, Anna Pia. 2007. 'Mondi femminili ed altre tragedies canadesi: le poesie di Gianna Patriarca'. *Oltreoceano. Percorsi letterari e linguistici* 1: 29–38.

———— 2013. 'Lo specchio dell'io: ritornando da scrittrici'. *Oltreoceano. Donne al caleidoscopio. La riscrittura dell'identità femminile nei testi dell'emigrazione tra l'Italia, le Americhe e l'Australia*, 7: 45–55.

DeMarco, William. M. 1981. *Ethnics and Enclaves: Boston's Italian North End*. Michigan: UMI Research Press.

De Rogatis, Tiziana. 2023. *Homing/Ritrovarsi. Traumi e translinguismi delle migrazioni in Morante, Koffman, Kristof, Scego e Lahiri*. Siena: Università per stranieri di Siena.

Dewaele, Jeana Marc. 2002. 'Psychological and Sociodemographic Correlates of Communicative Anxiety in L2 and L3 Production'. *The International Journal of Bilingualism* 1: 23–28.

Dewaele, J. M., Housen A. and Li, Wei. 2003. *Bilingualism: Beyond Basic Principles*. Clevedon: Multilingual Matters.

Dewaele, J. M. 2004. 'Blistering barnacles! What language do multilinguals swear in?'. *Estudios de Sociolingüística* 5(1): 83–106.

Dingle, Hugh, and Drake, Alistair. 2007. 'What is Migration?'. *Bioscience* 57(2): 113–121.

Doubrovsky, Serge. 1977. *Fils*. Paris: Galilée.

Drozdzewski, Danielle, De Nardi, Sarah, and Waterton, Emma. 2016. *Memory, Place and Identity: Commemoration and Remembrance of War and Conflict*. Abingdon: Routledge.

REFERENCES

Duranti, Francesca. 1976. *La bambina*. Milan: La Tartaruga.

——— 1978. *Piazza mia bella piazza*. Milan: La Tartaruga.

——— 1984. *La casa sul lago della luna*. Milan: Rizzoli.

——— 1991. *Ultima stesura*. Milan: Rizzoli.

Ekman, Paul and Davidson, Richard J. 1994. *The Nature of Emotion: Fundamental Questions*. New York: Oxford University Press.Erichsen Skalle, Camilla. 2017. 'Nostalgia and Hybrid Identity in Italian Migrant Literature: The Case of Igiaba Scego'. *Bergen Language and Linguistics Studies* 7: 73–86.

Evans, Dylan. 2001. *Emotion: The Science of Sentiment*. New York: Oxford University Press.

Facchinello, Monica. 2005. 'Sceptical Representations of Home: John Banville's *Doctor Copernicus & Kepler*'. In *Global Ireland. Irish Literatures for the New Millennium*, edited by OndYey Pilný and Clare Wollace, 109–121. Prague: Litteraria Pragensia, pp. 109–121.

Fitch, Brian T. 1988. *Beckett and Babel: An Investigation into the Status of the Bilingual Work*. Toronto: University of Toronto Press.

Frank, Søren. 2008. *Migration and Literature: Günter Grass, Milan Kundera, Salman Rushdie, and Jan Kjærstad*. New York: Palgrave Macmillan.

Fussell, Susan R. and Moss, Mallie M. 1998. 'Figurative Language in Descriptions of Emotional States'. In *Social and Cognitive Approaches to Interpersonal Communication*, edited by in Susan R. Fussell and Roget J. Kreuz, 1–30. Mahwah, NJ: Erlbaum, pp. 1–30.

Gardner, Katy. 2002. *Age, Narrative, Migration. The Life Course and Life Histories of Bengali Elders in London*. Oxford: Berg Publishers.

Gasparini, Philippe. 2008. *Autofiction: Une Aventure Du Langage*. Paris: Éditions du Seuil.

Gedalof, Irene. 2003. 'Taking (a) Place: Female Embodiment and the Re-grounding of Community'. In *Uprootings/Regroundings. Questions of Home and Migration*, edited by Sara Ahmed, Claudia Castañeda, Anne-Marie Fortier and Mimi Sheller, 91–112. Oxford: Berg.

Giachetti, Ismène. 1992. *Plaisirs et préférences alimentaires*. Paris: Polytechina.

Giorgio, Adalgisa. 2002. 'Writing the Mother-Daughter Relationship. Psychoanalysis, Culture and Literary Criticism'. In *Writing Mothers and Daughters*, edited by Adalgisa Giorgio, 11–45. New York: Berghahn Books.

Giuliano, Bruce B. 1976. *Sacro o Profano? A Consideration of four Italian-Canadian Religious Festivals*. Ottawa: University of Ottawa Press.

Glick Schiller, Nina, Basch, Linda and Szanton Blanc, Cristina. 1995. From Immigrant to Transmigrant: Theorizing Transnational Migration'. *Anthropological Quarterly* 68(1): 48–63.

Gnisci, Armando. 1998. *La letteratura italiana della migrazione*. Roma: Lilith.

——— 2003. *Creolizzare l'Europa: letteratura e migrazione*. Roma: Meltemi.

Grutman, Rainier. 1998. 'Auto-translation'. In *The Routledge Encyclopedia of Translation Studies*, edited by Mona Baker, 17–20. 1st edn. London: Routledge.

——— 2009. 'Self-translation. In *Routledge Encyclopedia of Translation Studies, edited by Mona Baker and GabrielaSaldanha, 257–260. 2nd edn. London: Routledge.

——— 2013a. 'Beckett e oltre: autotraduzioni orizzontali e verticali'. In *Autotraduzione e riscrittura*, edited by in Andrea Ceccherelli, Gabriella Elina Imposti and Monica Perotto, 45–61. Bologna: Bononia University Press.

——— 2013b. 'A Sociological Glance at Self-translation and Self-translators'. In *Self-Translation: Brokering Originality in Hybrid Culture*, edited by Anthony Cordingley, 63–80. London: Bloomsbury.

152   VOICES OF WOMEN WRITERS

Grutman, Rainier and Van Bolderen, Trish. 2014. 'Self-translation'. In *A Companion to Translation Studies*, edited by Sandra Bermann and Catherine Poter, 323–333. Oxford: Wiley Blackwell.

Gumperz, John. 1982. *Discourse Strategies*. Cambridge: Cambridge University Press.

Haller, Hermann W. 2011. 'Varieties, Use, and Attitudes of Italian in the U.S. The Dynamics of an Immigrant Language Through Time'. In *Sprachen in Mobilisierten Kulturen: Aspekte der Migrationslinguistik*, edited by Thomas Stehl, 57–70. Potsdam: Universitätsverlag Potsdam.

Hirsch, Marianne. 1989. *The Mother/Daughter Plot: Narrative, Psychoanalysis, Feminism*. Bloomington: Indiana University Press.

––––––– 1999. 'Projected Memory: Holocaust Photographs in Personal and Public Fantasy'. In *Acts of Memory: Cultural Recall in the Present*, edited by Mieke Bal, Jonathan Creve and Leo Spitzer, 3–23. Hanover: University Press of New England.

Hoffmann, Charlotte. 1991. *An Introduction to Bilingualism*. New York: Longman.

Hokenson, Jan Walsh and Munson, Marcella. 2007. *The Bilingual Text: History and Theory of Literary Self-Translation*. Manchester: St. Jerome Publishing.

Hokenson, Jan Walsh. 2013. 'History and Self-translation'. In *Self-Translation: Brokering Originality in Hybrid Culture*, edited by Anthony Cordingley, 39–60. London: Bloomsbury.

Hull, Philip V. 1987. *Bilingualism. Two Languages, two personalities*. Ann Arbor, MI: University of Michigan Press.

Humpál, Martin, and Březinová, Helena. 2022. *Migration and Identity in Nordic Literature*. Charles University: Karolinum Press.

Hutcheon, Linda. 2019. 'Italian Canadian Writing: the Difference a Few Decades Make'. *Oltreoceano. Geografie e letterature: luoghi dell'emigrazione* 15: 25–40.

Iacovetta, Franca. 1992. *Such Hardworking People: Italian Immigrants in Postwar Toronto*. Montréal: McGill-Queen's University Press.

Iuliano, Susanna, and Baldassar, Loretta. 2008. 'Deprovincialising Italian Migration Studies: An Overview of Australian and Canadian Research'. *Fulgor* 3(3): 1–16.

Jansen, Clifford. 1988. *Italians in a Multicultural Canada*. Lewiston: E. Mellon Press.

Jo Bona, Mary. 1999. *Claiming a Tradition: Italian American Women Writers*. Carbondale: Southern Illinois University Press.

Jones, Owain. 2011. 'Geography, Memory and Non-representational Geographies'. *Geography Compass* 5(12): 875–885.

Jonsson, Carla. 2010. 'Functions of Code-Switching in Bilingual Theater: An Analysis of Three Chicano Plays'. *Journal of Pragmatics* 42(5): 1296–1310.

Jung, Verena. 2002. *English-German Self-Translation of Academic Texts and its Relevance for Translation Theory and Practice*. Frankfurt am Main: Peter Lang.

Kaplan, Alice. 1994. 'On Language Memoir'. In *Displacements. Cultural Identities in Question*, edited by Angelika Bammer, 59–70. Bloomington: Indiana University Press.

Kellman, Steven. 2020. *Nimble Tongues. Studies in Literary Translingualism*. West Lafayette: Purdue University Press.

Kippur, Sara. 2015. *Writing it Twice. Self-translation and the Making of a World Literature in French*. Evanston: Northwestern University Press.

La Gumina, Salvatore. L. 1973. *Wop! A Documentary History of Anti-Italian Discrimination in the United States*. Toronto: Guernica editions.

Lahiri, Jumpa. 2016. *In Other Words*. London/New York: Bloomsbury.

Lentz, Carola. 1999. *Changing Food Habits: Case Studies from Africa, South America, and Europe*. Amsterdam: Harwood Acad.

REFERENCES

153

Lepschy, Anna Laura and Lespschy, Giulio. 1988. *The Italian Language Today*. 2nd edn. London – New York: Routledge.

Lepschy, Giulio. 2002. *Mother Tongues and Other Reflections on the Italian Language*. Toronto: University of Toronto Press.

Lipsky, John. 1982. 'Spanish-English Language Switching in Speech and Literature: Theories and Models'. *Bilingual Review* 9(3): 191–212.

Longhurst, Robin, Johnston, Lynda, and Ho, Elsie. 2009. 'A Visceral Approach: Cooking 'At Home' with Migrant Women in Hamilton, New Zealand'. *Transactions of the Institute of British Geographers* 34(3): 333–345.

Loriggio, Francesco. 2021. 'Italian Canadian Italophone Fiction: The Works of Nino Famà'. *Forum Italicum* 55(3): 805–824.

Maestri, Eliana. 2018. *Translating the Female Self across Cultures*. Amsterdam/Philadelphia: John Benjamins Publishing Company.

Martin, Biddy and Mohanty, Chandra Talpade. 1988. 'Feminist Politics: What's Home Got to Do with It?'. In *Feminist studies/Critical Studies*, edited by Teresa de Lauretis, 191–211. London: Macmillan.

May, Rachel. 1994. *The Translator in the Text: On Reading Russian Literature in English*. Evanston: Northwestern University Press.

Mayblin, Lucy, and Turner, Joe. 2021. *Migration Studies and Colonialism*. Cambridge: Polity Press.

Mazzara, Federica. 2015. 'Spaces of Visibility for the Migrants of Lampedusa: The Counter Narrative of the Aesthetic Discourse'. *Italian Studies: Cultural Studies* 70 (4):449–64.

Mccarthy, Angela. 2007. *Personal Narrative of Irish and Scottish Migration, 1921–65: 'For Spirit and Adventure'*. Manchester: Manchester University Press.

Mey, Jacob L. 2001. *Pragmatics: An Introduction*. Oxford: Blackwell.

Michelut, Dôre 1989. 'Coming to Terms with the Mother Tongue'. *Tessera* 6: 63–71.

––––––– 1990. 'Il Lei: Third Person Polite'. *Tessera* 11:109–116.

––––––– 1990. *Linked Alive: Sets of Renga*. Montréal: Éditions Trois.

––––––– 1994. *Loyale à la chasse*. Montréal: Édition Trois.

Michelut, Dôre, Alonzo, Anne-Marie, Douglas, Charles, Savoie, Paul, Maracle, Lee and Black, Ayanna. 1990. *Liens*. Montréal: Editions Trois.

Michelut, D. 1993. *A Furlan Harvest: An Anthology*. Montréal: Éditions Trois.

Milroy, Lesley and Muysken, Pieter. 1995. 'Introduction: Code-switching and Bilingualism Research'. In *One Speaker, Two Languages: Cross-disciplinary Perspectives on Code-switching*, edited by Lesley Milroy and Pieter Muysken, 1–14. Cambridge: Cambridge University Press.

Moslund, Sten Pultz. 2010. *Hybridity. The Different Speeds of Transcultural Changes*. Basingstoke – NY: Palgrave Mcmillan.

Myers-Scotton, Carol. 1993a. *Social Motivations for Codeswitching, Evidence from Africa*. New York: Oxford University Press.

Nannavecchia, Tiziana 2014. 'There is No Home to Go Back to. Life Across Boundaries: An Italian-Canadian Literary Perspective'. *Diffractions* 2: 1–17.

––––––– 2016. *Translating Italian-Canadian Migrant Writing to Italian: A Discourse Around the Return to the Motherland/Tongue*. Ph.D. School of Translation and Interpretation, University of Ottawa. Unpublished.

Nasta, Susheila. 2002. *Home Truths: Fictions of the South Asian diaspora in Britain*. London: Palgrave Mcmillan.

154 VOICES OF WOMEN WRITERS

Nikolau, Paschalis. 2006. 'Notes on Translating the Self'. In *Translation and Creativity, Perspectives on Creative Writing and Translation Studies*, edited by Manuela Perteghella and Eugenia Loffredo, 19–32. E. London: Continuum.

Nilep, Chad. 2006. ' "Code Switching" in Sociocultural Linguistics'. *Colorado Research in Linguistics* 19: 1–22.

Nyman, Jopi. 2009. *Home, Identity, and Mobility in Contemporary Diasporic Fiction*. Amsterdam – New York: Rodopi.

Opitz, Bertram and Degner, Juliane. 2102. 'Emotionality in a Second Language: It's a Matter of Time'. *Neuropsychologia* 50: 1961–1967.

Ortíz Cuadra, Cruz Miguel. 2013. *Eating Puerto Rico: A History of Food, Culture, and Identity*. Translated by Russ Davidson. Chapel Hill, NC: University of North Carolina Press.

Ortony, Andrew. 1975. 'Why Metaphors Are Necessary and Not Just Nice'. *Educational Theory* 25: 45–53.

Oustinoff, Michaël. 2001. *Bilinguisme d'écriture et auto-traduction, Julien Green, Samuel Beckett, Vladimir Nabokov*. Paris: L'Harmattan.

Ożańska-Ponikwia, Katarzyna. 2013. *Emotions from a Bilingual Point of View: Personality and Emotional Intelligence in Relation to Perception and Expression of Emotions in the L1 and L2*. Newcastle upon Tyne: Cambridge Scholars Publishing.

Padolsky, Enoch. 2005. 'You Are Where You Eat: Ethnicity, Food and Cross-cultural Spaces'. *Canadian Ethnic Studies* 37(2): 19–31.

Palsson, Gisli. 2014. 'Personal Names: Embodiment, Differentiation, Exclusion, and Belonging'. *Science, Technology, & Human Values* 39(4): 618–630.

Parati, Graziella. 2005. *Migration Italy: The Art of Talking Back in a Destination Culture*. Toronto: University of Toronto Press.

Parati, Graziella. 2011. *The Cultures of Italian Migration: Diverse Trajectories and Discrete Perspectives*. Fairleigh Dickinson University.

Patriarca, Gianna. 2015. 'La langue à l'intérieur de mes langues'. *Interfrancophonies* 6: 93–96.

———— 2016.'To Be or Not To Be "Still" Italian: Notes from a Canadian Writer'. In *Exploring Voice: Italian Canadian Female Writers*, edited by Venera Fazio and Delia De Santis, 241–243. Toronto: Frank Iacobucci Centre for Italian Canadian Studies.

Pavlenko, Aneta and Lantolf, James. 2000. 'Second Language Learning as Participation and the (Re)construction of Selves'. In *Sociocultural Theory and Second Language Learning*, edited by James Lantolf, 155–177. Oxford: Oxford University Press.

Pavlenko, Aneta. 2001. *Language Learning Memoirs as a Gendered Genre*. Oxford: Oxford University Press.

———— 2005. *Emotions and Multilingualism*. Cambridge: Cambridge University Press.

———— 2006. *Bilingual Minds: Emotional Experience, Expression, and Representation*. Clevedon: Multilingual Matters.

———— 2008. 'Emotion and Emotion-laden Words in the Bilingual Lexicon'. *Bilingualism: Language and Cognition* 11(2): 147–164.

Peñalver, Recuenco María. 2011. 'Más allá de la traducción: la autotraducción'. *Trans. Revista de traductología* 15: 193–208.

Perin, Roberto and and Sturino, Franc. 1989. *Arrangiarsi. The Italian Immigration Experience in Canada*. Lancaster: Gazelle Book Services Ltd.

Perteghella, Manuela and Loffredo, Eugenia. 2006. 'Introduction'. In *Translation and Creativity. Perspectives on Creative Writing and Translation Studies*, edited by Manuela Perteghella and Eugenia Loffredo, 1–16. London: Continuum.

REFERENCES

Pfaff, Carol W. 1979. 'Constraints on Language Mixing: Intrasentential Code-switching and Borrowing in Spanish/English'. *Language* 55(2): 291–318.

Pivato, Joseph. 1985. *Contrasts: Comparative Comparative Essays on Italian Canadian Writing*. Toronto: Guernica Editions.

———— 1990. 'Nothing Left to Say: Italian Canadian Literature'. In *Writers in Transition: The Proceedings of the First National Conference of Italian-Canadian Writers*, edited by Dino Minni and Anna Foschi Ciampolini, 27–41. Montreal: Guernica.

———— 1998. *The Anthology of Italian-Canadian Writing*. Toronto: Guernica Editions.

———— 2020. 'Self-translation as Problem for Italian-Canadian Authors'. *Oltreoceano. Del tradurre: aspetti della traduzione e dell'autotraduzione, edited by Silvana Serafin and Anna Pia De Luca* 16: 15–30.

Podnieks, Elizabeth, and Andrea O'Reilly. 2010. 'Maternal Literatures in Text and Tradition: Daughter-Centric, Matrilineal, and Matrifocal'. In *Textual Mothers, Maternal Texts. Motherhood in Contemporary Women's Literature*, edited by Elizabeth Podnieks and Andrea O'Reilly, 1–27. Waterloo, Ontario: Wilfred Laurier University Press.

Polezzi, Loredana. 2012. 'Translation and Migration'. *Translation Studies* 5(3): 345–356.

Ponzanesi, Sandra and Merolla, Daniela. 2005. 'Introduction'. In *Migrant Cartographies: New Cultural and Literary Spaces in Post-Colonial Europe*, edited by Sandra Ponzanesi, S. and Daniela Merolla, 1–52. Oxford: Lexington Books.

Ramirez, Bruno. 1989. *The Italians in Canada*. Ottawa: Canadian Historical Association.

Ratnam, Charishma. 2018. 'Creating Home: Intersections of Memory and Identity'. *Geography Compass* 12: 1–11.

Recalcati, Massimo. 2015. *Le mani della madre. Desiderio, fantasmi ed eredità del materno*. Milan: Feltrinelli.

Romaine, S. 1995. *Bilingualism*. 2nd edn. Oxford: Wiley-Blackwell.

Romoli, Vittoria, Cardinali, Paola, Ferrari, Joseph, and Migliorini, Laura. 2021 'Home Away from Home: Comparing Factors Impacting Migrants' and Italians Sense of Psychological Home'. *International Journal of Intercultural Relations* 86, 14–25.

Rorato, Laura. 2018. 'Narratives of Displacement: The Challenges of Motherhood and Mothering in Semi-fictional Works by Laura Pariani, Mary Melfi, and Donatella Di Pierantonio'. *International Journal of Comparative Literature & Translation Studies* 6(1): 75–82.

Rushdie, Suzanne. 1991. *Imaginary Homelands*. London: Granta Books.

Saidero, Deborah. 2008. 'Plurilinguismo e autotraduzione nelle opere di Dore Michelut. In *Itinerranze e Transcodificazioni: Scrittori migranti dal Friuli Venezia Giulia al Canada*, edited by Alessandro Ferraro Anna Pia De Luca, 87–95. Udine: Forum.

———— 2011. 'Self-translation as Transcultural Re-inscription of Identity in Dôre Michelut and Gianna Patriarca'. *Oltreoceano: rivista sulle migrazioni* 5: 31–40.

———— 2013. 'The Transcultural Rewriting of the Italian Ethnoscape'. *Oltreoceano. Donne al caleidoscopio. La riscrittura dell'identità femminile nei testi dell'emigrazione tra l'Italia, le Americhe e l'Australia* 7: 57–66.

———— 2018. 'Women and Religion in Italian-Canadian Narratives'. *Oltreoceano. La dimensione religiosa dell'immigrazione nel Nuovo Mondo* 14: 105–120.

———— 2020. 'Self-Translation as Translingual and Transcultural Transcreation'. *Oltreoceano: rivista sulle migrazioni* 16: 31–42.

———— 2021. 'The Quest Motif in the Travelogues and Memoirs of Migrant Writers'. *Oltreoceano Erranze tra mito e storia* 17: 71–78.

Santoyo, Julio César. 2005. 'Autotraducciones: una perspectiva histórica'. *Meta* 50(3): 858–867.

—— 2006. 'Blank Spaces in the History of Translation'. In *Charting the Future of Translation History*, edited by Georges L. Bastin and Paul F. Bandia, 11–43. Ottawa: University of Ottawa Press.

Sciorra, Joseph, and Giunta, Edvige. 2014. *Embroidered Stories: Interpreting Women's Domestic Needlework from the Italian Diaspora*. Jackson: University Press of Mississippi.

Seccia, Maria Cristina. 2018. 'Reading Literature through Translation: The Case of Antonio D'Alfonso in Italian'. In *Comparative Literature for the New Century*, edited by Joseph Pivato and Giulia De Gasperi, 153–173. Montreal: McGill-Queen's University Press.

Sennet, Richard. 1998. 'Disturbing Memories'. In *Memory*, edited by Patricia Fara and Karalyn Patterson, 10–26. Cambridge: Cambridge University Press.

Skalle, Camilla 2017. 'Nostalgia and Hybrid Identity in Italian Migrant Literature: The Case of Igiaba Scego'. *Bergen Language and Linguistics Studies 7: 73–86*.

Sobrero, Alberto. 1993. *Introduzione all'italiano contemporaneo*. Roma – Bari: Editori Laterza.

Spagnuolo, Elena Anna. 2019. 'Italian Mothers and Italian-Canadian Daughters: Using Language to Negotiate the Politics of Gender'. *Genealogy* 3(24): 1–19.

Spunta, Marina. 1999. 'The food of tolerance in Francesca Duranti's Sogni mancini'. *The Italianist* 19(1): 228–250.

Steele, Claude M. and Aronson, Joshua. 1995. 'Stereotype Threat and the Intellectual Test Performance of African Americans'. *Journal of Personality and Social Psychology* 69(5): 797–811.

Stock, Femke. 2010. 'Home and Memory'. In *Diasporas: Concepts, Intersections, Identities*, edited by Kim Knott and Sean McLoughlin, 24–28. London-New York: Zed Books.

Strelkova, Natalia. 2012. *Introduction to Russian-English Translation: Tactics and Techniques for the Translator*. New York: Hippocrene Books.

Stroud, Christopher. 1998. 'Perspectives on Cultural Variability of Discourse and some Implications for Code-switching'. In *Code-Switching in Conversation: Language, Interaction and Identity*, edited by Peter Auer, 321–348. London: Routledge.

Tajfel, Henry and Turner, John C. 1986. 'The Social Identity Theory of Intergroup Behaviour'. In *Psychology of Intergroup Relations* (2nd ed.), edited by William G. Austin and Stephen Worchel, 7–24. Chicago: Nelson-Hall.

Tamburri, Anthony J. 2003. 'Beyond 'pizza' and 'nonna'! Or, what's bad about Italian/ American criticism?'. *Melus* 28(3): 149–174.

Tanqueiro, Helena. 2000. 'Self-Translation as an Extreme Case of the Author-Translator-Dialectic'. In *Investigating Translation*, edited by Allison Beeby, Doris Ensinger and Marisa Presas, 55–63. Amsterdam: John Benjamins.

Venuti, Lawrence. 1995. *The Translator's Invisibility. A History of Translation*. London: Routledge.

Vogt, Hans. 1954. 'Language Contacts'. *Word* 10(2&3): 365–374.

Weston, Daniel and Gardner-Chloros, Penelope. 2015. 'Code-switching and Multilingualism in Literature'. *Language and Literature* 24(3): 182–193.

Wierzbicka, Anna. 2004. 'Bilingual Lives, Bilingual Experience'. *Journal of Multilingual and Multicultural Development* 25(2&3): 94–104.

Wilson, Rita. 2009. 'The Writer's Double: Translation, Writing, and Autobiography'. *Romance Studies* 27(3):186–198.

—— 2012. 'Parallel Creations. Between Self-translation and the Translation of the Self'. In *Creative Constraints. Translation and Authorship*, edited by Rita Wilson and Leah Gerber, 47–65. Clayton, Victoria: Monash University Publishing.

REFERENCES

—— 2020. 'Pens that Confound the Label of Citizenship': Self-translations and Literary Identities'. *Modern Italy* 25(2): 213–224.

Yildiz, Yasemin. 2012. *Beyond the Mother Tongue. The Postmonolingual Condition.* New York: Fordham University Press.

Yuval-Davis, Nira. 2006. 'Belonging and politics of belonging'. *Patterns of Prejudice* 40(3): 197–214.

Zucchero, Jim. 2013. 'Ways of Writing Home'. In *Writing Our Way home*, edited by Licia Canton and Caroline Morgan Di Giovanni, 43–54. Toronto: Guernica Editions.

Websites

Athabasca University. *English-Canadian Writers: Gianna Patriarca* (Last Updated 12 February 2015). Available at: http://canadian-writers.athabascau.ca/english/writers/gpatriarca/gpatriarca.php (Accessed: 11/01/2023).

Athabasca University. *English-Canadian Writers: Dôre Michelut* (Last Updated 12 February 2015). Available at: http://canadian-writers.athabascau.ca/english/writers/dmichelut/dmichelut.php (Accessed: 11/01/2023).

Association of Italian Canadian Writers. Available at: http://www.aicw.ca/ (Accessed: 11/01/20123).

Accenti. The Magazine with an Italian Accent. Available at: http://www.accenti.ca/ (Accessed: 11/01/2023).

Canton, Licia. (2005). 'La lingua del Belpaese in Canada'. *Bibliosofia. Letteratura canadese e altre culture.* Available at: http://www.bibliosofia.net/files/belpaese.htm (Accessed: 11/01/2023).

Letizia Tesi (2012). 'Gianna Patriarca. Versi che rompono il silenzio', *Panoram Italia: Living Italian Style*, 12 August. Available at: Panoram Italia Toronto Vol. 2 No. 4 by Panoram Italia Magazine - Issuu.

Printed in the USA
CPSIA information can be obtained
at www.ICGtesting.com
JSHW020010130923
48245JS00001B/5